Confederate Mobile

Confederate Mobile

ARTHUR W. BERGERON, JR.

University Press of Mississippi
Jackson & London

Copyright © 1991 by the University Press of Mississippi
All rights reserved
Manufactured in the United States of America
Designed by Sally Hamlin

Library of Congress Cataloging-in-Publication Data

Bergeron, Arthur W.
    Confederate Mobile / Arthur W. Bergeron, Jr.
      p.   cm.
    Includes bibliographical references and index.
    ISBN 0-87805-512-6
    1. Mobile (Ala.)—History—Civil War, 1861–1865. I. Title.
F334.M6B47 1991
976.1'2205—dc20   91-15776
                                                       CIP

British Library Cataloging-in-Publication data available

For
Geoffrey Scott Bergeron
1971 – 1989

Contents

Introduction

Upon its formation, the Confederate States of America adopted the four elements of traditional coastal defense employed by the United States before the Civil War: "fixed defenses [fortifications], a navy, a professional army supplemented by well-organized militia, and an efficient system of interior land and water transportation and communication." The new nation lacked a navy but had some success in creating one. Building on existing coastal forts, Confederate engineers erected elaborate defensive positions. In addition, the states raised troops to form a national army. At first, each state was allowed "to defend its own coastline according to its particular interests."[1] The Confederate government could provide only professional officers to command and supervise military, naval, and engineering operations, but it did try to coordinate the total effort. The states were expected to furnish troops and laborers. By later 1861 and early 1862, because of a series of defeats both along the coast and on interior rivers, the Confederacy had to abandon its initial decision to protect its entire coastline. From about February 1862 until the end of the war, the South followed a policy of defending only essential areas under direct enemy threat and keeping minimal forces in unthreatened areas until they came under attack. The focus of this study is the operation of the Confederacy's policies in actual practice in a particular location.

The people of Mobile, Alabama, supported the secession of their state from the Union in January 1861, and thousands of its able-bodied men served in the Confederate army from 1861 to 1865. Recognizing the city's strategic importance as a port and major railroad center connecting the eastern and western sections of the new nation, the Confederate government moved quickly to provide adequate defenses for Mobile. Confederate soldiers occupied and began to strengthen Fort Morgan and Fort Gaines, which guarded the main channels leading into Mobile Bay. The Confederate Navy Department converted several steamers into gunboats and began construction of ironclads, all designed to support the land defenses of Mobile.

As the war progressed, Union land and naval forces moved into the Gulf of Mexico, and the Confederate authorities realized that Mobile required more defensive works than the two forts at the mouth of the bay. Engineers, using slave labor, designed and constructed earthen forts along the bay shore near the city and on various islands at the mouths of the rivers that emptied into the bay. These batteries were expected to protect the water approaches to Mobile should an enemy naval force run past Fort Morgan and Fort Gaines. To protect the city from a land attack, the engineers erected a series of earthen redoubts connected by infantry entrenchments around Mobile. By war's end, three separate lines of forts and trenches surrounded the city. Mobile's fortifications were surely as extensive and strong as those of almost any city in the Confederacy, and because of them, the city was "the last important place in the Confederacy which was captured."[2]

Confederate President Jefferson Davis personally chose for assignment as commanding general at Mobile men whom he knew were qualified to supervise the construction of the defensive works and to conduct a successful defense against an enemy attack. Confederate brigades, regiments, and artillery batteries moved in and out of the city throughout the war. Although the garrison at times shrank in size to levels that alarmed its commanders, the Confederate military authorities in Richmond made a commitment to supply enough men to occupy the fortifications so that an enemy attack would meet stiff resistance. The War Department also always made sure that the territorial command to which Mobile belonged, whether a department or a district, had the defense of the city as a chief objective.

The Union high command did not seriously contemplate an attack against the Mobile defenses until relatively late in the war. Although strategic objectives in other areas were one reason for the Union delay in moving against Mobile, the strength of the defenses around the city played a part in the decision. A naval demonstration against an earthen fort at Grant's Pass in February 1864 resulted in little damage to that work. Admiral David G. Farragut successfully led a squadron of monitors and wooden gunboats past Fort Morgan and Fort Gaines in August 1864 and captured the lower bay defenses, but the commitment of land forces elsewhere prevented a naval campaign against Mobile itself. Such a campaign finally got under way in March 1865, but its primary objective was defensive works on the eastern shore of the bay because of fear that the lines around the city were impenetrable. After brief sieges conducted by overwhelming numbers of Union troops, these Confederate fortifications fell. Faced with possible encirclement, Mobile's commander evacuated the city on April 12, 1865, and the city's government authorities surrendered Mobile to the enemy that same day.

My interest in the role of Mobile in the Civil War arose out of research on a Louisiana military unit stationed there late in the conflict. I discovered that several persons had written on limited aspects of Mobile's story, but no book presented a comprehensive treatment of the defense of the city during the entire war. The only book on the subject ever published describes the final campaign against Mobile in 1865 and was printed in 1866. Civil War historians acknowledge the importance of the blockade of the Southern coast in the defeat of the Confederacy, yet there are modern published monographs concerning the defense only of the ports of New Orleans and Charleston. I hope that my book helps to fill that gap.

I owe a special debt to the late Professor T. Harry Williams, who encouraged me to pursue this topic and provided valuable assistance in the early phases of research and writing. I also wish to express my sincere gratitude to Professor William J. Cooper, Jr., who read and made many excellent suggestions for several revisions of the manuscript. Professor Cooper also provided constant encouragement in my efforts to get the manuscript published. Charles East of Baton Rouge, Louisiana, read one revision and pointed out ways to strengthen and improve it. Numerous people assisted me in various phases of my research, but a few of them deserve special thanks. Michael Musick of the Navy and Old Army Branch of the National Archives proved invaluable in making available pertinent manuscripts in that repository. Likewise, Caldwell Delaney of the Mobile Museum Department assisted not only in researching that collection but in suggesting other useful sources. Dr. Thomas McMillan of Mobile graciously allowed me to make use of his personal collection of manuscripts several years before he deposited those papers with the Mobile Museum Department.

It has been a pleasure to work with Seetha Srinivasan and her staff at University Press of Mississippi. The outside readers for the press made invaluable suggestions for improvements. I especially wish to thank Trudie Calvert, who edited the manuscript for the press, for the superb job she did.

Confederate Mobile

CHAPTER 1

Mobile 1861,
Strategic Port and Rail Center

Mobile on the eve of the Civil War was the leading city of Alabama and one of the most important cities in the South. The French, under Pierre LeMoyne, Sieur d'Iberville, had established a settlement there in 1711. From then until 1814, when it fell to General Andrew Jackson, Mobile belonged successively to the French, British, and Spanish governments. When the Americans took possession, the population numbered a mere handful, but it grew steadily and stood at 29,258 persons in 1860.[1] One observer described the city in 1861: "With a population of thirty thousand the city contains many pleasant residences, embowered in shade trees, and surrounded by generous grounds. It is rendered attractive by its tall pines, live oak, and Pride-of-China trees."[2] Located on a sandy plain near the northwest corner of Mobile Bay, the city enjoyed excellent drainage and had no problems with mud. The inhabitants found this sand difficult to cross, however, so they established over the years a system of oyster-shell roads. These roads became a favorite carriage route and were well-known throughout the Gulf South.[3]

Both because of the various countries that had owned the area and of its status as a major port, Mobile's population contained a signifi-

3

cant number of foreign-born persons. The 1860 census recorded 7,733 foreigners in the city, one-fourth of the total population and 37 percent of the white population.[4] A visitor to Mobile considered its society "more cosmopolitan than that of any city in the South, save perhaps, New Orleans."[5] When British correspondent William Howard Russell made a brief visit to the city in May 1861, he wrote in his diary that on his arrival he saw "a fringe of tall warehouses, and shops alongside [the wharf], over which were names indicating Scotch, English, many Spanish, German, Italian, and French owners." Later Russell found the market "crowded with Negroes, mulattoes, quadroons, and mestizos of all sorts, Spanish, Italian, and French, speaking their own tongues, or a quaint lingua franca, and dressed in very striking and pretty costumes."[6]

In 1860 the Medical College of Alabama and Spring Hill College were located in or near Mobile. The former was a branch of the University of Alabama, the latter a private school run by the Jesuit order. Mobile had seven public schools and several private academies, all of which had reputations for their fine academic standing. The city's five hospitals provided excellent care for the sick. The Protestant Orphan Asylum, the Catholic Orphan Asylum, the Female Benevolent Society, the Samaritan Society, and the Can't-Get-Away-Club constituted the city's charitable institutions. Twenty-four Christian places of worship and two Jewish synagogues ministered to the spiritual needs of the populace. Mobile also had one of the finest fire departments in the South, consisting of eight engine companies and one hook-and-ladder company.[7]

Mobile prospered primarily because of its status as a center for trade and commerce. As a port, Mobile stood second only to New Orleans in the South. More than 330 vessels cleared and over 200 vessels entered the port in 1860. The value of articles exported totaled $3,670,183. Foreign imports amounted to $1,050,310. Thus "Mobile had the worst export-import imbalance of all antebellum ports."[8] Much of Mobile's trade moved up and down the rivers that converged on the city, primarily the Tombigbee and Alabama systems. Alabama is said to have had "more navigable river miles than any state in the nation," and most flowed into Mobile Bay. Alabama produced more cotton than any other Southern state except Mississippi by 1860, and the majority of these bales were sold in Moblie. In exchange for this cotton coming down the rivers, Mobile's merchants sent to the planters and farmers of the interior such goods as pork, corn, flour, and whiskey.[9]

Mobile never served as a center of Southern radicalism during the antebellum period. Its commercial ties with the North and fairly large population of foreigners seemed to argue for continued ties with the North. In the presidential election of November 1860, Mobile County voters cast 1,823 votes for Stephen A. Douglas, 1,629 for John Bell, and 1,541 for John C. Breckinridge—a better than two-to-one majority against the secessionist candidate.[10] The election of Abraham Lincoln, however, pushed Mobilians toward the secessionist camp. On December 7, 1860, the city's leading newspaper stated: "The rapid progress of events within the last few weeks leaves little ground for hope that the Union can be preserved upon any basis, just, equitable, and satisfactory to the Southern people." The paper expressed the hope that the separation of the states would be peaceful.[11]

Mayor Jones M. Withers of Mobile issued a proclamation on December 8 in which he stated, "We are in the midst of a revolution, and are invoking the sovereignty of our State against wrong and oppression."[12] Two days earlier Governor Andrew B. Moore had issued a call, in accordance with a resolution of the General Assembly, for an election of delegates on the twenty-fourth to a state convention to consider the course Alabama should follow. In meetings at Temperance Hall, the secessionists nominated their delegates, and the cooperationists (who wanted the Southern states to work together and leave the Union as a unit) met at Odd Fellows Hall to select their slate.[13] The news of the secession of South Carolina reached Mobile late on December 20 and, "though not unexpected, caused considerable excitement, and a salute of 100 guns was fired . . . in honor of the event."[14] The arrival of this news just before the election of delegates in Alabama undoubtedly affected the vote in Mobile.

Clarence P. Denman wrote of the secession of Alabama, "The returns [of the state convention delegates election] from Mobile County came as quite a surprise to those who regarded the cooperationist party as the successor of the Bell and Douglas parties." Those returns showed 2,297 votes cast for the secessionists and 1,229 for the coop-

erationists: a majority of 1,068 for the former. In analyzing these results, Denman concludes: "The cooperationists of the county had
advocated a method of withdrawing so closely akin to straight-out
secession that they should have received the votes of all those not
strongly in favor of separate state action; therefore, the large majority
for the straight-outs indicates that the people of Mobile County were
in harmony with the interior of the state."[15]

The most recent study of antebellum Mobile explains that the
people supported secession because of the extreme trade imbalance
and "the extent of the commitment to the cotton trade," which put
Mobile in "the most extreme position of colonial dependency within
the national economy." Northern businessmen handled most of the
marketing of the cotton flowing through the city because it was destined for either Northern or European textile mills. Additionally, the
majority of Mobile's imports came from New York. Mobilians, therefore, hoped that a new southern nation "would, among other things,
end their colonial relationship to the North and spur urban growth in
their city."[16]

The Alabama convention began its meetings in Montgomery on
January 7, 1861. Four days later the delegates voted sixty-three to
thirty-nine to take the state out of the Union. Business establishments
in Mobile had closed down awaiting the decision of the convention.
During the afternoon of the eleventh, the news of secession became
public, and celebrations broke out. The militia fired one hundred guns
in salute, and bands struck up joyful tunes. All of Mobile's military
companies turned out to parade through the streets. That night the
citizens lit lamps and candles in homes and businesses and tar barrels along Government Street so that the revelry might continue. A
huge fireworks display in Bienville Square highlighted the night
celebration.[17]

The city's leading daily newspaper, anticipating the formation of a
Southern nation, recommended that Mobile be made the capital of
the Confederacy. The article suggested that the Confederacy would
eventually expand to include Mexico and the West Indies, which
would make Mobile the best place for the center of government: "Mobile is, to a degree, the convenient center of the present and the
geographical center of the future, is a seaport susceptible of impreg-

nable defence, is healthful, and in every respect eligible for the honor of being elected the capital city of the South."[18] The paper's second choice was Montgomery.

Before the secession convention met in Montgomery, Governor Moore had begun seizing federal installations and property near Mobile. On January 3, he called out six Mobile companies of the First Alabama State Troops to accomplish that task. Two companies moved by steamer on January 4 to seize Fort Morgan and Fort Gaines at the mouth of Mobile Bay, while four companies moved at the same time against the Mount Vernon Arsenal, thirty miles north of Mobile. Ordnance Sergeant S. Patterson turned over the property under his supervision at Fort Morgan to Colonel John B. Todd. Not until January 18, however, did Colonel Todd take formal possession of Fort Gaines from Lieutenant C. B. Reese of the United States Corps of Engineers. Both forts were still unfinished, and United States engineer troops had been working to strengthen them. The property seized included some five thousand shot and shell.[19]

After the seizure of the forts, Mobile's citizens continued to form military companies, and the newspapers urged them to consider the possibility of war. At least one paper suggested that the city's fire companies follow Charleston's example and organize themselves for military duty. The fire companies were already enlisted, were accustomed to obeying orders, and could adapt quickly to drill. They would act primarily as a home guard, keeping their present uniforms. The paper expected that no more than one-third of the men would be called for duty outside the city at one time. The firemen did organize for home defense, forming a Fire Brigade and using the various engine houses as armories.[20]

Governor Moore acted quickly after Alabama seceded to provide for the defense of Mobile, the point most likely to come under enemy attack in a war because of its coastal location. On his own authority, he gave permission to his assistant quartermaster, Colonel Duff C. Green, to make a draft of $10,000 against the Executive Department to strengthen the forts below the city. Neither the General Assembly nor the secession convention had appropriated funds for that purpose. Green wrote to Moore that the people of Mobile intended to raise an additional $100,000, which could later be reimbursed by the state.

Moore wrote that "Mobile must be defended at whatever cost," but he urged his military subordinates to use public monies economically and efficiently.[21]

Planters in the interior of the state offered the services of some of their slaves to help construct defenses. At one time in early 1861, the engineers employed as many as 150 laborers at Fort Morgan. On another occasion, the authorities expected some 400 slaves to arrive in the city. The volunteers and laborers cleaned the cisterns in the fort so they could hold fresh rainwater. The men mounted all the artillery pieces they could on the available carriages and used sandbags to sod the ramparts facing the ship channel. Eventually, the entire fort would receive the same treatment, but for the time being, the men cut grass sod for the outer faces. After trenches were dug at the base of the scarp, water from the soil filled them, adding a little to the defensive posture of the fort.[22] But Fort Morgan was far from ready to withstand an attack.

The new Confederate government became involved in the defense of Mobile almost immediately. The city seemed particularly vulnerable because Pensacola, Florida, some sixty miles to the east, remained in Federal hands. The Confederate government did not yet have troops of its own to send but did begin acting in other areas of defense. Secretary of War Leroy Pope Walker telegraphed Colonel John H. Forney at Barrancas Barracks near Pensacola on February 26 and asked if he could spare any columbiads (large siege artillery pieces) from Fort McRae for use in Fort Morgan. When Forney replied that he could spare two such guns, Walker told him to make the transfer "without delay, so as not to excite suspicion and report."[23] Forney reported on March 4 that he had sent to Fort Morgan that day two eight-inch columbiads, with complete carriages, chassis, equipment, and implements.[24] On March 7, the military authorities at Mobile received by rail two ten-inch columbiads from the Tredegar Iron Works in Richmond, Virginia. With their mile-and-a-half range these guns were the most powerful ones at the fort.[25]

On March 18, 1861, the Confederate War Department assumed supervision of Fort Morgan, assigning Colonel William J. Hardee to command the post. Hardee, author of the standard text on infantry tactics, would have the services of two artillery officers to help train the local troops.[26] Nine and a half companies, about eight hundred men, constituted the garrison. Hardee found that the officers and enlisted men alike had had little instruction and lacked discipline. He began a program to correct these deficiencies but could do little by himself. On March 28 he wrote to Secretary Walker to request officers capable of conducting both infantry and artillery instruction, warning that if such services were not provided, in battle the Alabama volunteers would "disgrace themselves and the Confederacy." A visitor to the fort reported shortly afterward that Hardee seemed to have put the place "in thorough repair and readiness."[27]

As Hardee's force at Fort Morgan grew, he moved most of the men outside the fort into tents for fear that in such crowded conditions yellow fever or some other epidemic sickness might strike. The only tents available were small, however, and the men had to remain out in the hot sun much of the time. To provide clear fields of fire in case of attack, Hardee had ordered the men to level the sand hills and to cut down the few trees near the fort. An observer called the result "a huge, unbroken waste of sand, nearly as white as snow and intensely hot." By this time units from the northern part of the state had relieved most of the south Alabama companies. These new troops were not accustomed to such exposure. The same observer recommended that the government provide larger tents equipped with flies so the sea breeze could blow through.[28]

Mobile's defenses suffered other problems as well. Some people thought Fort Morgan could repel a naval attack but not a land assault. More serious, however, the approaches to Mobile from Mississippi Sound through Grant's Pass were completely unprotected. The closest work to the pass, Fort Gaines, had no garrison and could not have prevented light-draft vessels from using the approach. Robert H. Smith, Mobile's representative in the Confederate Congress, suggested that Hardee's command be extended to include Fort Gaines, Grant's Pass, and all other approaches to Mobile.[29]

About this same time, Major General Jeremiah Clemens of the Alabama militia suggested that guns from Fort Morgan be placed in defensive works on Dauphin Island and Sand Island at the mouth of the bay and at Spanish River and Choctaw Point near the city.[30] The Confederate authorities responded quickly. Major Danville Leadbetter, a noted engineer officer, received orders to inspect the defenses and make a full report. General Samuel Cooper, adjutant general of the Confederacy, authorized Hardee to transfer guns to the points suggested by Clemens, saying that they would be replaced by others from the arsenal at Baton Rouge, Louisiana. Finally, Cooper extended Hardee's command to include Fort Gaines, Grant's Pass, and all approaches to Mobile. Hardee would also have the services of the city's fledgling navy: the revenue cutter *Lewis Cass*.[31]

On April 16, following the outbreak of war at Fort Sumter, South Carolina, President Davis issued a call for volunteers for Confederate service, and four Mobile companies—the Mobile Cadets, Gulf City Guards, Mobile Rifles, and Washington Light Infantry—offered their services to Governor Moore. On April 23, he ordered them to move to Montgomery for formation into a regiment. Crowds filled the streets, balconies, wharves, and boats in the harbor to watch the young soldiers march off to war. Late in the afternoon the first two companies paraded through the streets to the wharf. Instead of the bright uniforms they had worn in the past, the men now "were clad in a stout, serviceable gray, specially selected for a rough campaign."[32]

The men enjoyed a brief rest at the wharf. One recalled later: "Then came the last leave-taking of mothers, sisters, sweethearts, wives; the hand-shakings of friends and companions, the blessings of old men, the final exhortation of father to son, the sobs and tears of agonized women." Then the two companies boarded the steamer *St. Nicholas* for the journey upriver to Montgomery. As the vessel pulled out into the stream, church and ships' bells rang, an artillery unit fired a salute, and the crowds cheered and waved farewell. As one of the volunteers recognized, "the city of Mobile had lost the *elite* of her youth."[33]

During succeeding months many more troops left Mobile, traveling by boat and train, wearing a variety of uniforms, and carrying different flags. There are no figures on how many men Mobile furnished to the Confederate armies. By July 1861 some 2,000 men had gone into service, but many had enlisted for only one year. Mobile County's white male population between the ages of fifteen and forty in 1860 was 8,053. If the white males between forty and fifty are added, the total number of men liable to military service during the war was approxi-

mately 9,682.[34] Some sixty companies from Mobile County served in
the regular Confederate army, and men from the county made up parts
of at least five other companies.[35] Assuming a strength of from 75 to
100 per company, Mobile County's contribution to the regular army
would have been at least 4,500 to 6,000 men. Those who served in
home guard, militia, or reserve units may have raised total enlistments
by as many as 1,000 men.

On the same day that Mobile's war volunteers left for Montgomery,
Major Danville Leadbetter sent a report of his inspection of the city's
defenses to Colonel Hardee at Fort Morgan. Leadbetter also made
several recommendations for strengthening the defenses. He suggested
that a floating battery commanded by a naval officer would suffice to
protect Grant's Pass. Leadbetter's concern focused primarily on Fort
Gaines and the main ship channel between Gaines and Fort Morgan.
He urged the placement of heavy guns in Gaines but recognized that
they would not be able to defend the bay entrance. This area was three
and a quarter miles wide, and no cannons in the forts could completely cover the middle of the approach. Leadbetter recommended
locating a floating battery of strong timber covered with iron bars in
the center of the channel. This battery, along with the guns of the
two forts, should prove sufficient to prevent enemy vessels from entering the bay.[36]

At this early stage of the war, the Confederate command gave no
thought to defensive works near Mobile itself. Leadbetter wrote Hardee that proper protection of the bay entrances would prevent an
enemy force from approaching the city from anywhere except overland from a point on Mississippi Sound. He thought the troops at
Mobile could not prevent such a landing on the coast. The only answer to such a movement would be strong defense by "the stout hearts
and strong arms of the military forces which can be concentrated at
the city." Leadbetter felt that the urgency of the situation required
that he begin work on his recommendations "without waiting for formal authority." Hardee forwarded Leadbetter's report to Montgomery
and told the secretary of war that he had ordered Leadbetter to work
on the defenses at Fort Gaines.[37]

Many of the leading citizens of Mobile were concerned about the
safety of their city, and they began to write to the Confederate War

Department about their fears. The consensus of the communications seemed to be that the city was defenseless and likely to come under attack by Northern forces. A three-man committee appointed by the citizens of Mobile traveled to Montgomery to ask Walker for arms and ammunition. These men also protested an order directing the only field artillery unit in Mobile to move to Pensacola. Colin J. McRae, Mobile's representative in the Provisional Confederate Congress, urged Walker to do something to calm the fears of the people. He suggested that cannon from Fort Morgan be mounted in batteries at Choctaw Point, Grant's Pass, and the western end of Dauphin Island.[38] The young Confederate government responded favorably but slowly to these requests.

William H. Russell visited Fort Morgan and Fort Gaines, and his impressions evidence the weaknesses of these works. He described Gaines as "a shell of masonry" and noted that to defend the fort the small garrison had only a few small cannon set up on the beach and sand hills nearby. Morgan seemed only slightly stronger because the Confederates had mounted cannon of varying calibers. Russell was impressed with the men of the garrison, the Second Alabama Infantry Regiment, and the unit's commander, Colonel Henry Maury. But he felt that the magazines were vulnerable to enemy fire, and in a heavy bombardment Morgan would suffer great damage. Recalling his observations of Fort Sumter after its fall, he recommended that the fort's garrison destroy the wooden buildings and barracks to avoid fires.[39]

Toward the end of June 1861, Mayor John Forsyth and some of the city's government leaders gathered a large quantity of artillery pieces and small arms for the use of the Mobile militia. Five hundred muskets came from the state authorities and an additional five hundred from the Confederate government. The Confederate authorities also informed Forsyth that as many as six hundred more muskets would be available if needed. Plenty of powder and musket balls existed to supply these and other weapons in the city. In addition to these muskets, Forsyth obtained between twenty-five and thirty artillery pieces, most of them smoothbores but some rifled guns. The mounting of the artillery proceeded slowly, but the authorities believed that half of the cannon would be on carriages and ready for action by early July.[40]

A meeting of prominent citizens of Mobile resulted in resolutions supporting the efforts of Forsyth and other civil authorities. On June 29 a committee of five men presented the resolutions to the meeting at Odd Fellows Hall. These men recognized that the city government might have to "take the responsibility of exercising unusual powers" and pledged themselves to support "all such measures as they may deem proper and necessary for the efficient defense of Mobile." A Committee of Safety was created to assist the civil authorities, and the city fathers were authorized to use the Harbor Improvement Fund or any other funds, to levy taxes, and to accept contributions for defense of Mobile. The citizens hoped the Confederate government would repay all expenditures but expressed willingness to have the city bear the burden. Forsyth, the aldermen, and the Common Council received authority to hire or purchase transportation, laborers, tools, and equipment and to construct necessary fortifications. Those men attending the meeting promised to use their influence to gain the support of the entire city population for the measures they had adopted.[41]

Mobile's militia units spent short periods of time in camps of instruction to improve their training and discipline. One of these camps, located at Bayou La Batre on the coast southeast of the city, bore the name Camp Garnett. Camp Moore, named for Alabama's governor, was established by the First Alabama State Volunteers of the Fire Brigade about one mile from the city on the north side of the road to Spring Hill. One soldier at Camp Moore reported that they drilled by companies during the afternoon. This soldier recognized that the camp's proximity to Mobile created a problem: "After drill, all want to go home. It is difficult for a man to realize the necessity of sleeping on hard boards in a tent, when his home, family, and a comfortable bed, are within a few minutes walk; therefore, it is but natural that he should want to 'go home,' and enjoy his domestic comforts, or go and see his sweetheart."[42] Commanders of Mobile would experience similar problems with troops stationed near their homes throughout the war, thereby weakening the Confederacy's coast defense system.

Part of Mobile's value to the Confederacy during the war years lay in the railroad connections that were one element of its defense. Just before the firing on Fort Sumter, the Mobile and Ohio Railroad opened its line to traffic. This road connected Mobile with Columbus,

Kentucky. At Corinth, Mississippi, it crossed the Memphis and Charleston Railroad, which ran east and west. The Alabama and Mississippi Rivers Railroad was the other east-west line that connected with the Mobile and Ohio, the tie-in being located at Meridian, Mississippi. From Meridian, the Alabama and Mississippi Rivers Railroad ran eastward to the Tombigbee River at Demopolis, Alabama, and westward through Jackson to Vicksburg.

This road was incomplete, however, when the war began. No bridge crossed the Tombigbee, and steamboats had to ferry people and goods over several miles of river between Demopolis and McDowell's Bluff. Even then, gaps existed between Demopolis and Selma and between the latter town and Montgomery. Despite attempts to complete construction on the line, it remained incomplete at war's end and could not be relied on for transporting men and supplies. Farmers in Alabama and Mississippi began switching from cotton to corn production as the war progressed, and the pig population in those two states grew at the same time. In fact, Alabama became a major bacon producer during the conflict. Much of this corn and bacon had to travel on railroads through Mobile for consumption by civilians and soldiers alike.[43]

On November 15, 1861, the Mobile and Great Northern Railroad began operations, completing Mobile's rail connections between the western and eastern theaters. This railroad ran from Tensas Landing to Pollard, Alabama, where it joined the Alabama and Florida Railroad to provide service to Montgomery to the north and Pensacola to the south. The Alabama and Florida line was not complete when the Confederate government was formed in March 1861. Its owners received an emergency loan from Alabama's state government and had trains running between Pensacola and Montgomery by May 6. The Mobile and Great Northern had been constructed fairly quickly. The workers laid the first rails at Tensas Landing on March 28, 1861, and the company promised that it would be finished by September.[44]

By early October, however, the work was still incomplete. Company president William D. Dunn wrote Withers that although grading, bridging, and laying of cross ties was complete, half of the rails remained to be put down. The company had exhausted its money supply, and Dunn requested a loan of $15,000, which he believed would make it possible to finish the road between November 10 and 15. Dunn hoped Withers would use his influence with the government to get the loan approved. Dunn also contacted Congressman McRae to ask for his assistance. The government approved the loan, and, as promised, the road opened on November 15. Major General Braxton Bragg assessed the strategic importance of the Mobile and Great Northern in moving troops and concluded, "It is equal to 3,000 men at each end."[45] After the fall of Corinth to Union forces in early 1862, the Mobile and Ohio–Mobile and Great Northern systems made Mobile the only rail link between Confederate armies in the East and West. The sole problem in the system was that men and supplies had to be detrained and transported by steamer between Mobile and Tensas Landing. Even so, steamers could complete this trip in about one and a half to three hours.[46]

The importance to the Confederacy of Mobile's strategic interior transportation lines was demonstrated in the summer of 1862. In what one author calls "the largest single Confederate troop movement by rail," twenty-five thousand men of the Army of the Mississippi moved in railroad cars from Tupelo, Mississippi, through Mobile to Chattanooga, Tennessee. A smaller troop transfer preceded this movement by about a month. Following the occupation of Corinth by Union forces, Major General Don Carlos Buell's Federal army began operations aimed toward Chattanooga. Major General Edmund Kirby Smith, whose Confederate department included Chattanooga, asked Bragg, then commanding the army at Tupelo, to send troops to help defend the Tennessee city. Bragg responded by ordering Major General John P. McCown's division to report to Kirby Smith by rail via Mobile. The three thousand men of this division left on June 28, 1862, and their lead elements reached Chattanooga on July 3. Transit through Mobile went smoothly, but the men encountered difficulties between Montgomery and Chattanooga, which slightly delayed their arrival.[47]

By late July 1862, Bragg had decided that he could not invade middle Tennessee from Tupelo as he desired and that Kirby Smith could not hold Buell out of Chattanooga. Knowing that this city and its railroad connections through eastern Tennessee were strategically more important than northern Mississippi, Bragg determined to go to

Kirby Smith's aid. On July 21 he ordered the infantrymen of the three divisions of the Army of the Mississippi to proceed by rail through Mobile to Chattanooga. He sent his artillery and wagons overland through central Alabama. To get troops to Chattanooga quickly, Bragg also ordered available units at Mobile and Pollard to start for the city. These latter troops departed on July 22, and Bragg's first units left Tupelo the next day. The Mobile units reached Chattanooga on the twenty-seventh, but the lead units of the Army of the Mississippi did not arrive for several more days.[48] If Mobile had not still been in Confederate hands, the transfer of Bragg's army from Tupelo in time to save Chattanooga would not have been possible, nor could the subsequent Confederate campaign into Kentucky have occurred as it did.[49]

Subsequent troop movements, though on a lesser scale, confirmed the importance of Mobile's rail connections. These transfers did not always go as smoothly as the movement of Bragg's army, however. In December 1862, for example, it took more than three weeks for a nine-thousand-man division to travel from middle Tennessee to Vicksburg. Most of the delays in this case occurred at points other than Mobile. In early 1865 Confederate authorities had to concentrate the remnants of the Army of Tennessee, then in northern Mississippi, with forces opposing Major General William T. Sherman's Union armies in the Carolinas. The initial troop contingents attempted to travel through Demopolis and Selma to Montgomery, but delays and other problems resulted in the rest of the troops being routed through Mobile to Montgomery. Mobile thus became the scene of the "last major troop move by rail in the Southern Confederacy."[50]

Mobile possessed at least one foundry that would provide assistance to the war effort. Skates & Company, also known as the Mobile Foundry, manufactured iron machinery, steam engines, and gin gearings before the war. The company signed contracts to produce cannons but probably cast only two bronze guns. On April 2, 1862, a newspaper reported: "The Government has copper enough in Mobile to make four or five brass cannon, but it cannot for the want of tin, which cannot be had, or at least is very scarce. . . . The foundries at Mobile can make no brass cannon at present. Their whole time is devoted to making more useful articles namely iron cannon and shot and shells and rifling cannon."[51] There is no evidence that any foundry in Mobile cast iron cannons. Skates & Company did cast artillery projectiles and coehorn mortars. The firm also added reinforcing bands and rifling to old heavy artillery pieces shipped to Mobile from other points. In August 1863, the commander at Mobile reported that the foundry "turns out one banded 32-pounder or 42-pounder per week."[52] The banding and rifling made these cannons much more effective when mounted in the city's fortifications.

The Confederate government recognized Mobile's importance to the war effort and felt obliged to protect it from capture by the enemy. The army generals and naval officers selected to command at Mobile and the military department to which the city belonged were to be vital in the city's protection and its integration into the overall strategy of coastal defense.

CHAPTER 2

An Array
of Military Commanders

The Confederate government early on assumed an active role in the defense of Mobile. On May 27, 1861, the War Department assigned southern Alabama to Department No. 1, commanded by Major General David E. Twiggs, who had his headquarters in New Orleans.[1] The day before, Lieutenant Colonel Franklin Gardner had assumed command of Fort Gaines following receipt of orders on May 7 to report to Hardee. Gardner inspected his new post and sent a report to Hardee. He endorsed the recommendations and plans for improving Gaines's situation made by Leadbetter in April and believed that as soon as the work was completed and some heavy guns were mounted, the fort would be "in a tolerably fair state for defense." Gardner requested at least two companies to reinforce his small garrison. Hardee forwarded Gardner's report to Montgomery, saying that he had no men to send Gardner and asking that the government order additional companies to Fort Gaines.[2] The government had no regular troops to send to Mobile but did provide supervision and material.

Hardee did not exercise command at Mobile for long. On June 17, 1861, he was ordered to go to Memphis, Tennessee, where he was promoted to brigadier general and assigned to command troops in northern Arkansas. This action did not reflect discredit on Hardee's performance at Mobile but grew out of the government's desire to place a firm hand over a critical border area.[3] Cooper's order to Hardee informed him that Gardner would succeed him at Mobile. Two days later, Colonel Henry Maury telegraphed Cooper questioning Gardner's assignment because he outranked Gardner. Cooper replied by ordering Maury to assume command at Fort Morgan and Gardner to retain his command at Fort Gaines.[4] These orders, though having no great ill effect, and the loss of Hardee did not help Mobile's defensive situation. Maury was described by Russell as "an ingenious and clever officer" but was at best an average commander. Later in the war he was arrested and tried for drunkenness. Evidence indicates that as commander at Fort Morgan, Maury did not exercise responsibility for the rest of the bay defenses as Hardee had before him. Mobile's defenses would lack a unified command for several months.[5]

At this time no one commander had charge of the overall defense at Mobile. The area belonged to Twiggs's Department No. 1, but that general concentrated his attention on New Orleans. On September 3, 1861, Congressman Smith recommended to Secretary Walker that Brigadier General Jones M. Withers, the former mayor of Mobile, be assigned to command the city's defenses. The War Department responded by creating the District of Alabama and assigning Withers as its head.[6] Although he had graduated from West Point and had served in the Creek and Mexican wars, Withers's chief qualification for this command seems to have been his familiarity with the city. News of his assignment reached Mobile before the War Department issued formal orders. Some people in the city expressed dissatisfaction with the assignment, but Mayor Forsyth and others spoke out in favor of Withers, and he seems to have entered his command without major opposition from the citizens.[7]

On October 7, 1861, the War Department realigned the command structure of the Gulf Coast by extending Major General Braxton Bragg's command at Pensacola to include the entire state of Alabama, designating the new entity as the Department of Alabama and West Florida. Bragg announced his assumption of command on the fourteenth and chose to keep his headquarters in Pensacola. He retained Withers as head of the District of Alabama. Withers thought his command was an independent department and wrote to Richmond that he felt "humiliation and mortification" when he learned he had been placed under Bragg's command. Because of "this sudden manifestation of change in estimate of my fitness for the position to which I was then assigned," Withers asked to be relieved of duty.[8] After several visits with Bragg and assurances from Davis that no one questioned his competency, Withers withdrew his request.[9] Because of the proximity of Mobile to Pensacola, this new command situation seemed a logical step in the Confederacy's defensive strategy.

The authorities in Richmond had placed Mobile and the rest of Alabama under Bragg partly to placate him. He had grown tired of the stagnant situation at Pensacola and desired a more active field so he could prove himself as a commander. Bragg wrote to a friend that Davis had promised him command of the Gulf Coast from Pensacola to New Orleans. When Twiggs announced that he would retire, Bragg expected Davis to "show his sincerity and confer this command on me."[10] Instead, the president gave New Orleans and Department No. 1 to Major General Mansfield Lovell, a Northerner who had recently joined the Southern cause. Bragg was naturally upset. In a letter to Governor Thomas O. Moore of Louisiana he complained: "The command at New Orleans was rightly mine. I feel myself degraded by the action of the government." In a series of letters Bragg spoke harshly of Lovell, saying the "eleventh-hour" convert had been "purchased in the open market by the highest bidder."[11] Yet Bragg determined to make the best of the situation and do well in his new command.[12]

Bragg complained soon after the creation of the new department that the officers in charge at Fort Morgan and Fort Gaines, Maury and Gardner, were "very competent, but sadly addicted to drinking, and therefore unsafe for those exposed positions." Hoping to find abler commanders for the forts, he recommended several officers for promotion to brigadier general. Gardner received orders relieving him of duty on November 14. Bragg misjudged the man in this instance. Gardner later became commander of the Confederate garrison at Port Hudson, Louisiana, and performed excellently in defending that position against vastly superior odds in a forty-eight-day siege. To replace him, the War Department promoted William L. Powell to colonel in

the provisional army and ordered him to Mobile. Bragg assigned Powell to overall command of both forts and Grant's Pass.[13]

On December 27, 1861, Secretary of War Judah P. Benjamin wrote
Bragg about a contemplated change of command. It is possible that
Bragg's expressed desire for more active service or the hope of assuag-
ing his feelings about not being given command over New Orleans
and the Gulf Coast prompted the secretary of war's action. Benjamin
stated that he and Davis had been looking for someone to go to the
Trans-Mississippi region and take charge of all Confederate troops in
Missouri and Arkansas. Bragg was their choice, and Benjamin asked
if he would agree to the assignment. While this letter was en route,
Davis received a letter from Mayor R. H. Slough and other prominent
citizens of Mobile asking that he establish Bragg's headquarters in
their city. They feared an attack and stated: "The presence of General
Bragg here would greatly inspire our troops and people, and would
consolidate and bring to perfection our military organization."[14]

Bragg declined the offer. The troops in the Trans-Mississippi area
were largely unorganized and undisciplined and there seemed little
prospect for success there. His argument centered, however, around
his concern for Mobile. A large enemy force had landed on Ship Island, and the people of Mobile had expressed alarm for the safety of
their city. Because of the lack of military resources and troop strength,
Bragg, too, was concerned about the city's safety. His influence with
the people and troops was such that he did not think "any other could
now fill my place to their satisfaction." Benjamin learned of the
enemy landing before he got Bragg's letter and quickly wrote Bragg
telling him to disregard the offered command. He informed Bragg of
the petition from the citizens of Mobile but left to him the choice of
headquarters location. After receiving Bragg's letter turning down the
offer, Benjamin responded, "The people there would have every reason to complain of your withdrawal under such circumstances, and
the dissatisfaction would be such as to produce a very bad state of
feeling as regards their defense."[15]

Bragg issued orders on January 27, 1862, changing the command
structure in his department. He placed Brigadier General Samuel
Jones in charge at Pensacola so that he could move the department

headquarters to Mobile. The troops in and around Mobile were designated the Army of Mobile, with Withers as commander. The army would have responsibility for defense of the Gulf Coast between the Pascagoula and Perdido rivers. Relieving Walker of command of the infantry brigade at Mobile, Bragg ordered him to Montgomery and transferred Brigadier General Adley H. Gladden from Pensacola to take over the brigade. Bragg expected Gladden to correct the demoralization and drunkenness in Walker's brigade through discipline and instruction, areas in which Gladden had demonstrated his competence while at Pensacola. On February 5 Bragg arrived in Mobile and established his headquarters.[16]

The departure of Bragg and Withers in March for active duty in northern Mississippi deprived Mobile of two able generals. Withers served capably as a division commander in the Army of Tennessee until late summer 1863, when failing health forced him out of active duty. His performance in several battles was praised by Bragg and Lieutenant General Leonidas Polk.[17] Although his tenure as commander of the Army of Tennessee proved to be an almost continuous record of failure, Bragg's service at Mobile can hardly be faulted. Bragg had been a hero in the Mexican War and an outstanding artillery officer in the old army. His appointment as a general in the Confederate army had received widespread applause because of his reputation and achievements. Davis demonstrated his confidence in Bragg by assigning him to command at Pensacola, where action might be expected because the Federals held Fort Pickens. Bragg recognized Mobile's strategic significance and pushed the defensive preparations there. He won the respect of his men and the people of the city. Bragg's advocacy of holding Mobile probably caused the War Department to decide not to abandon the city. He remained interested in the city's welfare until the end of the war. His command at Mobile could be criticized only for his underestimation of the importance of entrenchments around the city. He delayed construction of earthworks, but the delay had no adverse effects.[18]

Bragg had no misgivings about turning over to Samuel Jones the command of the Department of Alabama and West Florida. A native of Virginia, Jones graduated from West Point in 1841 and received a commission in the artillery corps. For seven years he served as an instructor at the Military Academy and taught courses in tactics and artillery. Jones's first Confederate service came as chief of artillery to General Pierre Gustave Toutant Beauregard at First Manassas, and his performance brought him a promotion to brigadier general. His experience as an artillery officer undoubtedly led Davis and Benjamin to choose him to go to Bragg in January 1862. That experience impressed Bragg, as did his "high character as an officer." After observing Jones for a short time at Pensacola, Bragg had confidence in his abilities and gave him "the most important command in this army . . . and the one on which the general [Bragg] considers the safety of our cause depends."[19]

The *Mobile Advertiser and Register* declared that Bragg's leaving would probably stir up the "croakers and panic makers" even though there was no cause for alarm.[20] Jones had assumed command shortly after Bragg left, but he kept his headquarters at Pensacola. Perhaps hoping to reassure the people of Mobile, Bragg on March 4 issued an order at Jackson, Tennessee, resuming command of the Department of Alabama and West Florida and adding to his jurisdiction the troops in northern Mississippi and southwestern Tennessee. This order apparently never took force, but Jones and other commanders at Mobile continued to correspond with Bragg and seek his advice or ask for instructions.[21] Further to calm the fears of Mobilians, Jones ordered an experienced unit from Pensacola to man the batteries protecting the upper bay, and he ordered reinforcements to Fort Gaines.[22]

Bragg soon requested that Jones send John B. Villepigue to report to him at Jackson. In complying with Bragg's telegram, Jones felt compelled to go personally to Mobile and assume command there. He ordered Villepigue to Tennessee, and the latter officer turned over command of the Army of Mobile to Colonel Powell at Fort Morgan until Jones could reach the city. Jones arrived on March 14 and almost immediately telegraphed General Samuel Cooper in Richmond asking that Davis declare martial law in and around Mobile. He assured the adjutant general that "the best citizens desire it and have petitioned that it be done."[23] Secretary of War Benjamin informed Jones on March 23 that Davis had approved his request. The next day Jones proclaimed martial law in Mobile and Baldwin counties and that part of Jackson County, Mississippi, east of the Pascagoula River. His order suspended "the jurisdiction of the civil courts . . . so far only as it may conflict with the military requirements of the Government."[24]

The command situation at Mobile remained in flux during late March 1862. On March 24 Bragg instructed Jones to turn over command to Colonel Powell and report to him in Tennessee. When word of this order got out, Governor John G. Shorter and the Mobile Committee of Safety requested Benjamin to allow Jones to remain. Benjamin telegraphed back that Jones would receive orders to remain but sent no instructions to Jones. William M. Dunn, chairman of the Committee of Safety, told Jones of this telegram, and the general determined to stay in Mobile and await official confirmation of Dunn's telegram. After several days with no word from Richmond, Jones decided to join Bragg. He turned over command of the Army of Mobile to Brigadier General Thomas J. Butler, commander of the Ninth Brigade, Alabama Militia. After a day or so with Bragg at Corinth, Jones received orders to return to Mobile. Bragg may have sent him back to be sure a competent officer was in charge of the department. Jones resumed command of the department and the Army of Mobile on April 2, but his position remained unsettled.[25]

More confusion then intruded upon the army's command arrangements. Brigadier General John H. Forney, having received orders nine days earlier to report to the city, arrived in Mobile on April 11, 1862. The War Department intended to replace Jones with Forney so that the former could join the army at Corinth. It seems clear that the government in Richmond hoped Forney's assignment would give him time to recover from a wound and wanted to give Jones a chance to prove himself as a field commander. Forney, however, still suffered from his wound and poor health, and he applied for and received a fifteen-day leave to recuperate. Jones felt compelled to remain in command.[26]

Forney returned to duty from sick leave and assumed command of the Department of Alabama and West Florida on April 28. Jones then reported at Corinth and received command of an infantry division. Forney's main qualification for command at Mobile was his experience at Pensacola early in the war. Governor Moore had appointed him as a special aide with the rank of colonel and sent him to the Florida town in January 1861 to assist in drilling the Alabama troops there.

He later received a commission as colonel of the First Regiment of Artillery, Army of Alabama, and commanded a portion of the troops at Pensacola. When Bragg assumed command there in March, he assigned Forney to duty as acting inspector general and had him superintend the construction of works and the mounting of artillery. In June 1861, Forney left Pensacola to take command of an Alabama infantry regiment on its way north to Virginia. He led his unit at First Manassas and in a skirmish at Dranesville in December, receiving a severe wound in the latter action. Both General Joseph E. Johnston and Brigadier General James E. B. Stuart recommended Forney for promotion because of his bravery in the skirmish. Forney was in Alabama recovering from his wound when he received his promotion and orders to report to Mobile.[27]

In late May and again in late June 1862, the War Department attempted to improve the command situation in the West and to reorganize the departments there. Beauregard at Corinth had requested a clear definition of the boundaries of his Department No. 2. The War Department responded by placing those parts of Mississippi and Alabama north of the thirty-third parallel, east of the Mississippi River, and west of Alabama's eastern boundary in Beauregard's command. After Bragg succeeded Beauregard, Richmond extended the eastern boundary of the department "to the line of railroad from Chattanooga via Atlanta to West Point, on the Chattahoochee River, and thence down the Chattahoochee and Apalachicola Rivers to the Gulf of Mexico." Four days after the War Department issued this last order, the new secretary of war, George W. Randolph, informed Bragg that his department included all of the state of Alabama. Mobile was thus in a new command, and the city's status would soon be clarified.[28]

Bragg assumed command of the extended Department No. 2, also referred to as the Western Department, on July 2, 1862. He reorganized several of the subdivisions of his new department, one of which became the District of the Gulf, consisting of the territory between the thirty-second parallel and the Gulf from the Pearl River to the Apalachicola River. Forney at Mobile commanded the new district.[29] The District of the Gulf remained the territorial command responsible for the defense of Mobile until the end of the war, although for a brief period the War Department upgraded the district to a department.

The district's boundaries changed slightly several times, but the protection of Mobile and Mobile Bay stood as top priority of the generals in charge of the district. As commander of a subdivision of a larger territorial unit, Mobile's general in chief lacked complete control over the troops in his district but could draw supplies freely from other areas in the department. District status connected with the states of Alabama and Mississippi seems to have been best for Mobile because the area surrounding the city could never furnish enough foodstuffs. The War Department would always see that Mobile had a sufficient garrison if it came under attack.

While engaged in shifting troops from Mobile to Chattanooga and from Tupelo to Mobile in July, Bragg planned to change commanders at Mobile. Forney apparently wanted to be relieved so that he could resume duty in the field. It is well-known that Bragg had little confidence in many of the major generals and brigadier generals under his command. Perhaps for that reason, Bragg ordered Samuel Jones, now a major general, to relieve Forney in command of the District of the Gulf. What position Bragg had in mind for Forney is unknown, but he probably would have succeeded to command of Jones's division. Word of this planned change reached Richmond (and possibly Mobile) before Bragg issued the order. Jefferson Davis telegraphed him: "The confidence felt in General Forney, at Mobile, and the knowledge he has acquired as the successor of General Jones, render the propriety of withdrawing him very doubtful. Please reconsider your purpose in that regard." Bragg revoked his order and left Forney in command at Mobile.[30]

Forney's health apparently began to fail in late October 1862. Dr. Josiah C. Nott and former mayor John Forsyth wrote to Bragg expressing concern for Forney and the safety of the city. Forsyth also addressed a letter to Davis. Nott felt that Forney's wound and the weight of his responsibilities had proven too much for him. Forney's personal physician and many of his officers believed that "he is not in condition for such an important command, & ought to be relieved from command until his health is restored." Forsyth intimated that Forney might be suffering mental as well as physical problems. The lack of proper direction from the top had apparently thrown affairs in and around Mobile into a state of near chaos: "The town is full of officers

& soldiers; the rifle guns are rusting in the batteries; 1200 cavalry on both sides of the bay are doing nothing. . . . Every thing is wrong & full of peril." Forsyth concluded: "Mobile is lost if the existing administration lasts until the enemy comes."[31]

Bragg began looking for assistance for Forney after receiving these reports. James E. Slaughter, the senior general serving under Forney, also apparently suffered from some illness and could not provide the support Forney needed. Bragg wrote to Cooper that for a general assigned to duty at Mobile "acquaintance with artillery and engineering is essential."[32] He had hoped to order Brigadier General Johnson K. Duncan, recently exchanged after his capture at Fort Jackson, Louisiana, to Mobile, but Duncan was also ill. In mid-November, Bragg asked for and received the services of Brigadier General William W. Mackall. Mackall had graduated eighth in his class at West Point and entered the artillery corps; he had experience with both artillery and engineering as commander of Island No. 10. At Mobile, he assumed command of the former Army of Mobile, now a division consisting of Slaughter's and Alfred Cumming's brigades.[33] On December 8 Bragg relieved Forney of command of the District of the Gulf, and the latter relinquished temporary command to Mackall on the fourteenth. Forney then began a much-needed leave to recover his health. He had served competently while at Mobile, but his failing physical condition restricted his effectiveness in his last days in command. Perhaps his major contribution to the defense of Mobile was his prosecution of work on the entrenchments around the city.[34]

Jefferson Davis needed a competent officer to replace Forney at Mobile, and he searched for such a man during a trip to the West in December 1862. While Davis visited Bragg's army at Murfreesboro, Tennessee, Hardee suggested Major General Simon B. Buckner, one of his division commanders. The desire to promote Brigadier General Patrick R. Cleburne at least partially motivated Hardee's recommendation. David did select Buckner and directed Bragg to appoint Cleburne as a major general to take over Buckner's division. Bragg issued the pertinent orders on December 14. He probably did not regret seeing Buckner leave the army. The Kentuckian seemed ready to join the growing number of Bragg's subordinates who were critical of his leadership.[35]

Despite Hardee's maneuvering and Bragg's personal feelings toward him, Buckner had excellent qualifications for command of the District of the Gulf. He had graduated from West Point, served bravely in the Mexican War, and taught tactics at the Military Academy. After resigning from the army in 1855, Buckner worked for a while as a construction superintendent. In Confederate service, he had led a division at Fort Donelson, gaining experience with field fortifications and in directing heavy artillery against naval vessels. Later, he participated in the Kentucky campaign and had a reputation as "an excellent organizer."[36] Mobile's new commander assumed his duties on December 23, 1862. A Montgomery newspaper, noting Buckner's arrival, stated: "He is well qualified for the position, and will inspire the utmost confidence in his ability, and military skill." In the next four months, Buckner more than lived up to those expectations.[37]

On April 27, 1863, the War Department ordered Buckner to turn over command of the District of the Gulf to his ranking subordinate and go to Knoxville to take over the Department of East Tennessee. The reason for this order is not clear, but the War Department possibly hoped Buckner would end the confused command situation in East Tennessee and work closely with Bragg in middle Tennessee. Major General Dabney H. Maury, who had just assumed command at Knoxville, received orders to await Buckner and then replace him at Mobile.[38] Buckner had improved the condition of the Mobile defenses and had provided needed stability and direction. Admiral Franklin Buchanan, no doubt expressing the sentiment of many in Mobile, wrote to Richmond asking that Buckner's orders be revoked: "He has the confidence of all here . . . and his absence will cause much regret to the whole community." Others in Mobile accepted the loss of Buckner and asked Secretary of War James Seddon to assign Mackall in his place. They had found him "uniformly courteous, and always attentive to all his duties—and firm and prompt in their discharge."[39]

Governor Shorter made a final appeal on behalf of the citizens of Mobile for Mackall's appointment to replace Buckner. Seddon replied that the authorities in the capital had already chosen Buckner's successor before the receipt of the April 30 letter from the Mobile Committee of Safety or Shorter's telegram and that the decision would not be changed. Slaughter assumed temporary command of the District of the Gulf on May 8, 1863, when Buckner left by rail. The War Department instructed Slaughter to continue the organization of local defense troops while he awaited Maury's arrival. His only other action of consequence as temporary commander seems to have been to issue an order to obstruct the channel at Grant's Pass.[40]

On May 19, 1863, Maury assumed command of the District of the Gulf, a position he would retain until the end of the Civil War.[41] A native of Virginia, Maury graduated from West Point in 1846 and fought in the Mexican War. He began Confederate service as chief of staff to Major General Earl Van Dorn in Arkansas, then was promoted to brigadier general and led a division of the Army of the West at the battles of Iuka and Corinth. His division moved to Snyder's Bluff on the Yazoo River above Vicksburg in late December 1862 and defended that position against attacks by Union gunboats. In April 1863 Davis chose Maury to assume command in East Tennessee, desiring "an efficient officer of rank" for that "important command."[42] There is no evidence indicating why Davis so soon switched Maury and Buckner, but he clearly wanted Maury rather than any senior major general to take over at Mobile. Maury's primary qualification for the command was his experience in supervising heavy artillery against gunboats at Snyder's Bluff, but his record in Arkansas and northern Mississippi had marked him as an able general.[43]

Former Confederate congressman Edmund S. Dargan provided his home as a residence for Maury and his wife when they arrived in Mobile. In later years, Maury remembered his tenure at the city as "altogether an interesting and agreeable command."[44] He had not particularly wanted to go to Mobile and did not understand why the War Department had assigned him there. He had hoped to take over a division in his native Virginia. When he received orders for Mobile, however, Maury welcomed the prospect of leaving Knoxville. He wrote to the secretary of war: "I shall enter upon its duties with more satisfaction than I find here."[45] Maury became very popular with the people of Mobile and the soldiers under his command. As one of his men later recalled: "Our commander was Dabney H. Maury, 'every inch a soldier,' but then there were not many inches of him. The soldiers called him 'puss in boots,' because half of his diminutive person seemed lost in a pair of the immense cavalry boots of the day. He

was a wise and gallant officer."[46] Maury proved a competent, trust-
worthy commander of the District of the Gulf. He pushed the construction of Mobile's defenses and was agreeable when called upon to
send men or supplies to other points of the Confederacy. Maury recognized Mobile's place in the Confederacy's overall war strategy and
acted accordingly.

On June 8, 1863, Mobile's command designation changed again
when the Department of the Gulf, consisting of Mobile and the approaches to the city, was created. Technically the new department
remained under the jurisdiction of General Joseph E. Johnston's Western Department, headquartered in Mississippi. Governor Shorter and
the Mobile Committee of Safety had urged Richmond to make Mobile
an independent command and expressed their displeasure about its
status as a "mere dependency" of Bragg's Army of Tennessee, but
Buckner deserves most of the credit for persuading the War Department to take that step. After his arrival at Knoxville, he sent Seddon
a lengthy letter discussing Mobile's situation and recommending that
the city be separated from Bragg's command. He recounted command
problems that had occurred during his tenure at Mobile and stressed
the connection between the defense of Mobile and Vicksburg.[47]

Davis had created the Confederate department system "as a means
to organize and to administer military forces within every inch of
southern terrain." Each department was responsible for defending a
certain area or location. Davis allowed the department commanders
wide discretion in the defense of their areas, and they exercised virtually complete control over the units under them. This autonomy
was the only way the establishment of the Department of the Gulf
worked in Maury's and Mobile's favor. Davis had hoped that departments would supply their own needs for food and other supplies, but
the territory within the Department of the Gulf could not provide
enough food for Mobile and its army. Both Buckner and Maury had
difficulty obtaining supplies from other department commanders. Finally, the creation of a separate department at Mobile made it harder
to coordinate the city's defense with defense of the states of Alabama
and Mississippi.[48]

A final change in Mobile's command status began to take shape
when on January 28, 1864, the War Department created the Depart-

ment of Alabama, Mississippi, and East Louisiana. Both Maury and Polk, the department commander, assumed that the order did not affect the status of Maury's command. Maury continued to use the title "department" on his reports and returns, and on February 7 Polk issued orders defining the boundaries of the "Department" of the Gulf. The War Department informed Maury that his command was now a district in Polk's department and incorrectly stated: "There is no order constituting such a department [of the Gulf]." Even though the War Department had included Mobile and its environs in several descriptions of Johnston's massive Western Department while he held command, Johnston still referred to the area around Mobile as a department. This uncertain situation was finally resolved on April 6, 1864, when the War Department formally revoked the orders creating the Department of the Gulf and designated Maury's command as the District of the Gulf. This appellation remained in effect until the end of the war.[49] Despite the confusion caused by the War Department's January 28 order, it placed Mobile in its proper context within the strategy for the defense of the western Confederacy.

Early in the war the Confederate navy at Mobile consisted of a few small sailing vessels and launches, each armed with a single cannon. State authorities had seized the revenue cutter *Lewis Cass* and lighthouse tender *Alert* shortly after secession and converted them into gunboats. The navy turned over the *Lewis Cass* to the army in April 1861. The schooner *Alert* with her rifled thirty-two-pounder became the flagship of the Mobile squadron. Lieutenant James D. Johnston took charge of the naval station with the title "Keeper of the Light House." Johnston received his orders from Flag Officer George N. Hollins, the commandant of the station, who kept his headquarters in New Orleans because he also commanded that station and squadron. One army officer later labeled the little Mobile squadron "a most absurd and childish farce" and criticized Johnston and his subordinates, saying "I would not feed [them] for their services."[50] Yet Secretary of the Navy Stephen R. Mallory defended Johnston as "one of the best officers of the old service," and Johnston served capably with the Mobile squadron until he was captured in August 1864.[51]

Controversy between the army and navy at Mobile sprang up in late December 1861 and early January 1862. Early in December Withers had expressed open contempt for the small naval force: "The idea of our caricature gunboats being a protection to the coast trade is to me simply ridiculous. In truth I should look on our Navy Department as an amusing fancy sketch but for the waste of money and corruption for which it is the excuse." Bragg carried on the controversy, reporting to Richmond that Lieutenant Johnston refused to acknowledge Withers's authority. Shortly thereafter, Federal blockade vessels forced ashore a blockade runner and tried to capture her by sending in sailors on small boats. Fort Morgan's guns opened fire on the enemy boats, driving them off, and an unarmed Confederate steamer finally braved enemy fire to help the runner into the bay. Bragg was angry because the gunboat *Florida* had remained at Mobile "unoccupied and independent" and the gunboat *Alert* had been "lying in the harbor here utterly useless." [52]

In Richmond, Secretary Benjamin took Bragg's complaints to Davis, who agreed that there should be more harmony between the services. Benjamin recognized that he confronted a delicate problem of authority and advised Bragg that he would talk over the matter with Secretary of the Navy Mallory. When Benjamin referred Bragg's letter to Mallory, he suggested that it might be good policy to make small craft in coastal waters subject to the orders of the appropriate department commander. Then he made a telling observation: "As you cannot have chosen your best officers for *such unimportant commands*, I think it not improbable that there is ground for the complaints." Mallory answered Bragg's charges by saying that the *Florida* was in Mobile refitting after her recent engagement with enemy vessels and thus too far away to have lent aid and that the *Alert* was only a small schooner with one gun. He had confidence in Johnston and promised that the navy would cooperate in the future. [53] This controversy reveals a weakness in the Confederacy's system of coast defense which later contributed to the fall of New Orleans.

Captain Victor M. Randolph assumed command of the naval squadron at Mobile in February 1862, probably because of the controversy involving Lieutenant Johnston. Randolph's arrival probably also marked the establishment of a squadron independent of the flag officer in New Orleans. Early in the war Randolph had had charge of the Pensacola Navy Yard, and most recently he had commanded naval batteries on the York River in Virginia. Shortly after his arrival, two new gunboats joined Randolph's squadron: the wooden side-wheel steamers *Morgan* and *Gaines.* Johnston had helped initiate contracts for their construction at Otis's shipyard in the city. The vessels were launched in mid-February and received their machinery and armament later in the month. Each gunboat carried ten guns, but they had practically no armor except some iron plating to protect their engines. Randolph made the *Morgan* his flagship, and his entire squadron made a public procession on March 8.[54]

Mobile's naval squadron got a new commander in September 1862. Secretary of the Navy Mallory had relieved Flag Officer Randolph of command in August. Mallory expected Randolph's replacement, Admiral Franklin Buchanan, to be more active and aggressive than Randolph had been. The officers and men of the squadron welcomed the change, one officer calling Buchanan "a *man* and a *Commander.*"[55] Buchanan had been promoted to admiral on August 21, making him the ranking officer of the Confederate navy. A veteran of the Mexican War, he had served as first superintendent of the United States Naval Academy and commander of the Washington Navy Yard. In March 1862 he took the ironclad *Virginia* into Hampton Roads, Virginia, and destroyed two Federal frigates. A wound kept him out of the famous confrontation between the *Virginia* and the *Monitor.* Buchanan was the right man for the position, an "officer who embodied the daring, dash, and discipline of the old navy along with the professionalism of the new."[56] At Mobile Buchanan won the respect not only of his command but of the army officers as well. His good relations with the army command "fostered a spirit of cooperation between the services that was lacking in other areas [of the Confederacy]."[57]

Under Buchanan the Mobile squadron began more properly to fit into the Confederacy's coastal defense strategy. William N. Still, Jr., has corrected old assumptions by historians on the real objective of the Confederate navy. Rather than a force intended to destroy the Union blockade, the navy had as its primary goal the defense of the South's major rivers and harbors. The Confederates built their first five ironclads with the idea of breaking the blockade, but this strategy changed in 1862: "The first *Virginia*'s performance in Hampton Roads and the *Arkansas*'s success against Union naval forces on the Mississippi . . . resulted in the Confederate government's decision to concentrate on ironclad construction for river and harbor defense."[58] Historians have credited Secretary Mallory with this change in thinking, "which, of course, fitted in well with Jefferson Davis's overall strategy of defense."[59] The presence of even a weak ironclad such as the *Baltic* helped delay or prevent Union attacks. Buchanan kept his gunboats in the lower bay to help guard entrances to the bay and pushed the completion of ironclads under construction to strengthen his defensive capabilities.

The strategy of coastal defense at Mobile, as elsewhere, was essentially passive. Union army and naval forces would act as the aggressors along the Gulf Coast. Their strategic plans and tactical actions relative to Mobile would dictate Confederate responses.

CHAPTER 3

Failed Federal Hopes
of Attacking Mobile

Mobile and other Gulf Coast ports figured only indirectly in the North's early war strategy. President Abraham Lincoln adopted the famous Anaconda Plan of Lieutenant General Winfield Scott, which called for a tight naval blockade of the Southern coast while a combined land and naval force moved down the Mississippi River toward New Orleans. The conquest of the great river along with the cessation of foreign trade would, the Federals hoped, bring the war to a successful conclusion without a large expenditure of lives. Mobile, New Orleans, and Pensacola were the only three Gulf ports "which possessed rail or water connections with the interior [that] needed to be closed."[1] No one in the Union high command gave any thought to attacking any point on the Gulf Coast.

A board appointed by Secretary of the Navy Gideon Welles recommended against a campaign from the Gulf toward New Orleans, the South's most important city. Leading naval minds feared that wooden ships could not succeed in a battle with masonry forts like those that protected the lower Mississippi River and Mobile Bay. Eventually, political pressure and military victories caused the Federals to make plans for a movement up the Mississippi. The campaign down that river had gone nowhere by the fall of 1861, while midwestern farmers waited impatiently to get their crops to markets overseas. In August and November of that year, Union naval vessels bombarded and captured two Atlantic coast ports, proving that steam-powered ships could pass forts. Assistant Secretary of the Navy Gustavus V. Fox advanced a plan for attacking New Orleans, and Lincoln agreed to commit forces to the campaign. He had "begun to mature the notion of simultaneous advances," and the New Orleans proposal fit well into his strategic thinking.[2]

On December 3, 1861, Federal troops landed on Ship Island, located in Mississippi Sound about twelves miles off the coast of Mississippi. Confederate soldiers had evacuated the island in mid-September, and the Federal blockading fleet had taken possession of it. Occupation of the strategically located island by Union forces gave them an important anchorage and refueling station as well as a base from which to attack either New Orleans or Mobile. Flag Officer David G. Farragut received command of the West Gulf Blockading Squadron to lead the attack. Only after capturing the Crescent City would he try to take Mobile. Major General Benjamin F. Butler was ordered to occupy Ship Island with men from his command near Fortress Monroe, Virginia. Later the War Department would name him to command the land forces that would cooperate with Farragut, first against New Orleans and then against Mobile. The nineteen hundred men who went ashore on Ship Island on December 3 were the first of around thirteen thousand troops who would eventually serve under Butler on the Gulf Coast.[3]

The Federal campaign against New Orleans began in earnest on April 18, 1862. Through March and early April Farragut's vessels had begun entering the mouth of the Mississippi River. On April 18, his mortar flotilla began a bombardment of Forts Jackson and St. Philip, the masonry forts seventy-five miles below the Crescent City. Farragut hoped to silence the guns in the forts and open the way for his steam sloops to sail past them and up to New Orleans. A week's bombardment failed to achieve the desired result, so Farragut decided to run his squadron of gunboats past the forts at night hoping to minimize damage and casualties. At about one o'clock on the morning of April 24, the Federal vessels started upriver. After a brief engagement, the gunboats got past the forts and destroyed the small Confederate river defense fleet. Farragut's squadron proceeded to New Orleans, which its mayor surrendered to him the next day. Cut off from supplies and reinforcements and faced with a mutiny by most of the men in the garrisons, the commander of Forts Jackson and St. Philip surrendered on April 28. Butler's Federal troops occupied New Orelans on May 1. The Union forces had won a major victory early in the war with surprising ease.[4]

Once the Crescent City had fallen, Farragut began almost immediately to make plans to attack Fort Morgan, but before he could commit his gunboats to a bombardment of Fort Morgan, news from upriver caused him to change his plans. There were strong Confederate naval forces at Memphis, and an ironclad was being constructed near that town. Farragut realized that the Union gunboats moving down the Mississippi might need his assistance. He also hoped to prevent completion of the Confederate ironclad. Accordingly, he ordered his sloops northward. Farragut informed Secretary of the Navy Welles of his decision and concluded, "I will not have a sufficient force to attack Mobile until more gunboats arrive." Welles responded that Lincoln wanted Farragut to concentrate on opening the Mississippi River and to delay other naval operations until that objective was achieved.[5]

Although Farragut committed his sloops to the Mississippi River campaign, he had already sent Commander David D. Porter's squadron of mortar boats and gunboats toward Mobile. Porter hoped to find positions at which to station his mortar vessels and to place buoys in the channel to guide Farragut's gunboats when they made their attack. During these preparations, one of Porter's gunboats ran aground near Fort Morgan, and the Confederate gunners fired about ten rounds at her. The gunboat's commander succeeded in getting her afloat again without damage. Bad weather forced Porter to call off his operations, and subsequent events prevented him from returning to Mobile Bay. Porter's operation did have a positive result in one respect: the Confederates evacuated Pensacola.[6]

The failure of Union naval forces to capture Vicksburg in the spring and early summer of 1862 caused Farragut to reconsider an attack on Mobile Bay. His squadron, reinforced by ironclads that came downriver from Memphis, bombarded the Confederate stronghold for several weeks in June and July but could not force the defenders to retreat or surrender. Frustrated in his campaign and fearful that his vessels might be stranded by the falling water level in the Mississippi River, Farragut began looking toward the Gulf. On July 8, he wrote to Welles that he planned to send Porter's mortar schooners to begin operations against Forts Morgan and Gaines. The admiral went on, "I will follow as soon as possible with the vessels of my command." Since the army could not cooperate in an attack on Vicksburg, the Union high command approved Farragut's withdrawal to the coast. Welles informed Farragut of this and stated, "Nothing is to be gained by a contest with the batteries of the enemy."[7]

Farragut's squadron and the small infantry force supporting it left the Vicksburg area on July 24. The Union gunboats dropped the soldiers off at Baton Rouge and reached New Orleans on the twenty-eighth. Farragut spent several weeks at the Crescent City and then informed Welles that he was going to Pensacola and then to stand off Mobile Bay to plan his attack on the forts. By this time, however, the authorities in Washington had changed their minds on strategy in the Southwest. Welles wrote to Farragut on August 19 telling him that operations on the Mississippi River were more important than any elsewhere in the theater. The secretary ordered the admiral not to concentrate his gunboats at Mobile Bay and to "defer for the present any intention you may have entertained" for bombarding the forts. Farragut could keep a sufficient number of ships at Mobile "to repel any attacks from the enemy's vessels in that quarter and to maintain an efficient and stringent blockade." Fox reinforced these instructions in a letter to Farragut on September 9: "We only expect a blockade [at Mobile Bay] now and the preservation of New Orleans."[8]

Though ordered not to attack Mobile, Farragut did not abandon completely the idea of going after Fort Morgan and Fort Gaines. In late September, he had asked the Navy Department to send him two more gunboats because he thought he could capture the forts with cooperation from the army. Later, he requested troops from General Butler in New Orleans for an attack on Fort Gaines. The general had sent most of his available force on an expedition into south Louisiana west of the Mississippi River and could not send Farragut any assistance until that campaign was ended. In the meantime, Butler tried to persuade Farragut not to attack Fort Gaines but instead to send his squadron against Port Hudson, Louisiana, where the Confederates had begun erecting river batteries in August. Farragut eventually realized that he would receive no troops from Butler. He chafed at his inactivity and, in a letter to a friend on November 30, expressed his desire to attack Mobile despite the risk to his gunboats. Several days later, he wrote this same friend, "Would that I was not hampered by this wish of theirs [the Union high command] that I should not risk the ships."[9]

Farragut would not get a chance to risk his ships against the Mobile defenses for some time. On December 14, Major General Nathaniel P. Banks arrived in New Orleans and relieved Butler of command of the Department of the Gulf. Banks had originally been ordered to form an expedition aimed at invading Texas. Political pressure from the Northwest caused Lincoln to abandon that plan in favor of a new campaign up the Mississippi River. Major General Henry W. Halleck informed Banks: "The President regards the opening of the Mississippi River as the first and most important of all our military and naval operations, and it is hoped that you will not lose a moment in accomplishing it." The general brought with him orders from the Navy Department for Farragut to employ his squadron in cooperation with Banks's land forces. The admiral eagerly looked forward to an active campaign against the Port Hudson defenses. Mobile's defenses would be safe from a threat until Union forces had conquered the Mississippi River.[10]

In the summer of 1863, the Federal campaign to open the Mississippi River finally climaxed. After a march southward through northeastern Louisiana, an army under Major General Ulysses S. Grant crossed the river below Vicksburg on April 29. Grant's men marched northeastward toward Jackson, then turned west and by May 18 had surrounded John C. Pemberton's Confederate army in the trenches around Vicksburg. Banks's Union army in Louisiana began a siege of Port Hudson, which was defended by a small force under Major General Franklin Gardner, five days later on May 23. Both Union armies attempted two assaults on the Confederate earthworks, but the defenders defeated each attack, causing heavy losses. Grant and Banks then resorted to regular siege operations, which eventually starved out both Confederate garrisons. Pemberton surrendered to Grant on July 4, and Gardner surrendered to Banks on July 9. Thus the Union command had succeeded in dividing the Confederacy and gaining control of the Mississippi River.[11]

Union authorities again gave thought to an attack on Mobile. Sherman, after capturing Jackson, Mississippi, following the fall of Vicksburg, suggested to Grant that an attack be made on Mobile from New Orleans. When Mobile fell, he wanted to conduct operations against Selma. Banks in Louisiana also urged a move to capture Mobile: "The capture of Mobile is of importance second only in the history of the war to the opening of the Mississippi. . . . Mobile is the last stronghold in the West and Southwest. No pains should be spared to effect its reduction." Perhaps prodded by these missives, Grant telegraphed Halleck in Washington, suggesting an attack on Mobile from the vicinity of New Orleans. But the Union high command had other objectives in mind. Halleck informed Grant that the remaining Confederate armies in Mississippi, Arkansas, and western Louisiana should be broken up first. When these missions had been accomplished, the Union command would have enough men to go against either Mobile or Texas.[12]

Banks continued to press Washington about an attack on Mobile. He felt that the capture of the city and the occupation of much of Texas would practically end the war in the Southwest. Halleck told Banks that Texas was a more important objective. Lincoln had urged Halleck to send a force to eastern Texas. Still Banks persisted. In several letters he pointed out that his intelligence reported that Mobile was weak and not likely to receive reinforcements. He suggested that Grant send troops from his army and that the attack start from Portersville on Mississippi Sound. Banks anticipated a campaign of only thirty days and stated that Grant concurred in the operation. Diplomatic considerations arising from the French takeover in Mexico were uppermost in the minds of the Union high command, however. Halleck instructed Banks to forget Mobile for the time being and move immediately against some point on the Texas coast. Banks began making plans in accordance with Halleck's orders.[13] Again, more important Union objectives saved Mobile from an attack.

The Union high command had committed a serious blunder in failing to listen to the suggestions for a Mobile campaign. A recent study of Northern strategy stated that the "complacency" shown at this time by Lincoln and Halleck "proved a factor in the southern success in the Chickamauga campaign" and called their preoccupation with the Trans-Mississippi theater a "serious mistake." When the Union Army of the Cumberland threatened to outflank Chattanooga in late August 1863, Bragg frantically sought reinforcements from Virginia and Mississippi. Joe Johnston sent nine thousand men (almost half of his effective strength) from his army in eastern Mississippi to assist Bragg. If Banks's troops had moved against Mobile instead of Texas, Johnston would have had to have gone to Mobile's defense instead of reinforcing the Army of Tennessee. Without Johnston's men, Bragg could not have attacked the Union army at Chickamauga and defeated it. A strong force might have captured Mobile and moved up the Alabama River against the railroads, supply depots, and industries in the center of the state. Eventually, the Union force might have marched toward Atlanta to meet the Army of the Cumberland as it pushed Bragg (or his successor) back toward that city. The war might have come to a quicker conclusion if Lincoln and Halleck had approved the recommendations of Grant, Sherman, and Banks.[14]

Mobile figured only indirectly in Union plans for the early months of 1864. Throughout the fall of 1863, Grant continued to desire a movement against the city and into the interior of Alabama. He wanted Sherman to lead the attack and hoped that the campaign would result in the destruction of the rail lines and industries around Montgomery and Selma. At one point, he even hoped that Sherman's force could march toward Atlanta and connect with Major General William S. Rosecrans's army moving from Chattanooga through northern Georgia. But by January 1864 Grant had given up any hope of a winter campaign against Mobile. He had had to send men to eastern and western Tennessee to meet enemy threats, and large numbers of soldiers had gone home on reenlistment furloughs. Banks's army in Louisiana could not attack Mobile because Halleck had ordered him to prepare for an expedition up the Red River in Louisiana toward Shreveport. A raid by Sherman's army from Vicksburg to Meridian would be the only winter campaign in Mississippi and Alabama.[15]

Sherman's raid had as its objective the destruction of the railroad between Jackson and Meridian and of the lines leading north, south, and east from the latter town. A force of seven thousand cavalrymen under Brigadier General W. Sooy Smith would ride from Memphis through northern Mississippi and join Sherman's twenty-one-thousand man army at Meridian about February 10. Sherman anticipated that when he reached that place the Confederates would expect him to turn south against Mobile. He did not think he had enough men to attempt an attack on the Gulf city, however, and so would not go beyond Meridian. In fact, Sherman planned to return to Vicksburg by March 1 so that he could send ten thousand men to cooperate with Banks on the Red River. He thought the latter campaign would last only a month and "would be the death blow to our enemies of the Southwest."[16] The destruction of both Meridian and Shreveport would then free troops for a spring attack on Mobile.

When Ulysses S. Grant became lieutenant general and commander of all Union armies, he began planning for the spring 1864 campaign. Those plans included multiple raids into the South by the major Federal armies. Grant hoped to destroy the South's ability to sustain the war; his armies would wage a war of exhaustion. He intended that an assault on Mobile would take place in late April or early May to coincide with his own campaign to capture Richmond and with a movement through northern Georgia against Atlanta by several armies under Sherman's command. Banks's Department of the Gulf army would conduct the attack against Mobile. But Banks's men were committed to a raid up the Red River in Louisiana, which began in mid-March. Grant had ordered ten thousand of Sherman's men to assist Banks but wanted them returned to Sherman in time for the campaign against Atlanta. Grant's plan called for Banks to collect twenty-five thousand men from Louisiana, Arkansas, and Texas, which would be augmented by five thousand troops from Missouri. This army would threaten Mobile, preventing Polk from sending reinforcements to Joe Johnston from Mississippi or Alabama. Grant hoped that after the Mobile attack, Banks's army would move via Selma and Montgomery toward Atlanta. If successful, the campaign through Alabama would constitute a severe blow to the Southern war effort in the West, open up a secure supply line to Sherman, and again sever the Confederacy.[17]

Fortunately for Maury at Mobile, and probably for the entire Confederacy, this critical feature of Grant's plan never materialized. The Red River campaign got off to a late start. Banks committed blunders that led to the rout of his army in the Battle of Mansfield and to a strategic defeat in the Battle of Pleasant Hill. Shaken by these events and cognizant of Grant's orders to return the ten thousand men to Sherman by late April, Banks ordered a retreat toward the Mississippi River. Falling water levels in Red River forced a delay of several weeks while the Federals tried to extricate a fleet of ironclads trapped behind rapids in the river. By the time Banks's exhausted soldiers reached the Mississippi River, they were unable to comply with Grant's wishes. Since Sherman's men did not join him at Chattanooga, he had fewer soldiers to take against Johnston. The absence of a threat to Mobile allowed Polk to go to Johnston's aid with fourteen thousand men. These troops reached Resaca, Georgia, in time to cover the Army of Tennessee's retreat from that town. Sherman's drive toward Atlanta was thus slowed and the war prolonged for at least several months.[18]

Once the Red River campaign had ended in late May, Grant and Sherman again requested an expedition against Mobile. Sherman wanted only a feint to draw Confederate troops away from Georgia, but Grant still hoped the city might be captured so that Federal forces could use it as a base from which to supply Sherman's armies after they got deep into Georgia. Major General Edward R. S. Canby, who had superseded Banks as Union commander in the Gulf region, began making preparations and intended to send Brigadier General Andrew J. Smith's troops to make the attack. Canby had to abandon this plan when Major General Nathan Bedford Forrest defeated a Union force at Brice's Crossroads, Mississippi, and Smith's men moved to Memphis to help fight Forrest. Canby suspended subsequent plans when Grant ordered two divisions from Canby's army to protect Washington from a threat by Confederate Major General Jubal Early's army. This second delay meant that the Federals could make no move against Mobile until sometime in July at the very earliest.[19]

Throughout the war, intelligence reports reaching Union army and navy commanders along the Gulf Coast had kept them apprised of the condition of Mobile's defenses. They realized that the Confederates not only were strengthening the masonry forts at the mouth of Mobile Bay but were constructing impressive field fortifications around the city itself and at points on the upper bay. The Federals knew also of the Confederate efforts to establish and maintain a strong naval force at Mobile, particularly several ironclad vessels. All of these factors affected Union strategy.

CHAPTER 4

Strengthening Mobile's Defenses, 1862

Major Leadbetter reported on August 4 to Congressman Robert H. Smith about the status of Mobile's defenses and made recommendations for improving them. Fort Morgan, garrisoned by ten companies of the Second Alabama, seemed to be in good shape. Approximately seventy cannon were mounted in the fort, but few of them were heavy guns. Leadbetter did not think the fort would survive a regular siege. Fort Gaines remained weak. The garrison consisted of five companies of state artillerymen, but they had only ten serviceable guns, all thirty-two-pounders. Many more guns would have to be mounted before the fort would be in acceptable shape. One company of state artillerymen manned the three thirty-two-pounders that guarded Grant's Pass. Here, too, heavier guns were needed. No defenses existed to prevent an enemy force from landing on Mississippi Sound and marching into Mobile.[1]

Most of Leadbetter's recommendations dealt with the works guarding the bay entrances. To protect Fort Morgan from approach by land, he suggested extensive earthworks on the peninsula east of the fort to prevent long-range cannon fire from reaching the fort. Even at this early stage of the war Leadbetter anticipated that the United States would use ironclad steamers against the forts. He recommended a heavy chain supported by rafts as a means of blocking the main ship channel near Fort Morgan. For the channel near Fort Gaines, he felt that obstructions consisting of cribs of logs or timbers filled with stones, bricks, and other debris would suffice. Delayed by these obstacles, enemy ironclads could be destroyed or crippled by the fire of columbiads in the forts. Leadbetter suggested the construction of fourteen batteries connected by rifle pits in a semicircular line around the city to protect Mobile's land approaches. To cover the water approaches to the city, he favored strong batteries at Choctaw Point and the mouth of Spanish River. The cost of these defensive works would be tremendous, but Leadbetter concluded: "We must, if necessary, spend our all in this business, certainly hundreds of millions, and I know of no point more worthy the application of a half of one million than Mobile Bay."[2]

Congressman Smith passed Leadbetter's report on to the War Department, where it received immediate attention. Secretary Walker ordered sixteen ten-inch columbiads sent to Mobile as soon as the Ordnance Bureau could have them ready. He also wrote to Governor Henry T. Clark of North Carolina requesting that he send thirty thirty-two-pounder guns to Mobile. Walker authorized the rifling of the thirty-two-pounder smoothbores already at Mobile and their placement in the best positions to repel an attack. He asked Leadbetter to prepare cost estimates for each defensive site at Mobile. Finally, Walker wrote to Governor Moore and asked him to accept for active duty six companies of state troops which would go to Fort Gaines and strengthen its garrison.[3]

About this time Leadbetter received orders to go to Richmond to assume command of the Confederate Engineer Bureau. The War Department ordered Captain Samuel H. Lockett to Mobile to succeed Leadbetter as engineer officer.[4] Leadbetter addressed a long letter to Lockett detailing his recommendations for the Mobile defenses and making suggestions for possible action. Leadbetter also elaborated on his ideas for defensive works surrounding Mobile. He thought the line should be located approximately two and one-fourth miles out from the courthouse, which stood near the riverfront. The redoubts would be placed about one mile apart and would mount heavy guns. Redans

with smaller guns would be built between the redoubts. Entrenchments suitable for field guns and infantry weapons would connect the
line. Leadbetter expressed some doubt about his ideas for obstructions
in the ship channels and asked for Lockett's thoughts. In closing,
Leadbetter estimated that the proposed defenses would cost about
$500,000.[5]

Mobile's civic authorities recognized the deficiencies in the city's
defenses and expressed willingness to spend the money in the city
treasury to remedy the weaknesses. They proposed a voluntary tax to
raise $50,000 "for the purpose of placing the city in a posture of de-
fense." The proposal met so much opposition from the people that it
was dropped before it could come to a vote. The *Advertiser and Register*
ran an editorial entitled "Look to Our Homes" to call attention to the
city's weak defenses. This editorial emphasized the need for large, long-
range guns, which would be expensive. Richmond and Montgomery
could not furnish the necessary artillery so Mobile might have to purchase some guns itself. The paper warned: "The time may soon come
when those who smothered this appeal to the patriotism of the citizens
of Mobile will discover that they have been 'penny wise and pound
foolish' in mounting that favorite hobby of demagogues—resistance
to taxation." The following day, the *Advertiser and Register* renewed
the appeal to the people to put up $50,000 for "Home Defence," but
there is no evidence of a favorable response.[6]

Much of the correspondence between Mobile and Richmond during
the next month or so dealt with the defense of the city and attempts
to obtain and mount the artillery necessary to strengthen the forts and
batteries guarding the water approaches. Leadbetter frequently mentioned the thirty guns requisitioned from the governor of North Carolina, which he expected to be forthcoming. Governor Clark, however, had advised Richmond that he had no spare guns but that the
navy yard at Norfolk had some. Efforts by the Mobile authorities to
secure guns from that source failed. By early October, Leadbetter finally admitted defeat in a letter to Lockett: "From present appearances
I would not recommend you to rely on getting any more heavy guns
or carriages from this quarter. The demands from all directions are
urgent, and the Secretary says he cannot give what he has not got."[7]
The acute need for cannon at Fort Gaines is reflected in a report by

one of the units stationed there: "The company has two 6 pounder
Field Pieces one a U.S. Brass Gun patent 1845, the other an Iron 4
pounder Gun boared [sic] to a 6 Pounder captured from the British at
Fort Boyer [sic] in 1814 and made in 1777."[8]

Toward the end of September, the Confederates began constructing
the earthworks around Mobile which Leadbetter had proposed. The
city's Council of Defense issued an appeal to the citizens to furnish
one thousand slaves to help white volunteer workmen and Confederate engineers do the work. Although the owners would receive no
remuneration, the council offered to provide rations for the slaves.
The council asked the slaveowners to provide spades, shovels, and
picks, and whites had to furnish their own tools. Both the owners and
the white volunteers were assured that the laborers would work in
racially separate parties. As the construction got under way, the
Council of Defense again asked any whites "who wish work" to report
to the racetrack at the edge of town, where the laborers were being
organized.[9]

Braxton Bragg devoted much of his attention to Mobile after it
came under his jurisdiction. He sent his engineer officer on an inspection tour when he assumed command and made a visit himself from
October 23 to 27. At Mobile, Bragg found that Withers had halted
construction of the earthworks on the land side of the city. He concurred with Withers's decision and criticized the "grand scheme for
squandering money by digging ditches . . . which would have required
40,000 men to defend them." Bragg felt that more troops should be
ordered to Mobile to back up the essentially untrained and undisciplined forces there. To protect Mobile, Bragg decided to put his force
at Pensacola on the defensive and to concentrate men and material at
Mobile. Perhaps the best summary of Withers's position at Mobile lies
in Bragg's comment that "he has a hurculean [sic] task with most inadequate means."[10]

Bragg found shortcomings in both the troops and subordinate commanders at Mobile. The men suffered from measles, and Bragg felt
that their proximity to the city encouraged a lack of discipline. He
suggested that their camp be moved to a point fifteen or twenty miles
from the city. To improve their diet, he ordered that they receive ten
ounces of bacon or salt pork or sixteen ounces of beef as meat rations

and that "one gill [four fluid ounces] of good Louisiana Molasses will be added to the ration."[11]

In late October 1861, Bragg learned that an enemy expedition had the Gulf as its objective. He began looking around for troops to reinforce Mobile and Pensacola. Brigadier General Leroy P. Walker, who had recently resigned as secretary of war, commanded a new brigade at Huntsville, and Bragg requested that two of his regiments be ordered south. On arriving, the men would receive weapons of sick and wounded soldiers then on the coast. After receiving permission to use some of Walker's brigade, Bragg ordered one regiment to Mobile. He also ordered two armed regiments at Montgomery to Withers. When Bragg ordered a second of Walker's regiments to Mobile, that general wrote to Richmond that he, too, would go to Mobile. Secretary of War Judah P. Benjamin approved Walker's move. Walker reported to Bragg at Pensacola and received formal assignment to Withers's command.[12] In addition to these infantry units, a newly formed artillery company reported to Mobile, where it obtained guns and equipment. The Federal expedition did not go into the Gulf but attacked forts protecting Port Royal Sound, South Carolina.[13]

The Federal occupation of Ship Island in December, a move Confederate authorities had feared since their soldiers had evacuated the island, received attention when Benjamin asked Bragg whether he had taken any measures to prevent an enemy force from landing at Pascagoula and marching to Mobile. Benjamin feared now that the enemy had a foothold on Mississippi Sound he would land and march by night to surprise Mobile. Bragg replied that he had cavalry pickets on the coast where landings might take place. The infantry and light artillery not on duty in the forts were prepared to concentrate quickly to meet any threat. Bragg also expected that reinforcements from Pensacola could reach Mobile in ten hours. The War Department then issued orders transferring the area of Mississippi between Pascagoula and the Alabama state line from Department No. 1 to Bragg's department. Bragg assigned the area to Withers's district.[14]

That same month, the gunboat *Florida* joined the Mobile squadron and soon participated in the first naval engagement near the bay. The *Florida* had served as a packet vessel for the Mobile Mail Line between Mobile and New Orleans before the war. Governor Moore of Alabama requested that her owners turn her over for conversion into a gunboat. When they refused, Moore ordered her seized, and she was taken to Lake Pontchartrain north of New Orleans for the necessary restructuring. Workers cut down her sides and placed iron plating on her deck to protect her boilers. The *Florida* carried different numbers of guns of varying calibers during the war. Her armament in December 1861 probably consisted of four guns—one rifled and three smoothbores—mounted on pivot carriages and exposed on her open deck. The *Florida* had operated briefly with a small squadron on Lake Pontchartrain and in Mississippi Sound before she entered Mobile Bay through Grant's Pass.[15]

Although Bragg had shifted Walker's brigade to Mobile, he found that the unit had morale problems, most of them attributable to its commander. While his men remained in a crowded, unhealthy camp some miles from Mobile, lacking discipline and instruction, Walker lived in the city with his staff and ignored his brigade. Bragg had absolutely no confidence in Walker and thought him unfit for command. He wrote Richmond requesting proper generals for his troops. In response, the War Department ordered Brigadier General Samuel Jones to Pensacola from the Army of the Potomac and nominated Colonel John K. Jackson for promotion to brigadier general for duty at Mobile. Bragg seemed pleased with these moves. He wrote Benjamin that he planned to place Jones in command at Pensacola so that he could spend more time at Mobile himself. Even though Walker outranked Jackson, Bragg promised to employ both men to best advantage. The command at Mobile would soon see several changes in organization and subordinate commanders.[16]

About the time Bragg took over immediate supervision at Mobile, he had slightly more than seven thousand men present for duty. Most of these troops had only recently entered service, and none had faced enemy fire. Some units had only pikes as weapons, and others had no arms at all. Bragg ordered the First Louisiana Regulars from Pensacola, where they had fought in several actions, to Mobile and a raw regiment from Mobile to Pensacola. He also ordered a company of marines from the Florida town to Mobile. He expected these new troops to serve as examples of discipline for the men of the Army of Mobile.[17] Bragg thought he might soon need these experienced troops. He had received reports that a large Federal naval expedition had sailed for the Gulf and feared it might attack Mobile. Bragg admitted in a confidential letter that Fort Morgan and Fort Gaines could not "prevent their entrance of a dark night," and he pushed for the construction of water batteries near the city.[18] Actually, the Federal fleet then assembling at Ship Island under Farragut had New Orleans rather than Mobile as its objective.

Events in Kentucky and Tennessee soon intruded to break the relative calm at Mobile. Following the Confederate defeats at Mill Springs and Fort Henry, the War Department scoured the lower South for troops to reinforce General Albert Sidney Johnston's army. Bragg had to furnish at least four regiments, and he ordered two regiments each from Mobile and Pensacola to Knoxville.[19] These defeats, combined with several reverses along the Atlantic coast, caused the Confederate government to reevaluate its coastal strategy. It abandoned the politically expedient system of defending its entire coastline in an effort to protect private property everywhere and opted for selective defense of essential cities or areas. The War Department chose to keep small garrisons at unthreatened places and to rush reinforcements to them when they came under attack. Bragg's command faced no immediate threat, but the Tennessee line faced imminent disaster.[20]

Bragg took this opportunity to make some suggestions to the authorities in Richmond on the Confederacy's future strategy. His ideas contain perhaps the earliest considerations of the place of Mobile in the overall strategy of the Southern war effort. Bragg thought the Confederates should concentrate all their resources for an attack on the enemy in Kentucky. He advocated abandoning all points on the Gulf except Mobile, New Orleans, and Pensacola. He did not feel that the loss of the abandoned territory would prove significant. From this time on, Bragg continued to support the defense of the city because of the strategic significance of its rail and telegraph links with the eastern and western portions of the Confederacy.[21]

Events in Tennessee again caused a change in the command and troop situation at Mobile. After the fall of Fort Henry, Johnston retreated with his army from Bowling Green, Kentucky. Fort Donelson fell to Union forces on February 16, and once again Johnston's men retreated, evacuating Nashville and moving south toward the Tennessee River to unite with forces commanded by Beauregard. On February 18, 1862, Benjamin instructed Bragg to withdraw his forces from Mobile and Pensacola and "hasten to the defence of the Tennessee [River] line." He advised Bragg to abandon Pensacola but to leave garrisons in the forts in Mobile Bay. Benjamin hoped these garrisons would discourage an attack on Mobile. The Confederate high command did not agree initially with Bragg's advocacy of defending Mobile or his belief in its importance. Benjamin told Bragg "the risk of its capture must be run by us." Bragg did not receive these instructions until February 27. At that time he complied by ordering most of his infantry with Generals Withers and Gladden to Corinth, Mississippi. Colonel John B. Villepigue replaced Withers in command of the Army of Mobile. After arranging to turn over the department to Jones at Pensacola, Bragg left Mobile for Corinth on March 1.[22]

The defenses at Grant's Pass received renewed attention from the Confederate engineers. Lockett had staked out gun positions at Cedar Point to help protect the pass. Villepigue visited Cedar Point and revised Lockett's plan. Henry B. Warren, a civilian engineer with responsibility for erecting the battery, found an infantry company at the point, but the men were ordered to go to Corinth before he could put them to work mounting guns. Warren did get foundations laid for three guns but had to await the arrival of laborers to complete construction of the battery. By April, Warren had finished his task, and a company of the First Alabama Battalion Artillery had occupied the earthwork. Warren also began driving piles into the waters of the pass. He had the piles prepared on Dauphin Island and transported by steamer to the pass. The men assigned to this task drove some 250 piles into the water about a quarter of a mile out from Grant's Island. To protect the pile driver from enemy vessels, the Confederate command stationed a steamer nearby so it could pull the barge to safety if necessary.[23]

The manpower situation confronting Sam Jones in mid-April was not encouraging. In all, only about twenty-four hundred men were present for duty in the Mobile defenses, most of them stationed in Fort Morgan and Fort Gaines. Following the Confederate defeat in the Battle of Shiloh, Jones had sent several units to reinforce Beauregard's army at Corinth and would soon send several more. He felt that the forts at the bay entrances were in fairly good shape, and although he did not think the enemy would attack, Jones warned that if a strong assault were mounted, Mobile would be lost. To help defend the city, Jones requested that Richmond either send weapons to arm several thousand men to be recruited in Alabama or order troops from Corinth to Mobile. He also asked that a general officer be sent to Mobile.[24]

Forney inherited from Jones late that month a poor but apparently not discouraging situation. Mobile's defenses still remained weak. A private in Fort Gaines confided in a letter to his sister that if a large enemy force attacked the bay, "my opinion is we will not be able to hold the fort tho the officers think we can."[25] On assuming command, Forney directed that the engineers place obstructions on the Dog River bar to prevent enemy vessels from approaching the city if they should get into the bay. The engineers left a small passage over the bar for their own naval vessels, but the engineers could quickly close the gap by sinking a wrecked vessel in it. Forney also ordered "that all cotton at or near navigable waters within this Military Command shall be forthwith removed by the owner to some point in the interior of the country near to which no approach can be made by water, or shall be burned."[26] He hoped this action would discourage an enemy attack on Mobile. Any cotton not removed promptly would be burned without compensation to the owner.[27]

Following the fall of New Orleans, Forney feared that the Federals would attack Mobile. He evidently felt that the enemy fleet could pass Fort Morgan and Fort Gaines as it had Fort Jackson and Fort St. Philip on the Mississippi River. Obviously, if this occurred, much more than obstructions over the Dog River bar would be necessary to protect the city from attack. Accordingly, Forney revived the idea of defensive works near Mobile. On April 30 he ordered that entrenchments for light artillery and infantry be constructed to surround the city. The soldiers of the Army of Mobile would furnish the labor, but citizens were welcome to volunteer their services. Forney also instructed his men to strengthen the batteries that covered the Dog River obstructions and to erect other batteries to bear on the obstructions.[28] Cap-

tain Charles F. Liernur, whom Jones had assigned as chief engineer of
the department on April 15, took charge of the construction of these
defensive works and received assistance from other engineer officers.[29]

Others besides Forney were dissatisfied with the defensive posture of
the city. One resident wrote that things were "in a bad state" and that
"many families" had begun moving to the interior of the state.[30] Some
of the military men also expressed apprehension. The troops in Mobile
lacked sufficient arms and ammunition. Forney's exact feelings are difficult to discern, but the opinions of Flag Officer Randolph about the
naval force at Mobile seem clear. He did not expect his "cockleshell
gunboats" to survive an attack on the bay and thought the Confederate military would be forced to defend the rivers above Mobile. One
of Randolph's subordinates wrote home that the flag officer took his
squadron to the city whenever enemy vessels appeared off the bay.[31]
Although he thought of evacuating the city, Forney promised the
people that he would defend it. He asked them to furnish tools and
workers to build the entrenchments and appealed to the citizens to
avoid "all undue excitement" and to preserve "strict order."[32]

Work on the entrenchments began more slowly than Forney had
hoped. Units worked in shifts, one during the day, another at night.
Forney authorized his officers to impress white and black laborers alike
to speed construction. A private in the Alabama Cadet Corps wrote
his mother: "The officers send a squad of men in town and if they see
an idle man on the streets or more than one clerk in a store they order
him to 'Fall in,' and march him down and give him a hoe or shovel
and put him to work."[33] At least one reason for the lack of progress
seems to have been that many of the men laboring on the batteries
would leave work and go into the city. Liernur requested the provost
marshal in Mobile to set up a guard to prevent the men from leaving.
Forney soon issued an order requiring commanding officers to keep
their men at work and away from the city.[34]

To facilitate construction of the works, Liernur decided nearly to
strip the forts at the bay entrances of engineering property and laborers. He sent Captain William R. Neville to bring the "papers, maps,
furniture, building material (not needed for defence and which can be
used by the troops to restore breaches and damages during action),
horses, carts, provisions, tools, cooking utensils &c" to Mobile. Ne-

ville also had orders to transfer all Negro laborers to the city. Apparently some of the cannon and ammunition in the forts were to be moved as well because Forney mentioned them in Neville's instructions.[35] The owners of the Mobile and Ohio Railroad turned over some of their railroad iron to Liernur for use in bombproof shelters in the bay batteries. Again Forney aided Liernur by ordering Captain Junius A. Law's Company D, First Alabama Artillery Battalion, from the battery at Cedar Point to the city defenses.[36]

The government authorities and press of Mobile appreciated the efforts of Forney and Liernur. Recognizing the urgency of the work in progress, the *Advertiser and Register* appealed to the people of the city to provide the needed labor, which the military could not furnish alone. It urged the men to volunteer their services at Liernur's offices in the customhouse. The paper closed its editorial with the words: "The work will not admit of delay, and Gen. Forney will not permit it to drag when there are idle men in town capable of doing service."[37] The City Council passed a series of resolutions commending Forney and asking the populace to become involved in the defense of the city. The town fathers promised to help in every way they could. Their resolutions expressed determination "to stand by the authorities in their efforts to beat back the invading foe, and to hold the city to the last extremity."[38]

The Union navy's appearance at Mobile Bay in early May resulted in the Confederate evacuation of Pensacola. Anticipating the evacuation of the forts and naval yard, Colonel Thomas M. Jones had begun several months before to remove artillery, ammunition, and other property from the town. General Robert E. Lee in Richmond had advised Jones that if the enemy attacked Mobile he should move his forces to that city. When Jones received a telegram from one of Forney's staff officers saying that shots had been fired on Fort Morgan, he began withdrawing from Pensacola. The evacuation was completed on the night of May 9. Governor Shorter had opposed the evacuation ever since he had heard rumors of it two months before but had made preparations to assist with the movement of cannons and ammunition. As a result of his efforts, he succeeded in getting some of the artillery for the Mobile defenses when the Confederate troops withdrew from the Florida town. One historian has concluded: "His overall activities were invaluable to the war effort, and also allowed many private citizens to escape with their personal belongings."[39]

Forney maintained Jones's troops near Pollard, Alabama, as an "army of observation" to protect the railroad between Mobile and Montgomery. He originally assigned Colonel J. R. F. Tatnall of the Twenty-ninth Alabama Infantry to command the troops. Tatnall's men had instructions to remove the railroad iron between Pensacola and Pollard in addition to scouting the countryside. In late May, Forney assigned Jones, by then an acting brigadier general, to command the troops at Pollard.[40] From May 1862 until early 1865, the Confederates stationed troops at Pollard to watch the Union forces in Pensacola and to help protect Mobile from threats in that direction.

The Confederate authorities in Mobile remained concerned about the city's defensive posture. In late May 1862, Liernur was still working feverishly on the line of earthworks surrounding the city. He had only a small number of laborers, however, and appealed to the citizens to volunteer their "Negro Laborers, Cooks, and Waiters, who can be spared, to work on the entrenchments and perfect the works." The names of persons who contributed would be registered with the provost marshal along with the number of laborers furnished. To strengthen the armed forces around the city, Forney urged the men of Mobile and nearby counties to form military companies and arm themselves as best they could. These companies would form themselves into regiments, and once organized they would drill so as to be prepared for service when needed. Forney promised to try to provide ammunition for those who could not supply themselves.[41]

The Confederate command also began to give attention to the defensive situation along the rivers that emptied into Mobile Bay at its northeastern corner. Forney's plans for the area included something new to Mobile: a floating battery. In May 1861, the state authorities had seized the ship *Danube* from her owners. The Confederates later converted her into a floating battery mounting four forty-two-pounder cannon. Forney ordered her stationed at the point where the Blakely and Apalachee rivers diverged so that her guns would command the latter river. He also wanted a battery erected on the western bank of the Blakely River to protect that stream.[42] The Confederates needed defensive works covering these two rivers because if they were left unobstructed, enemy vessels could ascend them and then make their way through the maze of streams at the head of Mobile Bay to approach Mobile from the rear. Eventually the engineers built another earthwork to help prevent such an enemy move. The Confederates usually referred to the defenses in this area as the Apalachee Batteries.

Bragg again expressed his concern for the defense of Mobile when he moved his army through the city in July. Even though he ordered infantrymen from Mobile to reinforce Kirby Smith ahead of the Army of the Mississippi, he planned to leave "a sufficient garrison" at Mobile.[43] Four infantry regiments and a light artillery battery entrained at Mobile and proceeded to Chattanooga. Not only were these regiments closer to Chattanooga than Bragg's units, but they had more men present for duty. Bragg's regiments had suffered casualties at Shiloh and in the skirmishes around Corinth and had lost men to disease at both Corinth and Tupelo. To replace the units from Mobile, Bragg ordered three Alabama and two Louisiana regiments detached from the Army of the Mississippi. He also ordered a light battery from Columbus, Mississippi, to Mobile. The two Louisiana units moved on to duty at Pollard while the Alabama regiments remained at the city, where they could recruit.[44]

By October 1862, the Confederate troops stationed in Fort Morgan had settled into a regular routine of duties. With no signs of an enemy attack, daily life was uneventful. Before breakfast every morning the men drilled by company. They held guard mount at eight o'clock and then dress parade. Activities during the afternoon varied. On Monday, Wednesday, and Friday, the men of the Second Battalion, Twenty-first Alabama Infantry Regiment, went through battalion infantry drill, while the troops of the First Alabama Artillery Battalion drilled at the guns. On Tuesday and Thursday the battalions switched, the artillerymen drilling as infantry and the infantry as artillery. The only duty on Saturday was cleaning, and on Sunday company inspections of kitchens and quarters were held. Only about nine hundred to a thousand men occupied Fort Morgan, and at least some of the officers there thought their position was weak. Lieutenant Colonel Charles S. Stewart wrote to his wife that the fort could not prevent enemy ironclads from running through into the bay. He felt that only in cooperation with the Confederate ironclads under construction at Selma could the fort's garrison achieve any success against an attack.[45]

In mid-October, the Confederates feared that an attack on Mobile was imminent. Scouts near Pensacola sent word to Forney that thousands of Union troops had landed at the Florida town with the intention of undertaking a campaign into southeastern Alabama. Forney quickly sent requests for reinforcements to Richmond and to Lieutenant General John C. Pemberton, commanding in Mississippi. He did not think he had enough men to defend both Mobile and Pollard. Governor Shorter also asked Jefferson Davis to send more men to Mobile, saying, "General Forney is worn down and wants help." Pemberton sent a brigade to Meridian in case the enemy did advance on Mobile. The War Department promised Forney that Brigadier General Leadbetter would be ordered to report to Mobile as chief engineer and that the department would send a brigadier general to command some of Forney's troops. Military activities in other theaters left no troops available for transfer to Mobile unless an actual attack occurred. Davis authorized Forney to enroll for Confederate service all militiamen between the ages of thirty-five and forty. The fear of attack passed quickly, however, and Forney received no troop reinforcements.[46]

About October 20, 1862, Governor Shorter visited Mobile. After this trip he wrote Davis a lengthy letter in which he stressed the importance of Mobile and the problems he found there. First, Forney needed some regular army officers as subordinates. Second, the troops at Mobile were primarily "fresh, undisciplined, and unskilled." Third, and most important, the forces in the District of the Gulf seemed too weak in numbers adequately to protect the territory for which they were responsible. Shorter called Mobile "the only Gulf port of any importance which is left us and one of the most important lines of communication in the Confederacy." He reminded Davis that the fall of Mobile and its railroad connections would result in the isolation of the Trans-Mississippi Department. Shorter felt that no amount of money spent in the defense of the city would be excessive because the Confederacy would not survive long if it fell to the enemy. He advocated drastic action should Mobile face capture: "If Mobile is to fall, I earnestly hope that orders will be given that not one stone be left upon another. Let the enemy find nothing but smoking and smouldering ruins to gloat over."[47]

In replying to Shorter's letter, Davis concurred with the governor on Mobile's importance and the probable consequence of its fall but regretted the Confederacy did not have any spare troops to send there. Davis did not seem to think that Mobile was sufficiently threatened to increase its garrison. Although he said that the War Department was looking for men to send, he suggested that conscripts be used to fill the depleted Alabama units then at Mobile.[48] Davis's comments reflected the Confederacy's policy of coast defense. Forney did receive subordinate brigadier generals, however, when Alfred Cumming, who had already been ordered to Mobile, assumed command of a brigade of four regiments and James E. Slaughter was ordered to Mobile from Jackson, Mississippi. Forney assigned Slaughter to the command of the Army of Mobile, which then consisted of the troops in the city entrenchments and bay batteries, including Cumming's brigade. Forney was promoted to major general.[49]

Some of the people of Mobile did not trust the Confederate military authorities in the city. A few merchants thought that certain officers used their positions to favor individuals in the shipment of supplies on the railroads and riverboats. Other merchants and boat owners were reluctant to bring fuel and food to the city for fear that the military would impress the boats or articles aboard. As a result, trade slowed and prices of items such as firewood and corn rose sharply. Several persons wrote to Davis and the War Department to complain about the state of affairs. Acting Secretary of War James A. Campbell sent a long letter to Forney outlining the complaints he had received. Campbell advised that seizures of private property were justified only in cases of extreme necessity and warned against officers using their influence for personal gain. Before he received Campbell's letter, Forney had published a notice that he and the Confederate authorities did not contemplate the seizure of any boats or supplies, although railroads and steamboats would be expected "to give preference to the transportation of Government stores."[50]

Mayor Slough initiated a possible solution to the problem existing between the military and civilians. In early November 1862 he appointed a Committee of Safety for Mobile. The twenty-five-man group included such leading citizens as Price Williams, Peter Hamilton, Daniel Wheeler, and Dr. G. A. Ketchum. These men were to work with the governor and the Confederate authorities at Mobile to collect information relating to the city's defenses which the civilian populace should know about. The committee also had authority to make plans that would lead to cooperation between the civilians and the military if the enemy threatened the city. In announcing the formation of the committee, Slough reaffirmed that Mobile would be defended. He felt that as mayor he was compelled to let the people know what he expected of them. He pointed to the examples of Vicksburg and Richmond, where the people had cooperated with the armies in turning back enemy attacks. Slough felt sure Mobilians would "help save to the Confederacy one of the most important bases of military operations."[51]

On November 4, 1862, Leadbetter finally arrived in Mobile. He had received orders to go there in mid-October but had been delayed by ill health and still suffered from a cold and jaundice. Despite his sickness, he conducted a ten-day inspection of the defenses in the district. He was not pleased and began looking for means to strengthen the defenses. In a report to the War Department, Leadbetter stated that time was of the essence but that "the means available in anchors and chains for rafts and in iron for general use is extremely limited."[52] Obstructing the various channels near Fort Morgan, Fort Gaines, and the bay batteries became his first priority. He hoped that the obstructions would slow enemy vessels so that they would receive a pounding by artillery fire. Leadbetter also wanted to complete the line of defenses around the city, which remained unfinished and weak.[53]

Leadbetter began working in earnest in late November to upgrade Mobile's defenses. He assigned one of his engineer officers to place obstructions in the entrances to Mobile Bay. This officer began supervising the driving of wooden piles into the sea floor on the twenty-fourth. Although the work was difficult, he reported to Leadbetter that he hoped his crew could put in around fifty piles a day. Another of Leadbetter's subordinates supervised the erection of earthworks on the land (east) side of Fort Morgan and the sodding of the fort's walls.

Leadbetter asked Forney for permission to take up eight miles of the railroad between Pollard and Pensacola so that he could use the iron in the defensive works around Mobile. Forney gave his permission but furnished only a guard to protect the operation. Leadbetter had to provide the necessary laborers and transportation.[54]

Although Leadbetter could see some progress, shortages of men and material remained a problem. Leadbetter had to request more laborers from the state government because previous appeals had not resulted in a sufficient number. Governor Shorter promised to impress slaves and forward them to Mobile as soon as possible. Leadbetter also asked Shorter and the Confederate Engineer Bureau for more spades and shovels, but neither source had any to spare. A shortage of artillery pieces also plagued Leadbetter. The Mobile Committee of Safety wrote to Shorter asking him to use his influence to try to get more cannon from the Confederate authorities in Richmond. Shorter forwarded the letter to the secretary of war, reminding him that similar requests for guns had been made several times in the past. In closing his letter, the governor stated his conviction that if guns arrived they would surely enable the land and naval forces at Mobile to defend the city. The Engineer Bureau did send two heavy guns in response to Shorter's and Leadbetter's requests.[55]

To protect the interior of Alabama from invasion in case Mobile fell, Governor Shorter ordered construction of fortifications along the state's two major rivers. In the fall of 1862, soldiers and slave laborers began erecting earthworks at Choctaw Bluff on the Alabama River and at Oven Bluff on the Tombigbee River. Originally, this work was supervised by Captain Ebenezer Farrand of the Confederate navy, but in early 1863 the Engineer Office at Mobile assumed responsibility for the river batteries. Several engineer officers, including Major Victor von Sheliha and Colonel James W. Robertson, exercised control over construction at the two sites during the months that followed. Most of the work had been completed by the fall of 1863, and heavy guns, including several double-banded Brooke rifled pieces cast at Selma, were mounted in the fortifications. On June 17, 1863, Maury issued orders naming the two works Fort Stonewall at Choctaw Bluff and Fort Sidney Johnston at Oven Bluff. Confederate troops garrisoned the two sites until after the fall of Mobile. On April 15, 1865, Colonel William R. Miles, commander of both points, had his men blow up the magazines, and they then withdrew to Demopolis.[56]

The only events of consequence during Mackall's tenure as head of the District of the Gulf in December involved Grant's Pass. Leadbetter decided to erect a strong earthwork there to protect the vital entrance into the bay. The few guns placed there early in the war had been removed. To guard the pass, Confederate engineers had driven piles in the channel and stationed one or more gunboats there to bar passage by the enemy. Thomas H. Millington, a civilian engineer, took charge of the construction of an earthwork designed to mount at least three guns. He began work on a shell bank in Grant's Pass on December 7. Leadbetter instructed him to transport dirt from Dauphin Island or Mobile Point near Fort Morgan to use in the construction. Millington found it more expedient to use oyster shells and sand from the immediate vicinity, however, and by December 13 the battery was ready for guns to be mounted. The chief of artillery for the District of the Gulf had selected one ten-inch columbiad, one eight-inch columbiad, and one thirty-two-pounder rifled piece as armament for the work. Millington and his engineers worked unmolested until the construction was completed on December 17.[57]

CHAPTER 5

Defense Work Continues, 1863

No extraordinary events occurred in the Mobile defenses between the time Buckner arrived and the end of January 1863. The troops assigned to the various batteries and earthworks drilled several times a day as both infantry and artillery. Their officers expected them to keep their batteries and quarters clean and in good order.[1] The engineers needed more shovels for use in construction of the fortifications, and Buckner appealed to both the quartermaster general and the Engineer Bureau for them. The Engineer Bureau could furnish only about half the number requested. Many of the laborers available to the Confederate engineers had proved unsatisfactory. One officer complained, "The Irishmen sent me by the Bureau is a lazy set and I return them having only permitted them to work but one day."[2] The elements also created problems. For example, high tides and winds eroded away about ten feet of the front parapet of the Pinto Island Battery. The commander of the bay batteries recommended that pilings be erected in front of the battery to act as a breakwater.[3]

The Confederates conducted a minor foray against the Sand Island lighthouse on the last day of January 1863. Sand Island is situated near the main ship channel into Mobile Bay southwest of Fort Morgan, and a lighthouse on the island helped guide vessels into the bay. After the Union navy established the blockade off the bay in May 1861, the blockaders sometimes used the lighthouse to observe the movements of the Confederates within the bay. To deprive the enemy of this observation post, the engineer officer for the lower bay defenses, Lieutenant John W. Glenn, lead a small group of Confederates from Fort Gaines to the island by boat and set fire to five frame buildings near the lighthouse. Lookouts aboard the USS *Pembina* detected Glenn's activity, and the gunboat fired a few shots at the island. The Confederates withdrew after having destroyed only the buildings set afire, but Glenn planned to return to destroy the lighthouse.[4]

Work to improve the battery at Grant's Pass had continued since a skirmish there in December. Captain J. M. Cary's Alabamians replaced the carriage of their eight-inch columbiad to make it more serviceable. When they discovered the magazine leaking and covered with too little dirt, Lieutenant Glenn's engineers made the necessary repairs. To supply the garrison in the event of extended operations, the Confederates constructed a casemated storeroom for foodstuffs and water tanks to hold about thirty-eight hundred gallons. Cary recommended further improvements. He asked for a supply of timber to build a small hospital for his men. To protect them from the weather, he proposed that a building be erected as company quarters. Finally, he requested that the engineers build a wharf on the island to facilitate resupply and reinforcement of the garrison. In time the engineers completed all the construction Cary asked for.[5]

The Confederate engineers also worked on their defenses nearer Mobile as well as at Grant's Pass during January. Buckner had ordered a four-gun battery erected on Choctaw Point Spit because the earthen batteries near Choctaw Point could not effectively cover the main ship channel to the city or the Dog River bar obstructions. When the water covered the spit, the engineers would have to use crib work filled with dirt as the base for the battery. Leadbetter assigned this task to Liernur, whose men began driving piles for the crib work. The Confederates carried out minor improvements at the Pinto Island and Spanish River batteries. The former mounted six guns and covered Choctaw Pass and Spanish River. Spanish River Battery contained eight guns, the heaviest of which bore on the channel of Spanish River. Leadbetter also strengthened the line of obstructions from Choctaw Point to Spanish River. These piles stood in the water in eight rows five to ten feet apart. The openings left at the Spanish River and Choctaw Pass channels would be closed by rafts when necessary.[6]

Leadbetter's engineers also remained busy near the eastern shore of the upper bay. They had already completed Apalachee Battery on the west side of the fork of the Apalachee and Blakely rivers and mounted six guns in it. Leadbetter expressed dissatisfaction with the location and layout of the battery, however. He initiated erection of a four-gun work at the head of Apalachee Island. Here the Confederate artillerymen could cover the two rivers better than they could from the Apalachee Battery. Unfortunately, the engineers had no guns readily available to place in the new battery. Leadbetter planned to put the four forty-two-pounders then in the ironclad battery *Danube* in the work if no other cannon could be found. He did not think the *Danube* was strong enough to withstand heavy enemy fire. In the meantime, he directed that the *Danube* be stationed near Apalachee Battery for use if needed. Several lines of pilings were placed in the channels on each side of the new earthwork to obstruct passage.[7]

The entrenchments around the city occupied much of Leadbetter's attention. Work had ceased on the lines of fortifications begun by Liernur in 1862. By early 1863 that line stretched for nine miles. Buckner had concluded that he would not be able to obtain sufficient troops properly to man such extensive works. He ordered Leadbetter to build a second line of earthworks between Liernur's and Mobile. A shorter line would prove easier to man. Leadbetter planned to begin his work at Choctaw Point and extend the fortifications around to the mouth of One Mile Creek, where a series of earthworks and a swamp would block any enemy advance. In this line Leadbetter hoped to construct square redoubts approximately six hundred yards apart with trenches for infantrymen between each redoubt. In concluding his report of work done on these works, Leadbetter stated: "The line is too near the city to save it from bombardment, but such an attack would prove a lesser evil than the capture of the place. It is hoped that the line can be held until the place shall be relieved."[8]

In late February 1863 the Confederates completed the destruction of the Sand Island lighthouse. Even though the wooden buildings were gone, the men of the blockading squadron continued to land on the island and observe Confederate movements from the lighthouse. Writers in the past have given credit for destroying the lighthouse to Captain N. J. Ludlow, but Lieutenant Glenn actually carried out the mission. He and a small party of men proceeded by boat to Sand Island on the night of February 22. The next morning the Confederates placed a total of seventy pounds of powder at various places in the structure. By three o'clock that afternoon Glenn had completed his work, and he fired the charges. Then he and his men returned to Fort Gaines. In his report, Glenn described the results of his operation: "Nothing remains but a narrow shred [?] about fifty feet high & from one to five feet wide. The first storm we have will blow that down."[9]

During February the Confederate engineers continued to strengthen the Mobile defenses. Fort Morgan and Fort Gaines had required no great endeavor because they seemed practically complete. Leadbetter's men took up the iron rails from the road between Fort Morgan and Navy Cove for a floating battery under construction at Mobile. They laid wooden rails to replace the iron taken up. At Grant's Pass the engineers erected a wharf in accordance with Captain Cary's earlier request. Leadbetter continued work at the Choctaw Point Spit battery but felt the men should suspend construction because he did not think cannon were available to mount there, and he wanted to use the boats employed there to complete the new battery on Apalachee Island. The men had done a good deal of work at the latter battery, but they had to bring in earth by boat because little was available on the low, swampy island. The engineers placed no further piles in the channel near this battery during the month.[10]

Leadbetter's men conducted other engineering operations at the bay batteries and city entrenchments. They had practically completed Pinto Island Battery even though the tide eroded part of the parapet. At Spanish River Battery the engineers reinforced the parapet and expanded the flanks to contain two additional guns. They drove more pilings near these batteries to obstruct the channels. To help reinforce the earthworks, the Confederates moved a floating battery into the area. This battery mounted two ten-inch guns, and railroad iron covered its front. The gunboat Selma fired some of her guns at the battery to test the iron's strength, and although several shells broke on the hard surface, the iron was not damaged.[11] On Leadbetter's new line of entrenchments, the laborers began redoubts on either side of Government Street and worked outward from there. They completed each earthwork to the point that it seemed defensible and then moved on to begin a new work. They would add the finishing touches to the incomplete earthwork later. Leadbetter placed Colonel P. J. Pillans in charge of the construction of the city entrenchments.[12]

Buckner sent his chief of artillery, Major Victor von Sheliha, to Richmond to try to get more heavy artillery pieces for Fort Morgan, Fort Gaines, and Fort Grant. Leadbetter sent with von Sheliha a letter to Colonel Jeremy F. Gilmer, chief of the Engineer Bureau, pointing out Mobile's needs: "The liberality accorded in this behalf to the city of Charleston and the good effect of it, will plead in our favor."[13] In a letter to General Cooper complaining that the Ordnance Bureau had limited him to 175 rounds per gun, Buckner asked for more ammunition for his artillery pieces. Buckner also stated: "The object of the fortifications now in progress is to compel the enemy, should he appear in large force, to besiege this place, and reduce him to the necessity of making regular approaches. The works will be needless unless a proper supply of ammunition is provided. The requisition I send is for not exceeding a half-supply for a siege. It is indispensable to a good defence."[14] Secretary of War Seddon assured Buckner that he would receive enough ammunition to give him 200 rounds per gun. The supply bureaus in Richmond had no more than that at the time, but Seddon said he would keep Buckner in mind when supplies became more plentiful.[15]

During April 1863, Buckner lost several of his generals and many of his troops. Through the last two weeks of March, he received repeated requests from Pemberton in Mississippi to send one or two cavalry regiments to the northern part of that state to aid planters in getting their crops out of the region and to combat enemy raids. Union forces had been conducting numerous operations in the upper Yazoo River delta area looking for a route to approach Vicksburg from the north. Most of Pemberton's army had to remain near that town because of the presence of Grant's army in northeastern Louisiana so only a few units could oppose the delta raids. On March 28, Buckner finally agreed to send the Second Alabama Cavalry to Pemberton even though he did not feel he could spare any troops. The regiment reached Pemberton about April 29 with less than half of its men armed.[16]

President Davis telegraphed Buckner on April 7 asking what troops he could spare for Bragg in middle Tennessee. Reports of reinforcements reaching the Union army that faced Bragg caused the government to fear for the safety of that region. Because Confederate armies in Virginia and Mississippi could not spare troops, the garrisons along the Southern coast not threatened by the enemy had to be stripped of all available men to aid Bragg. Buckner replied that he could send Cumming's brigade of about twenty-two hundred men if Pemberton would reinforce Mobile in case of attack. By April 20 Buckner had sent Cumming's brigade of three regiments, one additional regiment, two infantry battalions, and a battery to Tullahoma—in all, about four thousand men. Buckner thus lost practically all of his infantry except for several regiments serving as heavy artillery.[17] In addition to General Cumming, who accompanied his brigade to Tennessee, Buckner lost General Mackall, who became Bragg's chief of staff. In response to a request for his services by General Edmund Kirby Smith, the War Department ordered General Slaughter to Texas, but it quickly revoked the order rather than deprive Buckner of his last brigadier. Slaughter retained command of the troops in the immediate vicinity of Mobile.[18]

Buckner's last action before departing for Knoxville in May was to issue a call for the citizens to organize themselves for local defense, an appeal that reflected the Confederacy's coastal defense policy. He urged the men to form companies, battalions, and regiments so as to be ready if needed. He turned the organization of the troops over to General Slaughter. After arriving in Knoxville, Buckner reported that his appeal "was responded to in a proper spirit, and with a promise of fair success."[19]

In a letter of May 23, 1863, President Davis reassured Governor Shorter that he was concerned for Mobile and explained the national government's policy on the defense of the area. Davis had recently received letters from Shorter and the citizens of Mobile expressing anxiety about the city's weak condition. He told Shorter that the government intended to protect the city because "any misfortune which should befall it would be deeply felt by the Confederacy." Davis explained that because of the enemy's numerical superiority, the Confederates could not leave large numbers of men in unthreatened coastal garrisons. All available men were needed in important places under attack or actually threatened. If the enemy attacked Mobile, troops would move there from other areas. Davis suggested that both state and city officials organize local defense troops to back up the regulars in the event of a sudden assault.[20]

The Confederate engineers continued work on the Mobile defenses during May 1863, although they had completed many of their tasks already. Little work was needed on the forts guarding the bay entrances. The engineers sodded the embankment at Fort Gaines and completed the wharf at Fort Grant. Leadbetter reported the Choctaw Point, Pinto Island, Spanish River, and Apalachee batteries all complete. He suspended work on the Choctaw Spit battery to put his full effort on the battery on Apalachee Island, which Leadbetter expected to complete in June. Despite a severe shortage of laborers, the Confederate engineers finished construction of most of Leadbetter's line of redoubts around the city. Fourteen redoubts stood ready for occupation, and Leadbetter planned only two more redoubts and several smaller works between some of the redoubts. His men mounted cannon in practically all of the defensive works. The only other work of consequence carried out by the engineers was to place additional obstructions between Fort Morgan and Fort Gaines and near Apalachee and Blakely islands near the eastern shore.[21]

A new weapon in Mobile's defensive arsenal made its appearance during May. Maury, having witnessed the effectiveness of torpedoes (mines) near Vicksburg, ordered that 150 of them be procured for placement in the waters around and in Mobile Bay. At Grant's Pass the engineers put 10 or 12 torpedoes in the channel west of the battery. Others were floated near the Spanish River Battery. Leadbetter informed Admiral Buchanan that he intended to place torpedoes in two locations not usually visited by naval or civilian vessels—the channels of Apalachee and Blakely rivers below Apalachee Island Battery and the area of Garrow's Bend near the city. Leadbetter also warned that he would eventually put the devices in the channel near Fort Morgan extending from the western edge of the channel toward

the fort to obstruct three-fourths of the passage. All vessels moving
through the area would need to sail close to the wharf at the fort.
Leadbetter advised Buchanan: "This will cause little trouble and may
prevent accidents."[22] By war's end, the torpedoes at Mobile had ac-
counted for the sinking of ten enemy vessels.[23]

In the summer of 1863, Admiral Buchanan received new vessels to
augment his small squadron. Two ironclad floating batteries, which re-
sembled ironclad rams, became operational: the *Huntsville* and the
Tuscaloosa. Two ironclad rams—the *Tennessee* and the *Nashville*—
also floated in the waters of the navy yard, where workmen labored to
complete their construction. Work on the floating batteries and the
Tennessee had begun in the fall of 1862 at Selma. Construction of
the side-wheeler *Nashville* had commenced at about the same time at
Montgomery. Buchanan had the *Huntsville*, *Tuscaloosa*, and *Tennessee*, all launched in February 1863, brought to Mobile to receive their
machinery, armament, crews, and iron plating. The *Nashville* reached
the city in June to go through the same process. At Oven Bluff on the
Tombigbee River, construction began on three more ironclads, but by
the summer of 1863 none had yet received their engines.

Buchanan was reluctant to send the two ironclad floating batteries
away from Mobile because their extremely slow speed made it difficult
for either vessel even to stem the tide of the rivers near the city. Each
of the floating batteries carried four heavy guns and could provide
powerful support to the earthwork bay batteries. When completed,
the *Tennessee* and *Nashville* would give the admiral two of the most
powerful ironclads in the Confederacy. Delays in getting the work
done and obtaining cannon, armor plating, and seamen, however,
meant that the two ironclads would not reach completion that summer as Buchanan had hoped. Still he looked forward to the day when
"he would have eight armored war-ships, counting the *Baltic*, to defend the bay."[24]

Maury renamed eight of the fortifications in his department in early
June 1863. All of these batteries received names of Confederate officers who had died in the line of duty. Apalachee Battery became Battery Tracy, named for Brigadier General Edward D. Tracy of Alabama,
who died in the battle of Port Gibson, Mississippi. The battery on
Blakely Island, sometimes referred to as Gindrat Battery, became Bat-

tery Huger, after Lieutenant Commander Thomas B. Huger, killed April 25, 1862, on the CSS *McRae* below New Orleans. Pinto Island Battery had its name changed to Battery Gladden in memory of Brigadier General Adley H. Gladden, who received a mortal wound at Shiloh shortly after leaving Mobile. Maury named one of the floating batteries for Brigadier General Lloyd Tilghman, who died at the battle of Champion Hill, Mississippi. The Light House Battery became Battery McCulloch for Ben McCulloch, killed at Elkhorn Tavern, Arkansas. Spanish River Battery was renamed Battery McIntosh to honor Commander Charles F. McIntosh, who died aboard the CSS *Louisiana* near New Orleans.[25]

News of the fall of Vicksburg impelled Maury to adopt new measures to improve his defenses. He was sure that enemy troops would attack the city now that they had control of almost the entire Mississippi River. In a circular to the citizens of Mobile and surrounding areas, he called upon able-bodied men to form local defense units and the owners of slaves to send laborers to work on the fortifications. Slaughter received the responsibility of organizing, issuing arms to, instructing, and making assignments for the new units formed. To Leadbetter Maury assigned the task of arranging employment for any slaves sent to the city. Leadbetter then took several measures to speed up work on the fortifications. First, he ordered that construction of the city entrenchments be carried on on Sundays as well as other days of the week. Second, under instructions from Maury, Leadbetter closed down construction at Choctaw and Oven bluffs and moved the laborers and tools to Mobile. In addition, Maury revoked the leaves of all officers, ordering them back to their units, and announced that only sick leave would be granted to officers in the near future.[26]

When he learned of the Port Hudson garrison's surrender, Maury became more concerned about a possible attack on Mobile. He realized that there was now little to prevent a Union army from moving against the city. The Federals had completed their campaign to gain control of the Mississippi River. In a letter to the War Department, Maury outlined the condition of his command. The forts at the bay entrances appeared defensible. Fort Morgan and Fort Gaines both had provisions for six months. Seventeen of the proposed nineteen redoubts in the city entrenchments were ready, and the two remaining would be ready soon. Maury anticipated that he would need twenty thousand men, plus appropriate ordnance supplies for his guns, to withstand a siege. But the defensive line was so close to the city that in an attack the city would suffer from enemy fire. Because of the active trade in Mobile and the city's status as a refugee center, Maury estimated that there were some fifteen thousand noncombatants whom he would have to evacuate. In response to Maury's letter, Davis instructed the War Department to push the collection of supplies for Mobile and study the reinforcement of the garrison in the event of an attack. He preferred to postpone removing noncombatants until an assault seemed certain.[27]

Unaware of actual enemy intentions, Maury remained apprehensive about an attack on Mobile, as did Joe Johnston. Both men attempted to get troop reinforcements for the city. Not only was Mobile's garrison relatively weak, but by early August 1863 Maury had only one general officer in his department. After several requests by Kirby Smith for his services in Texas, the War Department ordered Slaughter to the Trans-Mississippi Department. Slaughter left Mobile for Havana, Cuba, aboard a blockade runner and eventually got to Texas on another blockade runner.[29] Maury asked Cooper to return to Mobile the infantry brigade which Buckner had sent to Bragg in April—if Bragg could spare it. The War Department answered that no troops could go to Mobile from Tennessee then or in the foreseeable future. Bragg anticipated the Federals to advance against him at Chattanooga. Johnston wrote to Governor Shorter to request that he send troops to Mobile. Shorter replied that he had no volunteers or militia to send to the city. Few volunteers had responded to President Davis's June call, and the governor reported the militia severely depleted in numbers. There appeared to be no chance of reinforcements for Mobile.[29]

About the middle of August 1863, Maury again anticipated an attack on Mobile. Troop and ship concentrations at Ship Island were reported. He succeeded in pushing the work on his defensive lines because the planters had sent more laborers to the city than earlier in the year. Leadbetter ordered his men to strengthen the walls of Fort Grant and to place a rifled cannon there to improve the fort's firepower. A foundry in Mobile turned out two cannon per week, and

Maury planned to reopen another foundry that had closed. The Confederate command still needed a large amount of ammunition for the guns in the defenses, but Maury had accumulated food supplies sufficient for ten thousand men for four months. In response to Maury's news about a possible attack, Johnston made three of his brigades available if needed. He stationed one brigade at Meridian and the two others at Enterprise—all within easy reach of Mobile via the Mobile and Ohio Railroad.[30]

Though fearful of an attack, Maury remained confident of his ability to defend Mobile. Leadbetter had made good progress in strengthening the walls of the redoubts surrounding the city. Anticipating that the enemy would move by land either from the Pascagoula area or Pensacola, Maury believed that relief forces could cut the enemy's supply lines to either place and help check any attack. The Confederate command still needed long-range cannon at Mobile, and Maury asked Johnston for three twenty-pounder Parrott rifled guns which he had promised to send to the city. Maury did not want to employ one weapon—the land mine—in the defense of Mobile, however. In early August 1863, Brigadier General Gabriel J. Rains, who had designed these antipersonnel devices, had arrived in Mobile to confer with Maury about their possible use. After discussing the matter but accomplishing nothing, Rains proceeded under orders from Richmond to Charleston. Rains's ideas did not impress Maury: "General Rains has gone away with his gim-cracks; he was not at all practical; everything I received from him was vague and visionary."[31]

Despite Maury's expressed confidence, he still needed and attempted to get more troops for his garrison. He asked Johnston to send one of the brigades designated to go to Mobile as soon as possible. He argued that the new situation would prove healthier and more cheerful for the men. Maury did not want any Alabama troops sent to him if men from other states were available. Two of his Alabama regiments on duty at Mobile suffered from desertions, which Maury blamed on the influence of the men's despondent friends and relatives. He expressed particular interest in acquiring men of Louisiana units that had served the artillery batteries at Snyder's Bluff and Vicksburg. Many of these men had served under Maury at the former place, and he knew how good they were. As soon as the authorities declared these men exchanged, Maury wished them ordered to him: "The year of alertness and frequent practice at Vicksburg made them very dexterous in sinking ships." Johnston ordered Brigadier General Samuel B. Maxey's brigade of seven regiments from Enterprise to Mobile. Several of Maxey's regiments encamped at Hall's Mills, while the bulk of the brigade went to Portersville on the coast. The addition of these troops gave Maury approximately 6,400 men to defend the city. He wrote to Richmond: "With a proper garrison and a proper supply of ammunition I believe Mobile can successfully resist any attack of the enemy."[32]

In September 1863, Johnston reported to Richmond on the strength of the Mobile garrison. His estimate that ten thousand men were needed agreed with Maury's. In addition to the two brigades he had previously earmarked to support Mobile, Johnston told Cooper that two brigades at Newton, Mississippi, would also go to the city if the Federals attacked. These four brigades, along with 1,200 to 1,500 local defense troops, would give Maury a supporting force of approximately 6,750 men, which Johnston still did not consider adequate to combat a large besieging army. Maury asked the War Department to order Brigadier General John C. Moore to Mobile to command Maxey's brigade because Maxey had received orders to go to the Trans-Mississippi Department. He also repeated his request to Johnston to send Louisiana artillerists to man his heavy guns. Finally, Maury expressed a desire for the Missouri brigade that had served at Vicksburg. In requesting the Louisiana and Missouri troops, Maury stated again his conviction that it was "very important to have troops belonging to distant localities."[33]

The Mobile defenses appeared in satisfactory shape and required very little work during the month of September. Leadbetter's engineers enlarged Battery Gladden on its left flank so it could hold two more cannon. To honor the Missouri soldiers killed in the war, Maury ordered the Choctaw Point Battery renamed Missouri Battery. Along the line of works surrounding Mobile, the engineer laborers toiled to thicken the walls of the various redoubts. This work became so routine that the overseers and engineers allowed the slaves to slack off on their duties. Leadbetter ordered the engineers to remain at the fortifications throughout the workday and to threaten to recommend the overseers for conscription if they continued to neglect their duties. Near Fort

Morgan the engineers placed more torpedoes in the main ship channel. At Grant's Pass Lieutenant Glenn and his men expanded the walls of Fort Grant to accommodate six heavy guns and bombproof shelters for barracks and storerooms.[34]

On September 25, 1863, Colonel William Llewellyn Powell, commanding the lower bay defenses with headquarters at Fort Morgan, died in Mobile after a long illness. Powell's death saddened Maury, and he was at a loss to replace him. He praised Powell's ability and efficiency as an officer: "His loss is irreparable. He had peculiar qualifications for the position he occupied and was a man of very rare combinations of good traits."[35] During Powell's illness Maury had allowed the senior officer at Fort Morgan, Colonel George A. Smith of the First Confederate Infantry, to command Powell's brigade but wanted a permanent replacement. On the same day that Powell died, Brigadier General Francis A. Shoup arrived. Maury assigned Shoup to command Powell's brigade because of his experience as an artillery officer. Shoup had begun his Confederate service as a lieutenant of artillery and had commanded Hardee's artillery at Shiloh. But Maury did not intend Shoup's assignment to be permanent because he felt "the command is hardly equal to his rank."[36] In October Maury renamed the fort at Grant's Pass Fort Powell in memory of its former brigade commander.[37]

In early October 1863 Maury again needed a commander for the lower bay forts because Shoup became ill and had to relinquish his command. When Maury learned that Colonel Edward Higgins had been declared exchanged after his capture at Vicksburg, he asked Davis to promote Higgins to brigadier general and order him to Mobile to command both the lower bay and harbor defenses. Higgins had served as a midshipman in the United States Navy before the war and had entered Confederate service as a captain of artillery. As lieutenant colonel of the Twenty-second Louisiana Infantry he had commanded Fort Jackson and Fort St. Philip below New Orleans during Farragut's attack on the Crescent City. Later he commanded the defenses at Snyder's Bluff, and during the long siege of Vicksburg he had charge of the river batteries there. Maury thus thought his service had given him skill in defending fortifications against ships. During a visit by Davis to Mobile in late October, Maury again requested that the president promote Higgins and assign him to Mobile. On Maury's recommendation, Davis initiated the necessary orders, and Higgins assumed command by late November.[38]

The engineers conducted only limited operations in the Department of the Gulf during October 1863. The slowdown occurred at least in part because Leadbetter left Mobile to become Bragg's chief engineer and to superintend the construction of fortifications on Missionary Ridge southeast of Chattanooga. To replace him, the War Department ordered to the city Lieutenant Colonel Victor von Sheliha, a former Prussian army officer and most recently Buckner's chief of artillery. Von Sheliha would remain chief engineer at Mobile for most of the remainder of the war.[39] The engineers, with assistance from the infantry, began felling the trees between the two lines of earthworks surrounding the city and about one mile out from the first line of trenches. This tree removal would provide a clear field of fire for all of the redoubts and lesser works. One officer participating in this project wrote his wife: "It is only when I see all these hands chopping that I fully realize the expression, 'The forest disappeared beneath the settlers axe,' for I must say it is pleasant to see the trees falling all around."[40]

The engineering operations at Mobile cost the Confederate government a good deal of money. By October 1863 these expenditures had begun to cause some concern in Richmond. Leadbetter had estimated in January that he would need $700,000 to complete his work. At that time, however, the Engineer Bureau could send him only $50,000 because Congress had not acted on the bureau's appropriations request. Leadbetter's expenditures had reached $600,000 by June, and he still had not completed the defenses. For the next few months Leadbetter's estimates of funds required averaged $300,000. The Treasury Department notified the Engineer Bureau that it could place no more than $850,000 per month to the bureau's credit. Lieutenant Colonel A. L. Rives wrote Gilmer that because Mobile's appropriation took up more than one-third of this total he feared "the remainder will scarcely suffice to meet the expenditures necessary in other quarters." Rives told Leadbetter that the expenditures at Mobile had greatly exceeded those at Charleston, and he urged "the strictest economy in future opera-

tions."[41] Nevertheless, the monthly estimates of funds needed continued to average $300,000 for the remainder of the year.[42]

Troops once again left Mobile for another theater in late November
1863. Bragg at Missionary Ridge had been trying since late October
to get reinforcements for his army, then besieging Chattanooga. To
accommodate Bragg, Davis promised to get two brigades from Johnston in Mississippi and suggested that Bragg exchange troops with
Maury to obtain larger regiments. Johnston agreed to send two brigades to Bragg for temporary service. One of those chosen was that
of Brigadier General William A. Quarles, formerly Maxey's, then stationed at Mobile. Maury expressed willingness to send two of his regiments to Bragg if he could get some heavy artillerists to replace them.
He particularly wanted the First Alabama Infantry, which had manned
heavy guns at Port Hudson, and the First Tennessee Heavy Artillery.
Johnston, however, advised Maury against giving up any troops to Bragg
because replacements were probably not available. Maury heeded this
advice, and only Quarles's brigade departed from Mobile's garrison.
The remnants of the Tennessee artillery regiment did arrive in Mobile
in December and were assigned to the Apalachee batteries.[43]

In a letter written in late November 1863 Maury commented can-
didly that the city was very pleasant but because the situation there
was so quiet, men easily lost their soldierly habits. The people of the
city acted hospitably but had not really felt the war's impact. Maury
ventured the opinion that Mobile had been fortified at Vicksburg's expense. Heavy guns that could have been used at Vicksburg had gone to
Mobile, where they probably would receive little, if any, use. Maury
doubted that Mobile would be attacked because Banks's army was weakened from its repeated defeats in western Louisiana and Texas during
the fall and early winter and because the defenses around the city and
harbor could hold off any assault. He predicted: "I do not think they
will attempt Mobile until they have an army of 40,000 men, a large
fleet of ironclads and about ninety days liesure [sic] for them."[44]

Rumors of a planned attack on Mobile again reached the city in
December. Maury again asked Johnston to send him the artillerists
who had been taken prisoner at Port Hudson and Vicksburg as soon
as they were exchanged. He needed these experienced soldiers to gar-

rison his batteries rather than the infantrymen who then served the guns. If these regiments got orders for Mobile, Maury felt that their absentees would return and new recruits would fill their ranks. Besides his worry over the lack of veteran troops, Maury feared that he did not have sufficient food and ordnance supplies to withstand a siege. He admitted in a letter to Cooper that he expected the enemy fleet to run past Fort Morgan and Fort Gaines if an attack came. He expressed much the same feeling to Beauregard at Charleston but said he would do his best to obstruct the channel. Maury asked Beauregard to come to Mobile to help in the defense of the city if the situation at Charleston permitted him to get away. He recognized the success Beauregard had had in South Carolina and wished to use his knowledge in the defense of Mobile.[45]

In anticipation of the feared attack, von Sheliha pressed construction of Mobile's defensive works. The troops finished cutting down trees around the city redoubts and chopped the timber into firewood. Von Sheliha had enough Negro laborers coming in from the plantations that the small number of soldiers working on the defenses could return to their commands, but he hoped to get even more slaves. He knew he had to keep construction going to complete the defenses. Like Maury, von Sheliha realized that the masonry forts alone could not prevent a Federal fleet with ironclads from entering the bay. After written and verbal consultations with Maury, Gilmer, Buchanan, and Beauregard, von Sheliha decided to construct an earthwork battery on the west bank of the main ship channel between Fort Morgan and Fort Gaines. He also planned to obstruct the channel further with torpedoes, ropes, and sunken timbers. Continued construction on Fort Powell rendered that bay entrance secure. Closer to the city, von Sheliha's men reconstructed and expanded four bay batteries: McIntosh, Gladden, Huger, and Tracy. The line of city entrenchments appeared closer to completion, but it did not satisfy von Sheliha because of its proximity to the city. He began construction of a third line of fortifications between the two existing lines. This new line would include nine large redoubts, according to von Sheliha's plans. By late December, only Redoubts A and B, which flanked Stone Street Road, were in progress.[46]

CHAPTER 6

Defenses Deemed Inadequate

Again in early January 1864 an attack on Mobile was reported to be imminent. Maury contacted Polk, now commander in Mississippi, and Johnston, who had replaced Bragg after the Missionary Ridge disaster, to ask for reinforcements for his department. Polk immediately ordered two artillery units to Mobile and requested that Johnston return to him some of the brigades sent to the Army of Tennessee in November 1863. Johnston did not want to give up any men and referred the matter to Davis, who ordered two brigades—William E. Baldwin's and Quarles's—back to Polk for use in protecting Mobile. Maury also contacted Polk about obtaining supplies for his troops. Approximately three hundred cannon of various sizes stood in the Mobile defenses, but none had more than 250 rounds per gun. Maury had 130,000 pounds of salt meat and 400 beef cattle available but wanted more pork. He hoped to save as much of his current reserves as possible and bring in the pork when a siege seemed imminent.[1]

When Maury began to receive troop reinforcements, he endeavored to persuade noncombatants to leave Mobile. Even with the urging of Mobile's newspapers, the people did not depart in large numbers. Maury correctly realized that most civilians would not leave until the enemy actually began operations against the city.[2] The first reinforcements to reach Mobile were the men of Brigadier General Francis M. Cockrell's Missouri brigade. The First Louisiana Heavy Artillery Regiment followed shortly. These two units were assigned to the redoubts and entrenchments of the city works. Both units impressed Maury and the civilian population by their soldierly appearance and discipline demonstrated in a military review held soon after their arrival. The brigades of Baldwin and Quarles reached Mobile from Dalton, Georgia, in late January and moved into camp at Dog River Factory. With the addition of these troops, Maury had approximately twelve thousand men to defend Mobile.[3]

Von Sheliha continued to push his engineers to improve Mobile's defenses. He proposed to establish two ironclad floating batteries to obstruct the main ship channel into the bay rather than attempt to construct an earthwork battery as he had planned earlier. Von Sheliha hoped to secure the floating batteries on the western edge of the channel by anchoring them to flats which he would sink next to the channel. He had his engineers place floating rope obstructions in the channel while he worked on his plans, and he submitted his new proposal and other plans for the Mobile defenses to the chief of the Confederate Engineer Bureau, Major General Jeremy Gilmer. The latter did not think von Sheliha would succeed in establishing his floating batteries and cited the unstable sand bottoms, strong currents, and unmanageability of the structure as difficulties that might not be overcome. Although Gilmer did not strongly object to the effort, he urged von Sheliha to proceed cautiously and to test his floating batteries thoroughly. Gilmer suggested that von Sheliha erect the new line of redoubts around the city quickly and perfect them as time permitted.[4]

Gilmer arrived in Mobile on February 24, 1864, to serve on temporary duty under Maury. He had helped design many of the defensive works at Charleston, and his experience could prove very useful.[5] With Maury and Buchanan, Gilmer visited Fort Powell and Fort Gaines during the Union bombardment of the former. Later he reviewed the troops manning the city works and made a thorough inspection of the land defenses. He found the various forts and redoubts strong though still incomplete. Gilmer requested the War Department to order more engineers to Mobile to expedite completion of the works.[6] To strengthen the position at Grant's Pass, he ordered the construction of small earthwork batteries at Cedar Point and Little Dauphin Island. These works would prevent the Federals from erecting land batteries there to use against Fort Powell. Gilmer wanted the battery at Cedar Point built around the cedar trees located there to help conceal it. By the time Gilmer left on March 9, he expressed confidence that with a show of naval force to back it up, the outer line of defenses at Mobile could prevent the Federal fleet from entering the bay.[7]

Another new general, Brigadier General Richard L. Page, reported for duty at Mobile about this time to replace Higgins. The latter, whom Maury had assigned to command the outer defenses, became ill in early February and had to be relieved. Maury asked Seddon to promote Colonel Henry Maury of the Fifteenth Confederate Cavalry and assign him in Higgins's place.[8] Davis instead chose Page as Higgins's replacement and ordered him to proceed to Fort Morgan. Page held the rank of captain in the Confederate navy so Davis arranged his appointment as brigadier general. There is no evidence explaining Davis's choice of Page, but the new general's background seemed to qualify him for the position. A native of Virginia, Page had served in the United States Navy from 1824 to 1861. He resigned his commission when Virginia seceded and helped construct defenses on the James and Nansemond rivers. Later Page commanded shore batteries near Norfolk. When he received Davis's order, he had ably commanded the ordnance and construction depot at Charlotte, North Carolina, for two years.[9] Page reached Fort Morgan on March 12 and quickly made a favorable impression on the officers and men of the garrison. As one wrote: "We are very well pleased with our new general, although he hasn't found out the difference between a fort and a ship yet. He is a tall erect old fellow with the air of a man who has seen service and been accustomed to exercise command. A great disciplinarian, but very quiet and gentlemanly with it all. He is vastly preferred to his predecessor the irascible Higgins."[10]

Work on the various defensive positions continued while Maury moved some of his troops around, and the army and navy commanders attempted to maintain vigilance in case of another attack. Von Sheliha found it too difficult to transport heavy siege artillery to his Little

Dauphin Island battery and decided to arm the work with Parrott guns on field carriages. To give Fort Morgan further protection, von Sheliha began construction of a seven-gun water battery at the base of the fort's western face. The engineers completed three redoubts on the new land line near the city and moved guns into them. This engineering work required experienced men so the Engineer Bureau persuaded Seddon to continue the detail of three civilian engineers who had worked for the chief engineer at Mobile for several years.[11] Buchanan, meanwhile, kept his gunboats at the lower bay near Fort Powell, while he attempted to get the *Tennessee* over the Dog River bar. The poor condition of the *Baltic* caused naval constructor John L. Porter to recommend that workmen strip off her iron and place it on newer vessels. Buchanan continued to keep her in service despite Porter's recommendation and her own commander's opinion of her: "The *Baltic* is as rotten as punk, and is about as fit to go to sea as a mud scow."[12]

The specter of an attack on Mobile raised by Farragut's demonstration against Fort Powell in February 1864 caused von Sheliha to press his engineering operations, but a shortage of labor hampered him during much of April. About the twelfth of that month he had 250 men working on the city entrenchments. Companies of soldiers sentenced to hard labor by courts-martial supplemented the slave force but still could not conduct the construction quickly enough. Von Sheliha complained to the Engineer Bureau that although the yearly price paid planters for their hands ($360) seemed liberal, it probably would not satisfy the planters even if the government furnished clothing, quarters, and rations. He recommended conscription as the only sure way to bring in workers. Colonel George B. Hodge, in Mobile on an inspection tour for the War Department, echoed von Sheliha's conclusions.[13] By the end of the month, von Sheliha reported that his labor force had increased. He also received permission from the War Department to hire two thousand slaves, and agents moved into Mississippi and Alabama to obtain them. If he could not hire enough laborers, von Sheliha had the War Department's permission to impress slaves.[14]

Von Sheliha and his engineers conducted their operations as well as they could under the circumstances. They concentrated most of the work done along the lower bay line on Fort Morgan and Fort Powell because the Prussian believed Fort Gaines to be in satisfactory condition. At Fort Morgan, the engineers completed the water battery and had a redoubt east of the fort nearly complete. Recognizing the exposed position of the parapet guns in Morgan, von Sheliha ordered the erection of traverses between each gun to afford some protection for the gunners. The engineers added more sandbags to thicken the fort's magazine. They also completed the western face of Fort Powell so it was large enough to hold eleven guns. In the main ship channel, the engineers placed more torpedoes and the first of a series of timber obstructions. On the city entrenchments, von Sheliha's men laid gun platforms in four redoubts, continued strengthening three others, and began construction of a new redan. Hodge had high praise for the fortifications: "They evince a scientific proficiency in engineering unsurpassed, if equalled, by anything on this continent, and are themselves the most eloquent evidence of the educated skill of the engineer in charge, Lieut. Col. Von Sheliha." [15]

On April 13, 1864, Colonel Hodge reported to the War Department that he found the troops "well equipped and clad, and evincing in the precision of their drill and maneuvers a marked and most creditable efficiency." [16] Their weapons were in excellent shape. Hodge concluded, "The entire force compares favorably with any of similar numbers I have seen in the armies of the Confederacy." When Hodge began his inspection, Maury had five brigades numbering 9,300 men, but soon the garrison was reduced by 3,100 men. Baldwin's old brigade, now under Brigadier General Claudius W. Sears, left Pollard on April 11 for Selma, where it once again became part of Polk's field army. Polk was concentrating his men in north-central Alabama in response to a buildup of Federal troops at Huntsville and Decatur. He feared, incorrectly as it turned out, that the enemy planned an advance against the state's important coal and iron region. On the twentieth, James Cantey's brigade began leaving Pollard to join Johnston's army in northern Georgia. The War Department ordered this transfer so that Johnston might eventually gather enough men to enable him to assume the offensive into Tennessee. [17]

Hodge had both negative and positive comments about the supply departments at Mobile. He wrote critically of the quartermaster situation. The officer in charge of these supplies did not answer to Maury but was responsible only to the quartermaster general in Richmond, as was true almost everywhere in the Confederacy. Thus any time the army in Mobile requested quartermaster supplies, the requisition had to go to Richmond for approval. Hodge seconded Maury's complaint to Polk that the situation should be changed. The commissariat seemed in much better shape. Maury's warehouses held enough food to sustain the garrison for six months. On April 1 the rations issued to the men had been increased. One soldier commented later that the meat ration went up from one and one-quarter pounds to one and one-half pounds a day and bacon from one-third pound to one-half pound a day. At least one subordinate commander had established a fishery to add variety to his men's diets. Hodge found all of the foodstuffs to be of "excellent quality."[18]

The onset of the Atlanta campaign in May resulted in reductions in the strength of the Mobile garrison. On the first, Johnston requested that Brigadier General Alexander W. Reynolds's brigade at Pollard be ordered to join the Army of Tennessee. Maury complied by sending the brigade plus an Alabama battery to Dalton. To replace Reynolds's brigade at Pollard, Maury brought the First Alabama Infantry to Mobile from Fort Gaines and forwarded the regiment on to Pollard. There the First Alabama had to perform the guard and picket duty previously done by several regiments. Shortly after these troop movements, Polk ordered Maury to send two regiments to Selma. Maury forwarded not only these regiments but two field batteries as well.[19] Toward the end of May, Johnston needed more men to reinforce his hard-pressed army. The War Department ordered Quarles's Tennessee brigade from Mobile to northern Georgia. In addition to the Tennessee regiments, Quarles took with him the Thirtieth Louisiana Battalion at Fort Gaines and the First Alabama. Maury sent the Twenty-second Louisiana Consolidated Infantry from the city works to Pollard to replace the Alabama regiment. Not only did these soldiers go to Georgia, but Maury also ordered all spare horses and mules to Johnston.[20] The departure of these troops reduced Maury's force by approximately 2,000 men and left him with an army of slightly more than 4,300 men. But there was no immediate enemy threat to the city, and the loss of nearly one-third of his garrison had little real effect on Maury's situation.[21]

A shortage of competent engineer troops and laborers continued to plague von Sheliha during May. He still had officers traveling through Mississippi and Alabama trying to hire slaves. Von Sheliha complained to the Engineer Bureau that enrolling officers had conscripted many of his mechanics and other skilled white laborers. The bureau intervened with the War Department, requesting that the enrolling officers "interfere as little as possible with the mechanics, experts &c . . . necessary to the prosecution of the operations" of von Sheliha at Mobile. One company of engineer troops had already formed under Captain Leverette Hutchinson in the District of the Gulf. The War Department authorized a second company but refused to permit von Sheliha to organize a third. The department did allow him to recruit men into Captain Jules V. Gallimard's company of sappers and miners so that it could render efficient engineer service and suggested he call upon engineer companies organized in the army of the Department of Alabama, Mississippi, and East Louisiana when needed.[22]

During much of the month of June 1864 several Confederate officers feared an attack on Mobile. Maury reported that Captain James D. Johnston of the *Tennessee* expected Farragut's fleet to run into the bay and that every effort to obstruct the main ship channel had failed. General Page at Fort Morgan was also apprehensive and had no confidence in any of the Confederate warships except the *Tennessee*. From slaves who had escaped from the Federal lines at Pensacola, Page learned that the enemy planned to make an attack on June 18. When that day passed without an assault, he became convinced that the Federal move had only been postponed. He complained to a friend that he had only three hundred troops in the fort, not enough to man all of the guns, and saw no prospects of reinforcements. One of Page's subordinates at Fort Morgan did not share the general's pessimism and noted that the Federal fleet did not seem as strong as it had been earlier in the month. The officer concluded, "General Page persists in thinking an attack imminent and his mind is so peculiarly constituted that when once an absurd idea gets into it there is no getting it out except to make room for another equally absurd."[23]

The month of June 1864 proved a period of ups and downs for von Sheliha and his engineer operations. Early in the month, Colonel S. Crutchfield reported to the Ordnance Bureau in Richmond that on an inspection tour he found most of the ammunition magazines in the bay batteries and city works inadequate for proper storage. In almost every case he described the magazines as too small; a few were damp or poorly ventilated. Toward the middle of the month, the Engineer Bureau authorized von Sheliha to purchase the right to cut timber from land near the city works for use as lumber and fuel. Under orders from Maury, von Sheliha organized his engineer employees into a battalion for local defense, a move that would result in improved instruction and discipline. The War Department turned down von Sheliha's request that he be allowed to reorganize Gallimard's company of sappers and miners and increase its strength to one hundred men. He could raise the company's strength to only a total of sixty-four men. On June 25 von Sheliha wrote to Gilmer asking to be relieved from duty: "His reasons for making this application are that he receives no assistance whatever and yet is expected to accomplish more than any Engineer could possibly perform with the inadequate means at his disposal."[24] The War Department turned down von Sheliha's request, however, and he remained at his post in Mobile.

By July 1, 1864, Maury had few troops left in his command. Only 4,337 effectives remained in the entire District of the Gulf. Page's brigade, which garrisoned the three lower bay forts, numbered slightly more than 1,200 men, some 200 of whom were cavalrymen on picket and outpost duty. At Pollard, Colonel Isaac W. Patton had his own Twenty-second Louisiana Infantry, a cavalry regiment, and an artillery battery, in all about 1,100 men. This force was responsible for protecting the railroad to Montgomery as well as covering the approaches from Pensacola to Mobile. In early June, Higgins had returned to Mobile from sick leave and assumed command of the city works and bay batteries, also known as the artillery brigade. Under his command he had 1,100 artillerymen and 400 local defense troops. Most of Higgins's troops had manned water batteries at Vicksburg and were proficient in operating heavy artillery pieces. But because of their small numbers they had to perform a great deal of guard duty in addition to their normal routine. Besides being short of troops, Higgins had fewer artillery pieces than his predecessor. Maury had sent a large number of heavy guns and mortars to Atlanta for the earthworks there.[25]

On July 6 the First Louisiana Heavy Artillery and First Mississippi

Light Artillery regiments left for Meridian to act as infantrymen to assist in opposing a Union force marching eastward from Vicksburg. In speaking of the departure of the troops, one officer wrote in his diary: "Mobile is left almost without a corporal's guard."[26] Recognizing Mobile's weakened condition, Confederate authorities in Richmond sought to find additional troops for the garrison. Davis asked Governor Thomas H. Watts to organize state reserve units for Mobile, and General Cooper ordered Major General Jones M. Withers, commander of the Alabama Reserves, to send available units to the city. By mid-July, some forty to fifty companies of reserves had moved to aid Maury. Major General Stephen D. Lee, who had succeeded Polk in departmental command, briefly considered dismounting some of Forrest's cavalrymen and sending them to Mobile, but he realized that such troops would not be practical there. Maury, however, remained anxious to get his two artillery regiments back because of their experience "in preparing the redoubts, mounting guns, &c" and wrote Lee: "I know you will hasten them to me at the earliest moment at which you can spare them."[27]

Intelligence reports reaching Maury continued to indicate that the enemy would soon make an attack on Mobile, and he tried to prepare for the assault. He did not appear confident of success: "In view of the large naval preparations of the enemy we may expect Forts Morgan, Gaines, &c., to be cut off, and even reduced." Too many noncombatants still remained in the city. To Lee, Maury complained: "These people are not Virginians; they do not desire their city to be defended, and unless they see a pretty formidable force coming in here they will give me much trouble during my preparations."[28] Though a bit harsh, Maury's assessment seems to have been basically correct. The great majority of the people undoubtedly hoped some sort of defense would be made but not if it meant a bombardment of the city. An evacuation or bloodless surrender would allow them to continue their everyday lives relatively unaffected, and most of the population probably felt more concern about protecting their homes and livelihoods than occupation by the enemy. A few merchants and businessmen undoubtedly thought enemy occupation would benefit the city economically and looked forward to the day when the Stars and Stripes replaced the Stars and Bars.

The two artillery units Maury loaned to Lee returned to Mobile on July 18, 1864. These regiments had served as a reserve infantry force during the battle of Tupelo, Mississippi, on July 14 and were free to go back to Maury following the retreat of the Union army. Maury sent both units into the various redoubts in the city works. The men had occupied their stations for only two days when they received orders to report back to Lee at Meridian.[29] Only one regular army unit— Colonel Henry Maury's Fifteenth Confederate Cavalry—remained in the city. General Maury had moved this regiment from Pollard to Mobile, where it could reinforce Lee, protect the Mobile and Ohio Railroad, or guard the coast near Pascagoula. Detachments of the unit performed provost duty in the city in the absence of infantry or artillery troops. On July 22 the regiment left Mobile to return to Pollard. A Union raiding force had moved toward Pollard from Pensacola on the twenty-first, and Colonel Patton needed the cavalry unit to help repel the raid. No regular army units remained in Mobile to defend the city works. All guard duty fell on the shoulders of the local militia.[30]

On July 20, Confederate troops stationed at Fort Morgan witnessed the arrival of the monitor *Manhattan* to join the Union blockading squadron. The appearance of this monitor, the first of four that would eventually join Farragut, seemed a further indication that the Federals planned an attack. Page responded by ordering all noncombatants away from Fort Morgan. He and some of the other army officers believed that when the assault came Buchanan's squadron would be a weak spot in the defenses. Maury wrote Bragg that he did not count very heavily on the navy: "Their ships are inferior to those of the enemy, and the long period of inaction has not been promotive of energy and enterprise." A lieutenant at Fort Morgan voiced a more severe criticism of the navy in a letter to his sweetheart: "I have noticed one peculiarity about our naval men here, from Admiral Buchanan down to the last midshipman and that is an unlimited capacity for getting excited. They fly off the handle at the shortest notice and on the slightest pretext." This officer also thought the officers of the Mobile squadron had caused confusion in General Page's mind, hindering his ability to command the fort.[31]

Von Sheliha pressed his engineering operations in hope that the enemy would not find any weaknesses in Mobile's defensive positions. A continuing shortage of laborers and a shortage of tools made his work more difficult. At times during July as few as fifteen slaves made up the labor force in the city. Governor Watts responded to Maury's appeal for more slaves by saying that the planters would give them up only when troops arrived to take them. Von Sheliha did get to use three hundred slaves impressed from saltworks, but these men remained at Mobile for only nine days.[32] Even if von Sheliha had as many laborers as he desired, he admitted that he did not have enough tools for them to use. He had sent twelve hundred entrenching tools to the Army of Tennessee, leaving him with only fifteen hundred spades and shovels. Von Sheliha preferred not to use the three thousand picks at Mobile to break ground because plows did a better job. He tried to get a thousand shovels from the Quartermaster Department's stores in Montgomery, but the Engineer Bureau responded that only two hundred could be spared.[33]

The engineers made fair progress on the bay batteries and city works during July despite the shortage of labor and tools. Battery McIntosh required only repair of minor damages caused by heavy rains. Von Sheliha's men mounted a fifth gun in Battery Gladden and prepared platforms for two more guns expected to arrive from Selma. Because of the battery's isolated location, von Sheliha constructed a blacksmith shop there. To protect Battery Tracy and Battery Huger from an enemy approach from Pensacola, von Sheliha proposed the erection of defensive works near Blakely. The engineers conducted operations on six redoubts and three redans along the line of city entrenchments. Eight of the redoubts on von Sheliha's new line had guns mounted in them. The engineers had not yet begun work on four planned redoubts or several of the redans to be located between the larger forts. Von Sheliha had wanted to place infantry trenches between all of the redoubts and redans but could not do much construction of this type. In a midmonth report to the Engineer Bureau on the condition of the Mobile city defenses and bay batteries, von Sheliha stated that when he completed his plans, "Mobile will hold out as long as our provisions last."[34]

Von Sheliha's greatest concern was the condition of the three forts on the lower bay line, which would bear the initial brunt of the enemy naval attack. Von Sheliha assigned Captain Gallimard as engineer in charge of the entire lower line. The engineers mounted three guns on the east face of Fort Powell to protect the fort from attack from the rear if Farragut's fleet passed Fort Morgan and Fort Gaines. To strengthen the approaches to Powell from Mississippi Sound, the engineers constructed in the waters west of the fort a row of *chevaux-de-frise* (sharpened stakes driven at right angles through logs) made of railroad iron. Von Sheliha instructed Gallimard to cease work on batteries at Cedar Point and Little Dauphin Island because of the shortage of laborers. At Fort Gaines, Gallimard's men continued construction of a new wharf. The placement of torpedoes in the main ship channel continued. By the end of July, 180 torpedoes floated in three rows across the channel, but a gap of 226 yards still remained between Fort Morgan's water battery and the point at which the torpedoes commenced.[35]

An attack by a Federal gunboat on July 4 had amply demonstrated the weakness of Fort Morgan, and von Sheliha determined to try to strengthen the fort as much as possible. In the attack three shells hit the fort's outer wall, and one struck the west face of the citadel, a tall, octagonal brick structure in the center of the fort. Von Sheliha's conclusions drawn from his observation of the shells' effects seem prophetic: "From the depth to which these shots penetrated, from the size of the opening they produced, and from the amount of rubbish that fell, it is obvious that Fort Morgan, in its present condition, cannot withstand a vigorous bombardment. The guns on the west faces, if not dismounted by the reverse fire of the enemy, will fall with the casemates on which they are mounted. The high scarp-wall will be breached by curbated shot. The citadel will crumble to pieces from the effect of shot or shell, direct or reverse fire." The United States Army constructed Fort Morgan in 1833 when none of the heavy rifled guns used by Farragut's vessels had existed. With cannons like the hundred-pounder Parrott, the Federal fleet could stand out of range of the heaviest guns in Fort Morgan and pound the fort to pieces.[36]

In his instructions to Gallimard, von Sheliha made several recommendations for improvements to the fort. To protect the individual guns and their crews, he suggested the erection of heavy side and rear traverses. The engineers also had to build traverses around the bombproofs and magazines and in front of the main sally port. Von Sheliha wanted cribs filled with sand put up over all faces of the fort's walls that might receive direct fire from the enemy's fleet. This would prevent the walls from being penetrated by shot and broken into fragments, which would fly through the air like pieces of shrapnel, and also would prevent the walls from being pounded into rubbish and breached. Von Sheliha or one of his subordinates suggested that the citadel be cut down in height and bombproofed. One officer's opinion of this idea may reflect the judgment passed on all of the engineer operations in the fort: "All are agreed that if an attack is really imminent the work is most untimely." Finally, von Sheliha wanted the line of earthworks across the peninsula east of the fort completed. The engineers had already done some work on this line. In his report to Maury's chief of staff, von Sheliha predicted that if the work force were increased at Fort Morgan the laborers would complete the work in fifteen days. The slaves did not come in, however, and most of the critical improvements remained undone when Farragut's fleet ran past the forts on August 5.[37]

Chapter 7

Civilian Life in Wartime Mobile

Despite the extensive military preparations and troop movements going on around them, the people of Mobile attempted to maintain the life-style they had enjoyed before the war. To a great extent they succeeded. Many observers concluded that the war barely touched Mobile. One resident remembered after the conflict that "Mobile was called the Paris of the Confederacy, New Orleans having fallen so early in the fray, and gay indeed it was." Dances, parties, band concerts, and parades continued unabated. Although many soldiers and citizens enjoyed the social life at Mobile, others criticized the city for its "hideous reputation." A newspaper correspondent assigned to Mobile wrote: "I must say the country is likely to contrast the hard fighting and hard living of her brave soldiers in Tennessee, Virginia, and elsewhere, with these holiday doings at Mobile. Making obstreperous mirth over more than two hundred thousand newly made graves of our kindred and friends, and in the hearing of the poor sick fellows who crowd our hospitals in thousands, is not at all to my taste." In response to the criticism, Mobilians answered: "But while we worked and prayed for those who were actually doing battle for our cause, we felt that it was only right to make bright the lives of the soldiers and sailors stationed here, or on leave."[1]

This bright social life continued down to the last days of the war, but on occasion the citizens demonstrated that they did feel the impact of the war. Kate Cumming recorded in her diary in January 1865 that the city seemed as festive as ever. In the midst of the final siege of Mobile, a local soldier wrote to his girlfriend, "Our city is not at all changed in appearance."[2] A graphic portrayal of the chilling effect the war had on the community occurred in late 1862. There existed in Mobile a mystic krewe, called the Cowbellions, which paraded through the city every New Year's Eve. Young men made up most of the membership of the society, and they normally exhibited a great deal of cheerfulness and color. On the occasion in question, however, the mood was anything but cheerful. The few remaining members dressed in black, and they played the music of a dirge. They carried a transparent banner inscribed with the words "In Memory of Our Departed Associates." Witnesses to the somber spectacle were deeply affected and realized that "Mobile has had her share of sorrow."[3]

Soldiers and sailors found Mobile a very pleasant duty station or site for leave. A Missourian remembered that "a man could come nearer getting the worth of Confederate money there, than any other place in the department."[4] When members of Kentucky's famed Orphan Brigade passed through the city, they used a ruse to try to get around an order confining them to their camp and to obtain a meal of Mobile's noted oysters. The men found themselves face-to-face with their brigade commander as they entered the Battle House Hotel. To their excuse that they were looking for stragglers, Colonel R. P. Trabue observed: "'You are looking for straggling oysters. I know what you are up to.'"[5] Some soldiers got carried away by the city's atmosphere. One group of officers was said to have taken up quarters in the Battle House and "trained . . . on a diet of whiskey, music, and women."[6] Many young officers and enlisted men, including Brigadier General Thomas H. Taylor, married Mobile girls. On one day alone ten officers got married.[7]

The people of Mobile tried to aid the soldiers and sailors in ways other than providing social entertainment. In May 1861 Adelaide de

Vendel Chaudron and Ellen S. Walker organized the Mobile Military Aid Society. Originally this group of women made uniforms for soldiers in service. Later they supplied clothing and food to the families of men who were away at war. Eventually they provided assistance to needy soldiers passing through the city. The society initially did its work free of charge, but in time it had to accept government funds and private donations. Other women picked lint and made bandages for the wounded in nearby hospitals. Even in the final days before the fall of Mobile, its women were putting together boxes of provisions for the soldiers fighting in the trenches across the bay. The post chaplain, Reverend F. B. Miller, established the Soldiers' Library on Water Street, equipping it at his own expense and keeping it open throughout the war. In the library soldiers could find "a large assortment of reading matter, books, pamphlets, magazines and news papers, all conveniently arranged, and seats and tables for writing."[8]

The citizens extended charity to needy persons living in the city. In 1862 the Military Aid Society began providing food and clothes for the families of men away in service. Another group, the Female Benevolent Society, provided food, clothing, and quarters for soldiers' widows and children. A third group of women contributed clothing to needy children of soldiers.[9] To assure that the poor people of Mobile got food, a committee of the city's leading men established the Free Market in December 1861. They collected supplies both from Mobile County and from planters in the interior. The railroad and steamship companies provided free transportation for supplies coming from these planters. When the Free Market opened, approximately eight hundred people got food there. By early 1863 slightly more than twenty-five hundred people were taking advantage of the market. Even though goods became more expensive and in shorter supply as the war went on, the Free Market continued to serve the poor until Mobile's surrender.[10]

Life in Mobile remained relatively normal. The city government continued as usual except that the mayor and aldermen took on added responsibilities such as assisting the Free Market and aiding the thousands of refugees who crowded into the city. Throughout the war the courts in Mobile, such as the Confederate District Court for the Southern Division of Alabama, held regular sessions and scheduled special terms. All of the city's churches remained open, and their ministers, like the civil officials, assumed extra duties, visiting the wounded and the families of soldiers away at war and conducting numerous funerals. Mobile's public schools operated until the end of the war through liberal contributions by her citizens. The shortage of schoolbooks was lessened when Adelaide de Vendel Chaudron authored a set of readers and spelling books. S. H. Goetzel and Company printed these books and many others. In numerous instances the firm used wallpaper for parts of the books because regular paper was in short supply.[11]

The city authorities made every effort to keep Mobile as clean as possible throughout the war. Early in the conflict they ordered the razing of dilapidated buildings to make way for new construction. In August 1862 Mayor Slough appointed a committee with members in every ward to supervise the city's sanitary conditions. The City Council had passed an Ordinance to Secure Public Health, which empowered the committee to investigate anything that might endanger the people's health and required all property owners or occupants to keep their areas clean. The authorities did not always strictly enforce the ordinance. In February 1865 citizens reported to the city fathers that hogs running loose in the streets had damaged the sidewalks and other property. All stock owners received instructions to lock up their animals, and an inspector of animals supervised the enforcement of the regulations. One woman whose hog the inspector had seized had to pay $5 for an affidavit and $20 in pound fees to get her animal back.[12]

The people of Mobile exhibited a great deal of tolerance toward those among them who held divergent political opinions. A Northern-born Union man who lived in the city throughout the war wrote later that few acts of oppression occurred during the conflict.[13] One tense incident transpired in October 1862, when there were three cases of attempted arson. Fortunately, the fire department extinguished all of the blazes before they did great damage, but the need for vigilance was evident. In an editorial, the *Advertiser and Register* attempted to identify the guilty parties: "The majority of them are probably negroes, debauched by association with the viler strata of the white population, but there must be white men actively engaged in the nefarious schemes which are in operation." To aid the city police in patrolling the city, Slough organized groups of citizens to guard against mischief. For the most part, the city authorities prevented similar occurrences.[14]

Throughout most of the war, the civilian population of Mobile avoided large outbreaks of disease such as had happened before 1860. The efforts at keeping the city clean undoubtedly helped. A smallpox epidemic threatened to erupt in late March 1864, however. When the authorities discovered the presence of the disease, it was confined primarily to Negroes. The *Advertiser and Register* urged its readers to seek vaccination. O. Kratz, superintendent of vaccination, opened an office on Jackson Street to inoculate without charge anyone who so desired. Several days after this office was opened, the *Advertiser and Register* appealed to the people to take advantage of the free vaccinations, stating that smallpox appeared "very prevalent." Apparently Mobile's citizens heeded the advice because in mid-April it reported that the smallpox "is rapidly disappearing, and that the alarm which prevailed a few weeks ago has subsided."[15]

Both civilians and soldiers found good hospital facilities to treat diseases and wounds. The five hospitals in operation when the war began continued to operate. As the number of sick and wounded grew, the Confederate authorities constructed or transformed older buildings to create at least seven new hospitals for soldiers and sailors. The United States Marine Hospital opened on November 3, 1861, under the name of Ross Hospital after its appropriation by Confederate authorities. This facility, one of the finest hospitals in the South, could accommodate 250 patients. In November 1863 the city authorities turned over the City Hospital to the Confederate government to serve as a military hospital. The military set aside part of the building, now called Cantey Hospital, for civilians. The Sisters of Charity supervised the wards and acted as druggists and stewards. The three remaining prewar hospitals were for use by civilians only.[16]

In July 1862 the medical director at Mobile established a convalescent hospital at Spring Hill near the city. Between seventy and one hundred soldiers could receive care at the facility. One soldier reported that the food at Spring Hill consisted primarily of "poor beef, corn meal, coffee, grits, sour bread, small piece of bacon twist a week, also some pudding."[17] This soldier did have one complaint about his quarters: "There is one thing I have got acquainted with since I have bin here that is lice. . . . It is a hard matter to keep clean of them unless you shift your clothes twist a week. They are in the bedclothes. You are sertain to katch them."[18] The blockade and the needs of other hospitals limited the supply of medicine available for the Spring Hill and other facilities at Mobile, but the doctors had access to some medical supplies. Doctors and citizens used home remedies more often than they would have in normal times.[19]

On May 14, 1863, a hotel on Royal Street became the S. P. Moore Hospital. The Soldiers Rest Hospital opened on July 18, 1863, and one year later it was converted into a hospital for officers only. Several days after the opening of this latter facility, the Nott Hospital began receiving patients. Mobile's medical staff converted the Kennedy House Hotel into the Heustis Hospital on October 18, 1864. On November 23, 1864, the Mansion House Hotel became Nidelet Hospital, the last medical facility established by the military in Mobile. Both of the former hotels required extensive cleaning and renovation but became excellent hospitals.[20]

The women of Mobile gave generously to the patients in the military hospitals. In 1862 a group of women formed the Ladies' Supply Society to furnish food to the soldiers and sailors in Ross Hospital. Some of the members of this society took on additional duties such as cleaning floors, acting as practical nurses, and making beds. Dr. Josiah C. Nott, medical director of the Department of the Gulf, praised the society for its many good works. The Soldiers' Friend Society performed services at Moore Hospital similar to those conducted by the Ladies' Supply Society at Ross Hospital. One Mobile woman used her own money to establish and equip a convalescent hospital on the grounds of her home, where she spent many hours personally tending to the sick and wounded.[21]

The war interrupted and curtailed economic activities, prices rose drastically, and shortages existed. These interrelated problems made life difficult for all segments of the city's population. As a port city, Mobile's economy was based on its large merchant community. The blockade, the diversion of goods to the armies, and the use of river steamers and railroads by the military all reduced the trade the merchants had enjoyed before 1861. From time to time exhausted stocks and exorbitantly priced supplies forced stores to close. Merchants could do a booming business only following the arrival of a blockade runner bearing luxury food and clothing items. Naturally, the situation worsened as the war progressed and blockade running came to an end. Mobile never fully recovered from the effects of the war and never again was as important a port as before 1860.[22]

Mobile's civilians tried to adapt by finding substitutes for items in short supply. Homespun replaced finer fabrics for women's clothes. Old clothes were dyed to make them appear new. Referring to the clothing situation, one Mobilian wrote: "All the rag-bags have been emptied, and dresses turned and cut into all kinds of shapes. Any and every thing is the fashion; nothing is lost. The old scraps of worsted and flannel are carefully unraveled, carded, and spun, for making capes and nubies. The fact is, it is a kind of disgrace to have plenty of clothes. If any one has on a new silk or calico dress, kid gloves, or any thing that is foreign, they have to give an account of how they came by it."[23] Both women and men wore hats made from palmetto. Some men sported suits made of a mixture of cotton and doe hair, which was said to be waterproof. Sometimes wood became scarce, and the military impressed existing supplies. When lighting oil and candles became hard to acquire, many people burned pitch pine knots to provide illumination.[24]

Prices for all goods rose in Mobile as they did elsewhere in the Confederacy because of shortages and the decreasing value of Confederate currency. Speculators often took advantage of the situation to buy large quantities of supplies and sell them at exorbitant prices. In March 1862 a group of citizens asked General Samuel Jones to establish a tariff of prices to keep the speculators from asking too much for the goods they had for sale. Jones promptly established the tariff and prohibited large sales of foodstuffs to one individual or company. At first the *Advertiser and Register* protested Jones's order as unfair to the majority of honest merchants of the city, but when the general apprised the paper of the intent of the order, it came out in full support of his action.[25]

Once the crisis that had precipitated Jones's order had passed, the price tariff was abandoned. Later in the war the Alabama state government regulated prices of foodstuffs through a commission. None of these efforts succeeded, however, because prices for most items continued to increase. A currency bill passed by the Confederate Congress in February 1864 with the intention of increasing the value of currency had the effect of raising prices alarmingly in Mobile.[26] Molasses sold for twenty-eight cents a gallon early in the war but had gone up to seven dollars a gallon by the fall of 1863. Butter, valued at fifty cents a pound in November 1861, increased to five dollars a pound by June 1864. Perhaps the greatest rise was in the price of flour, which went from forty-five dollars a barrel in October 1862 to four hundred dollars a barrel in January 1865.[27] It is not difficult to understand why many people in Mobile were unable to furnish their families with needed food items even when those items were readily available in the city's stores.

Before the war the surrounding countryside could not supply all the food needs of the city's relatively large population. Nor were there large food surpluses in the interior of the state. Corn was about the only item that did reach the city from the interior in significant amounts. Mobile's major food imports—pork, wheat and flour, corn, beef, and whiskey—came from New Orleans through a well-developed coastal trade route. The Federal blockade cut off this coastal trade in the summer of 1861, forcing Mobile to look to Alabama and Mississippi for food supplies. But the plantations and farms of these states could not furnish pork, beef, corn, and wheat in quantities sufficient to meet the city's needs. That the population of Mobile ate as well as it did is a tribute to the merchants, planters, and farmers of Alabama and Mississippi.[28]

Necessary supplies were not always available. One of the more severe crises occurred in the winter of 1862 and early spring of 1863. On December 12, 1862, General Pemberton issued an order prohibiting the transportation of corn and fodder out of Mississippi. The necessity of supplying his army and the activities of speculators brought about this order. Because Mobile had drawn much of its corn from the counties of northern Mississippi via the Mobile and Ohio Railroad, the city stood to suffer as a result of the order. The *Advertiser and Register* quickly asked that Pemberton or higher authorities modify or rescind the order. At the same time, Governor Shorter, Mayor Slough, and the president of the Mobile and Ohio Railroad sent protests to Pemberton, General Johnston, and the War Department.[29]

Both the War Department and Buckner at Mobile referred the protests to Johnston, who was away in Tennessee and preferred not to interfere in such a distant situation. He suggested to Mayor Slough and Governor Shorter that Mobile look to southern Alabama for supplies. In view of Johnston's inactivity, Secretary of War Seddon suggested that Pemberton and Buckner try to work out the problem together.[30] Pemberton continued to insist that Mobile get supplies by way of the Alabama and Tombigbee rivers. His intransigence prompted Buckner to issue orders forbidding the shipment of supplies and provisions from his department and authorizing his chief of subsistence to impress cattle and other stores held by speculators. Buckner attempted to reassure the public: "It is not the policy of the Commanding General to make seizures of private property, or to prevent shipments from one portion of the District to another. Supplies evidently intended for private consumption will not be interfered with while in transitu within this District."[31]

The people of Mobile suffered from this conflict between military authorities, although evidence indicates that they found certain items in plentiful supply.[32] To help the populace subsist, the city's military commanders relaxed restrictions on fishing around Mobile Bay. Fishermen and oystermen normally could not go outside the confines of the bay, but General Mackall issued an order allowing them to go up to three miles west of Grant's Pass in search of their catches. All boats taking advantage of the order had to register with the army and comply with any regulations established by the naval commander at Mobile. Buckner received permission from the War Department to sell excess military supplies at cost to the needy in times of scarcity. At least a few enterprising citizens found ways to get around Pemberton's order. One man bought a quantity of bacon in Mississippi and devised an ingenious method of transporting it to Mobile without having it confiscated. He bought a six-foot pine box similar to those used to transport the bodies of soldiers to their families. Filling the "coffin" with bacon, he marked the box "John Shoat, 32nd Alabama Regiment, Mobile, Ala." A Montgomery newspaper reported: "The shoat, or shoats, came to hand without trouble, and in good order."[33]

Perhaps the most noted response to the supply difficulties was the formation of the Mobile Supply Association. A group of seventy-four prominent and wealthy gentlemen joined together to organize the association and used their own money to finance it. The association had as its goal the purchase of supplies and their sale at cost to people in the city. By selling goods at cost these men could keep prices of all goods down to a reasonable level. The *Advertiser and Register* urged other patriotic citizens to join the association so that its capital would increase and its operations could expand. At first, the agents of the association collected supplies only along the Alabama and Tombigbee river systems. The association's secretary, T. A. Hamilton, appealed to Johnston to permit the purchase of corn in Mississippi and its shipment on the Mobile and Ohio Railroad. Johnston approved the shipment of supplies for both the Supply Association and the Free Market. Eventually agents in many parts of the Confederacy were procuring necessities for Mobile's people.[34]

The supply shortage came to a head in late March and early April 1863. The inability of the military commanders to settle the matter, newspaper editorials complaining of the situation, and reports of signs reading "Bread or Peace" stuck on street corners in Mobile prompted Seddon to act.[35] He approved a plan put forth by Colonel Lucius B. Northup, commissary general and head of the Subsistence Department, which called for the creation of chief commissaries in each state to supervise the collection, storage, and distribution of supplies. In informing Buckner of his decision, Seddon wrote: "The course which under the circumstances I sought to adopt is what appears to me under any but very exceptional conditions the more regular and judicious. It is to confine each Commander, to subsidiary operations in obtaining supplies, to his own Department and to require of the Commissary General through the Bureau officers and agents to be active in all, collecting supplies, accumulating at Depots and preparing to distribute and meet requisitions from the various Armies according to their respective needs."[36] Northup's plan, the activities of the Mobile Supply Association, and improved crop harvests in Alabama eased Mobile's supply difficulties.

The "bread riot" of September 4, 1863, vividly demonstrated that some of the people of Mobile continued to suffer from shortages of food and other supplies. On the morning of that day, several hundred poor women, armed with hatchets, hammers, brooms, and axes, gathered on the Spring Hill Road. Carrying banners reading "Bread or

Blood" and "Bread and Peace," they marched down Dauphin Street into the city. Thousands of spectators watched as the women broke into stores, took food and clothing, and distributed their loot among their number. Available sources indicate that Jews owned most of the stores broken into, inferring a prejudice against them, and that most of the onlookers sympathized with the plight of these women. General Maury called out the Seventeenth Alabama Regiment to put down the riot, but the men of that unit refused to take action. The failure of the military to stop the women left the matter in the hands of the civil authorities. Mayor Slough made a speech promising to meet the needs of the rioters if they would disperse. A witness related the results of his effort: "[The speech] had the desired effect of disbanding the Amazonian phalanx and sending the women to their houses, well satisfied with the result of their foray."[37]

Slough quickly followed up on his promise to the bread rioters. On the same day that the riot occurred, the mayor addressed an appeal to the citizens of Mobile to come to the aid of the needy women: "Their own wants and those of their children are calculated to touch the hardest and least sympathetic heart. Let us then, my fellow citizens, see that these worthy objects of charity are placed above the reach of absolute destitution." Slough asked the people to contribute money to be used to purchase food and clothing for those needing assistance. To collect the money and distribute the supplies, he appointed a fourteen-man Special Relief Committee. The committee appointed a special agent to purchase goods from city factories for delivery to the poor and solicited contributions of money or material suitable for clothing. Selecting other citizens to form the Citizens' Relief Association and to aid in its activities, the Special Relief Committee surveyed the various wards of the city to locate poor families and determine their needs. In the following months, the committee succeeded in alleviating most of the distressing conditions afflicting Mobile's poor.[38]

Supply shortages continued until the end of the war, but nothing like the two crises just described occurred again. At various times meat, vegetables, and other items were hard to obtain. A scarcity of money or interruptions in the normal transportation system usually created these temporary shortages. In January 1865, for instance, the military impressed most of the river steamers to transport its own supplies, thus making it difficult to bring in goods intended for the citizens of Mobile. The army had not previously taken over river transportation, and only the exigencies of the time caused it to do so then. After the Federal fleet occupied the bay, its presence deprived Mobile of one luxury food—oysters. Oystermen could bring in a few of the shellfish from the upper regions of the bay, but high prices kept these few delicacies out of the hands of most people. The enemy occupation of the bay also almost completely cut off coffee imports. These shortages affected morale as well as stomachs: "Some who did not touch it [coffee] before the war, talk gravely about its loss as if their very existence depended upon it, and indeed they are quite melancholy about it."[39]

CHAPTER 8

Role of Blacks
in Mobile's Defense

Mobile's free blacks and slaves played an important role in the defense of the city. In 1860 Mobile County's population included 1,195 free blacks (50 percent of Alabama's total). Many of these people fell into a category called "Creoles" or the "treaty population." Their ancestors had been free during the colonial period and had received special status and citizenship rights under the 1819 treaty which ceded West Florida to the United States. The Creoles had formed their own fire company in 1830, and they had a school that provided an education other free Negroes and slaves did not enjoy. Nevertheless, during the war city authorities treated all free blacks the same and attempted to emphasize the differences between them and the slaves. Free blacks arrested for associating with slaves could receive fines as high as $25 in the Mayor's Court. City ordinances apparently restricted the freedom of movement of free blacks as well. In one case, the Mayor's Court sentenced "Alick" to ten days or a fine of $10 for being out after hours. The law protected both whites and free blacks from abuse by each other. The Mayor's Court fined "Dave" $50 and sent him to the City Court for slapping a white woman. When a white man struck a free black woman, he received a sentence of twenty-five days or a fine of $25. A free black woman accused by a neighbor of disorderly conduct had her case dismissed when witnesses and affidavits proved her "an honest, quiet and respectable girl."[1]

Many of Mobile's Creoles wanted to aid the Confederacy. On April 23, 1862, G. Huggins Cleveland wrote to Secretary of War George W. Randolph asking whether, if he were able to raise a regiment or battalion of Creoles, the War Department would accept it for Confederate service. Cleveland felt that as "a peaceable orderly class . . . as true to the South as the pure white race" these free blacks would perform good service in the Confederate army. He said the Creoles were eager to go to war and could form a regiment or battalion in a few days' time. Congressman Edmund S. Dargan of Mobile endorsed Cleveland's application: "I know the character of the population he proposes to enlist, and think they will render as efficient aid as any class we have." But the War Department denied Cleveland authority to raise his unit on the grounds that the "law does not permit the Department to accept any new corps."[2] Mobile's Creoles did not give up the idea of getting into Confederate service despite this rebuff.

On November 20, 1862, the Alabama General Assembly passed a bill authorizing the enrollment of Creoles between the ages of eighteen and fifty in Mobile as part of the state militia. Under this act, the mayor would accept interested men and form them into companies. The legislature mandated that he appoint white officers to command the units organized. As militia troops, the Creoles would serve exclusively in the defense of Mobile and its environs. Thus the free blacks of Mobile finally got the opportunity for military service which the Confederate government had denied them. In mid-December, Mayor Slough issued a call for Creoles to report for enlistment in accordance with the legislation. He instructed interested men to register with the chief of police. At least one company, called the Creole Guards, appears to have formed under the mayor's call. Little is known of the service performed by these men except that they helped guard warehouses containing government stores.[3]

In early November 1863 General Maury sought War Department approval to accept into Confederate service one or more companies of Creoles. The department had turned down a similar request several months earlier on the reasoning that blacks could not be organized as soldiers. Maury repeated his petition because he did not think the authorities in Richmond fully realized the status of Mobile's Creoles. He pointed out their special status and stated that most of the white people of the city did not look upon them as blacks. Maury intended to drill them as heavy artillerists, and he said they seemed anxious to enter regular service. Secretary of War Seddon replied that blacks could serve only as laborers or in support jobs. Political considerations dictated Seddon's stand: "Our position with the North and before the world will not allow the employment as armed soldiers of negroes."[4]

After the Federals captured the forts at the entrance of Mobile Bay in early August 1864, the Confederate commander at Mobile formed a special company of cavalry scouts to watch the enemy forces on Dauphin Island. Some of the men in this unit were blacks and may have come from Mobile's free black population. In October 1864 the Confederate command ordered the enrollment of the city's Creoles and other free blacks. There is no evidence to indicate whether this enrollment resulted in the formation of military units. When the Federals' final campaign against the city commenced in late March 1865, the post commander called for the organization of Creoles and free blacks into local defense companies. Maury assigned a person to organize the men reporting for duty and authorized these men to elect their own company officers, as long as they chose white men. By April 8, one company (known as the Native Guards) had formed. Although the city's assistant chief of police served as company commander, the other officers were Creoles. There is no evidence that this unit saw any active duty, and it probably disbanded when the Federals occupied Mobile.[5]

Slavery in Mobile apparently changed very little during the war years. By 1860 the proportion of slaves in the city's population had declined to just over 25 percent. Slave women outnumbered the men. A majority of the heads of families in the city owned slaves, but most owned only a small number of blacks who performed domestic duties. Businesses and corporations were the larger slaveholders in Mobile. Many of these slaves worked in the numerous cotton presses of the city. Other blacks performed assorted tasks such as driving cabs and railroad trains. During the war these slaves continued at their duties and large numbers of male slaves put in time as laborers on the city's fortifications. Available sources contain no evidence of slave unrest or of a dramatic increase in the number of runaways. In the waning days of the war, the Confederate authorities in Mobile attempted without success to get slaveowners to remove their blacks from the city. The reaction of the slaves to the occupation of the city by Union troops reveals the feelings they undoubtedly harbored during the conflict: "The *negroes* were *very* glad to see them. They shook hands with the Yanks telling them that they were glad they had come, for they (the negroes) had been 'waiting a long time for *their* time to come.' "6

The mayor, sitting as judge, continued to handle violations by slaves of city ordinances, and whippings continued to be the primary method of punishment. These whippings do not appear to have been any more severe than those inflicted before the war. The mayor sentenced slaves caught out after hours from five to thirty-nine lashes. If such a violation of curfew resulted from the owner's negligence, the mayor might fine the owner rather than punish the slaves. Theft might result in as few as twenty or as many as one hundred lashes, usually depending on the specifics of the crime. The mayor decreed thirty lashes "well put on" for one young slave who had a history of minor thefts. Even such seemingly minor offenses as smoking in the street brought the guilty party ten or twenty lashes. Editors of city papers recognized that blame often did not lie with the slave, but they supported the actions of the Mayor's Court: "Owners of slaves will take notice that all ordinances in reference to slaves will be rigidly enforced. Many slaves, if care be not taken, will be punished through the carelessness of their owners. This must be avoided—but the duty of His Honor is plain, and he will perform it."7

Slaves committed some violence against white citizens, but it is not possible to compare it with similar antebellum occurrences. Again, the punishment varied with the severity of the crime. The mayor sentenced one female slave to "25 lashes for two days for striking a little white girl." Most blacks convicted of assaulting whites received similar punishments. Occasionally slaves murdered whites or other blacks and paid with their lives. One widely publicized case involved an assault on a white woman and the murder of a black ferryman. After robbing and knocking out the woman, the three slaves left her for dead and attacked the ferryman. Before he died, the ferryman identified his assailants. Two other slaves eventually caught the criminals and turned them over to the police.[8] The law also protected slaves from attacks by whites. The mayor levied a fine against a boy for striking a black girl. In another case a young man received a sentence of twenty days or $20 for beating a slave who did not belong to him.[9]

Mobile's civil authorities tried to regulate social intercourse between whites and slaves. In October 1862 the editor of one newspaper issued a warning to women who sold whiskey to slaves, pointing out that the slaves had robbed and killed several such women. Hannah Ryan received a sentence of $50 or thirty days for allowing an illegal assemblage of slaves in her house. The mayor awarded the four slaves caught there with ten lashes each. The police arrested Ann Sullivan for receiving stolen goods and for illegal association with slaves. The one slave caught at her residence received a sentence of fifty lashes. Her punishment on the charge of associating with slaves amounted to thirty days or $50. The mayor turned her over to City Court for trial for receiving stolen goods. For harboring a runaway slave, Mary Ann Murray was sentenced by City Court to two years in the penitentiary.[10]

Petty theft was the most prevalent crime committed by slaves in Mobile. The problem became particularly bad in the spring of 1863, apparently because of the general food shortage then plaguing the city. After several instances of thefts of chickens and milk, the *Advertiser and Register* issued a warning about the lack of proper surveillance of slaves: "Too much liberty is allowed slaves—and it may happen some morning that somebody will wake up a nigger or two poorer than when he went to bed." Several weeks later the mayor began enforcing more strictly the curfew hours (9 P.M. to 4 A.M.) for slaves. He asked owners who were in the habit of sending servants to the market around 2 A.M. to cease that practice. The editor of the *Advertiser and Register* hoped the mayor would shut down slave balls and fairs and establish uniform dress regulations for slaves. The newspaperman feared that well-dressed blacks would incite unrest among the city's poor whites. Increased vigilance and more numerous arrests by the police and night patrols succeeded in reducing the number of thefts committed by slaves.[11]

Not until late 1864 did the Confederate government give serious consideration to arming slaves so they could help defend the South.

Some support for the idea had appeared in Alabama and Mississippi in the late summer of 1863, when it seemed that Federal armies might overrun both states. In August 1863 the Alabama legislature passed resolutions asking Congress to consider using slaves as soldiers. Congressman Dargan of Mobile even went so far as to support the idea of emancipating the slaves if such a course would bring strong European support for the Confederacy. Finally, in November 1864, Congress began debating the controversial issue. By early 1865 debate centered on bills that would tie emancipation to military service.

At first, Jefferson Davis publicly opposed using blacks as soldiers, though he had supported the idea of emancipating loyal blacks who served as laborers at the end of the war. Then he worked secretly to gain support for the bills before Congress. John Forsyth, the editor of the *Mobile Advertiser and Register,* gave his support to Davis, as did several other prominent citizens throughout the South. At a large public meeting at Temperance Hall on February 13, 1865, Mobilians passed resolutions calling on the Confederate government to arm one hundred thousand blacks for the armies. Congress passed a bill which provided for arming and emancipation of slaves, and Davis signed the bill into law on March 13. No evidence exists that any slaves in Mobile actually enlisted for military service under the terms of the law. The Confederacy could not fully implement the plan, coming as it did so close to the end of the war. Thus this radical measure did not affect the outcome of the conflict.[12]

Blacks' main contribution to the defense of the city was their labor on Mobile's many fortifications, but they had no choice in providing such labor. Early in the war Confederate authorities depended on owners to volunteer their slaves to work on the defenses, but in a few instances the military impressed blacks. Not until fear of an enemy attack in October 1862 did the civil and military authorities make a major push to obtain slave laborers. At that time General Forney asked Mayor Slough to furnish laborers. Slough, in turn, urged the citizens of the city to volunteer their services, and he announced that white laborers would receive $2.50 a day plus rations. Shortly after making this plea, Governor Shorter issued an appeal for six hundred slaves, one hundred each from Montgomery, Lowndes, Dallas, Marengo, Perry, and Wilcox counties, to work on the Mobile defenses.

The request read in part: "The owners will be allowed a dollar a day for each slave, to commence from his embarkation on river or railroad; transportation, subsistence and medical attendance will be furnished. Each slave must be provided with either a spade or shovel, axe or pick, clothing, bedding and provision to last to Mobile." Any owner who sent twenty-five slaves could also send a white man with them to care for them and help supervise their work.[13]

Shorter estimated that the defenses could be completed in about sixty days. Newspapers throughout Alabama and in other Southern states published the governor's appeal. The *Montgomery Daily Mail* urged the citizens of the capital city to give their aid cheerfully "in promoting a move so necessary for the protection and safety of our interests and our homes." The *Charleston Mercury* also expressed concern for the safety of Mobile but criticized Shorter for being too calm and too slow in acquiring necessary laborers. Why ask for only six hundred slaves, asked the paper, when several thousand could finish the work quickly? The *Mercury* also wondered "why in a vital matter of this sort, there should be any dislike to resort immediately to impressment."[14] Although Confederate authorities impressed increasing numbers of slaves, doing so remained a thorny political issue throughout the war.

The Confederate command at Mobile established a series of regulations concerning black laborers on January 26, 1863. Leadbetter ordered his superintendents to have overseers and laborers at work promptly at seven o'clock every morning. The overseers were to keep the men under their charge busy at all times so no time would be lost. Overseers could not excuse men from work without approval by a medical officer. The superintendents issued all tools to the overseers, who were responsible for them after issuing them to the work gangs. If the laborers damaged any property, such as flatboats, tools, pile drivers, or wagons, the superintendents had to report such damages to the engineer headquarters. Leadbetter expressed some concern for the health of the laborers. He wanted their rations to be as good as possible, and he ordered an assistant surgeon to check the men daily. How well these regulations would work had yet to be tested, however.[15]

The living and health conditions of the black labor force at Mobile underwent close scrutiny by both engineers and medical officers in early February 1863. Many of the workers suffered from illness much of the time, and rumors circulated that their mortality rate was very high. At least one engineer officer complained that he could not keep enough laborers to do the work he was ordered to do. Dr. D. E. Smith, the assistant surgeon in charge of the Engineer Hospital, investigated the blacks' living quarters and rations. He found that the food they were issued was insufficient for maintaining good health: "Upon investigation of their rations I find them to consist of Corn Meal, rice, Molasses, and fresh beef, the latter article often falling short and according to evidence of overseers for as many as five and six days in succession the negroes have lived upon Bread and Molasses. The Corn Meal is issued in sufficient quantities, but there being no lard or fat of any kind issued it makes very unpalatable bread. Bacon is issued for one day only in every fifteen days and salt meats are not issued at all." To correct these deficiencies, Smith recommended that the engineer commissaries issue the workers more salted meat and large quantities of fresh vegetables.[16]

Nor was Smith satisfied with the workers' quarters. Most of the blacks stayed in Hitchcock's Cotton Press, where they were crowded together in uncomfortable quarters. The press stood near the Choctaw Point swamps, a traditionally unhealthy area of the city because of dampness and mosquitoes. Dr. F. A. Ross, medical director of the District of the Gulf, had appointed three medical officers in addition to Dr. Smith at the hospital to attend to the laborers. According to Smith, the blacks suffered primarily from typhoid fever, measles, pneumonia, erysispelas, and "swamp fever." Ross admitted that the physicians had not been successful in treating some of the ill blacks but said they received the same care as the soldiers and there were fewer deaths among them than among a similar number of new recruits. Although Ross could do little about the food issued, he did recommend the erection of barracks for the blacks along the line of earthworks. The Confederates also constructed a larger hospital for the laborers who worked on Dauphin Island and the other lower bay defenses. In December 1864 an inspector reported on this facility: "I have never seen any place in which Negroes are congregated which presented the degree of cleanliness and neatness comparable with this establishment. The wards, out buildings, kitchen, bathroom, even the yard was policed as well as it was possible to do it."[17]

In June 1863 General Maury found the Mobile defenses short of black laborers. The Engineer Bureau in Richmond no longer encouraged the employment of soldiers on fortifications, possibly for fear of the demoralizing effects of doing the same work as slaves. Thus Leadbetter could rely only on slave labor and a small number of officers and men in engineer service. The planters of Alabama remained reluctant to send their slaves away when they needed them to work the fields. At one time Leadbetter had only about 150 slaves working on the city line of entrenchments. Maury authorized him to hire laborers for two dollars a day plus subsistence, but Leadbetter had little luck in hiring such men. When the engineer in charge at Choctaw Bluff asked for laborers to work there, Leadbetter wrote that he had none to spare. Toward the end of June Maury sent some of his troops into nearby counties to impress slaves. An officer who came from one of Alabama's hill counties enjoyed the impressment work he carried out near Greenville: "You can imagine that I have a good deal of fun. At first I thought it a very unpleasant business to impress Negroes, but the planters oppose it so much that my ambition makes it more a pleasure to take them than not."[18]

By early December 1863 Lieutenant Colonel von Sheliha found that insufficient rations had been issued to the black laborers at Mobile. The men received only three-quarters of a pound of beef a day, no corn meal, and little else. Von Sheliha recognized the necessity for larger rations and requested aid from the Commissary Department. After receiving assurances of increased supplies, von Sheliha issued orders that rations would include one pound of beef daily, one pound of pumpkins daily, one and one-quarter pounds of corn meal daily, ten pounds of rice per hundred rations eight days in fifteen, fifteen pounds of peas per hundred rations seven days in fifteen, and four and one-half pounds of salt per hundred rations daily. He ordered scales set up in each quarters area to weigh the rations. Von Sheliha charged his overseers with seeing not only that the slaves received proper rations but also that the food was prepared properly and distributed fairly. If the overseers failed to follow these instructions, commissaries had authorization to purchase necessary rations and deduct their price from the overseers' wages.[19]

Von Sheliha and his engineers received some criticism and complaints despite the good work they did on Mobile's defenses. Planters in the interior of Alabama voiced most of the complaints, which centered around the use and treatment of slave laborers. Von Sheliha answered these criticisms in a letter to Governor Thomas H. Watts. The planters alleged first that the engineers kept the slaves in Mobile beyond the sixty-day period for which they had been impressed. Von Sheliha pointed out that he retained no blacks longer than sixty days and that he had included the days spent in travel to and from Mobile in the impressment period. The second complaint was that the slaves were mistreated while in the city. Although he admitted to some abuses, von Sheliha referred Watts to orders he had issued setting standards for feeding the blacks. He also said that the cotton presses used as barracks had been improved and that workers made shoes and clothing for the slaves. In closing, von Sheliha hinted at a plan to replace the impressment system with a permanent engineering corps of black laborers, a plan that, if successful, would eliminate further criticisms of the engineers.[20]

Von Sheliha outlined his idea for a corps of black engineers more extensively in a letter to Senator Clement C. Clay of Alabama. He began by pointing out the disadvantages of the impressment system. The slaves left their plantations without necessary clothing and shoes. Many blacks were soon discharged because they were unfit for the duties required of them, while others were let go because of illness. The laborers who remained had to be instructed in the complicated tasks of military engineering, which took so much time that the slaves spent very little of the sixty-day impressment period in productive labor on the earthworks. Even during training and actual work, the process of acclimatization often reduced the amount of effective work the slaves could perform. In addition, the impressment system was expensive. The government paid not only for the transportation, hire, and support of the laborers but for the hire of agents and clerks to maintain the system and might have to compensate planters for slaves who died while at Mobile.[21]

Von Sheliha listed the advantages to be gained by the organization of an engineer laborer corps. First, such an organization would enable chief engineers to carry out their plans successfully. For example, von Sheliha estimated that if he had a proper standing labor force he could complete the work at Mobile so that it would "not only stand a most minute criticism" but would "stand any siege." Second, an engineer corps would work more efficiently than impressed laborers. Third, the government would save a considerable amount of money. Fourth, the creation of a labor corps would eliminate the shortcomings and hatred produced by the impressment system. Von Sheliha suggested that his idea also be extended to hospital nurses and teamsters. This would free many white men who could bear arms from what he called "an inactive, unsoldierlike service."[22] Von Sheliha's plan showed merit, and it is perhaps unfortunate that the Confederate authorities did not implement it.

The use of captured Union black soldiers became a controversial aspect of slave labor at Mobile in the closing months of the war. In his capture of Fort Pillow, Tennessee (April 12, 1864), and Athens, Alabama (September 24, 1864), Major General Nathan Bedford Forrest took prisoner some eight to nine hundred black soldiers, most of whom he sent to Mobile. General Maury put them to work on the fortifications after he received authorization from the War Department. More than half of the captured blacks ended up on duty with the ordnance, medical, and commissary departments rather than on regular engineer duty.[23] When they could identify the owners of the soldiers who had been slaves, the Confederate authorities paid compensation for the labor of these blacks. Several of the blacks escaped and reported to Union authorities that the Confederates had mistreated them while at work on the fortifications. Major General Gordon Granger lodged a protest with Maury and threatened to employ captured Confederate soldiers in similar work. After consulting with his superiors, Maury replied that the Confederate government did not consider these blacks prisoners of war but property of their owners. He assured Granger that the men received adequate food and supplies and were not abused. Though Granger still hoped to have these blacks exchanged as prisoners of war, the Confederates retained control over them until the end of the conflict.[24]

CHAPTER 9

Blockade Running into Mobile

Although Mobile occupied a strategic position in the Confederacy because of its railroad connections, of almost equal importance was the city's status as a major port for blockade runners. New Orleans outranked Mobile as a port early in the war, but the fall of the Crescent City in April 1862 made Mobile the leading port on the Gulf. The vessels that ran the blockade in and out of Mobile took their cargoes to and from Havana, Cuba, the best base in the Gulf for this trade. The trip between Mobile and Havana took about three days if the runner encountered no problems. Taking out of Mobile primarily loads of cotton, the runners exchanged their cargoes for both military supplies and items for consumption by the civilian populace of the Gulf South. Running the blockade was very dangerous, but attempts to get by the blockading squadron increased as the war progressed. Of the men who engaged in the trade, one author has written: "Some of the blockade runners were patriots who wished to aid the Confederacy, but many were in the business only for money, and they made profits equal their risk."[1]

Blockade runners did not find Mobile an easy port to enter and leave. Access to the bay was limited and difficult. Three entrances to the bay existed. One of these was a westward approach near Dauphin Island known as the Pelican Channel, but its shallow depth precluded its use. A second entrance, known as the Swash Channel, followed the shoreline from the east toward Fort Morgan. Although the channel was less than twelve feet deep at low tide, the runners used it a great deal because once they had gotten into it, the blockading fleet found it difficult to cut out the runner from the fleet's normal station. The main channel extended from near Fort Morgan five miles southward. At the lower end of this channel stood a bar covered by twenty-one feet of water. Blockading vessels stationed at these three entrances could cover them very easily. Confederate field artillery could keep the blockaders far enough away from the Swash Channel to keep it open most of the time, but the Confederates could do nothing to protect the other channels. By stationing vessels near the bar in the main channel, the Federals could maintain the blockade "more effectually and by a smaller force than at almost any other place of trade on the coast."[2]

The shallow waters in and around Mobile Bay also created difficulties for blockade runners. In the bay itself the two anchorages used by vessels had little depth. Only twelve feet of water covered the anchorage near the city and eighteen to twenty feet that near Fort Morgan. During the early years of the war, this lack of deep water limited the blockade-running fleet mostly to light-draft sailing vessels. These schooners and sloops had to depend on a fair wind to go in and out of the bay. Steamers engaged in the trade needed both fair wind and high tides. Naturally, many of the sailing vessels and steamers presented no match for the much faster Federal blockaders. By late 1863, however, new, light-draft, British-built steamers with engines designed for high speeds dominated the blockade-running business. These British steamers made frequent successful trips through the blockade. A contemporary observer noted that one of the vessels appeared "in her voyages almost as regular as a mail-packet in time of peace."[3]

In presidential proclamations of April 19 and 27, 1861, Abraham Lincoln established a blockade of the ports of the Confederacy from Texas to Virginia. The first Federal ship to appear off Mobile Bay was the steam frigate *Niagara*. She arrived in the area during the first week of May 1861. Her patrol area consisted of the entire coast between

Pensacola and the mouth of the Mississippi River so she did not always stand off Mobile Bay during the month of May. The USS *Powhatan* assumed the duties of blockading Mobile Bay on May 26. When she arrived near the main channel, her crew observed a welcoming signal on the flagstaff of Fort Morgan. The Confederate garrison had raised the United States flag, union down, on the flagstaff under the Confederate flag. To the editors of the *Daily Advertiser*, the incident seemed a "Joke on Lincoln," but the arrival of the *Powhatan* marked the permanent establishment of the blockade of Mobile.[4]

The Federals gave the ships then at Mobile approximately a month to leave the port with their cargoes before a rigid blockade became effective. Between May 4 and 27, thirteen vessels, most of them British ships bound for Liverpool, cleared the harbor. These vessels carried on them 28,182 bales of cotton weighing 13,507,240 pounds and 7,555 barrels of turpentine and resin. As the "last day of grace" neared, the acting British consul at Mobile, James Magee, arranged with the commander of the *Powhatan* to allow a tugboat to pull to sea the two remaining British ships. Magee then contracted with the captain of the steam tug *Baltic* to tow out the two vessels. These ships sailed out of the bay on May 31, after being boarded by the commander of the *Niagara*, which had relieved the *Powhatan* three days previously. From May 31 onward any vessel attempting to enter or leave Mobile Bay would be subject to seizure and the confiscation of her cargo by Federal authorities.[5]

From early June 1861 until the end of the year, little activity took place in and out of Mobile except for some coastal trade with New Orleans. Even this coastal trade had ended by June 24.[6] The Confederate government had not yet arranged to receive supplies from Europe so no English or other foreign ships attempted to enter Confederate ports during much of 1861. In fact, the first blockade runner to arrive in the Confederacy reached Savannah, Georgia, in September.[7] Besides this general lack of blockade running, the paucity of potential cargoes for export contributed to the inactivity at Mobile. Receipts of cotton from the interior fell off dramatically once the war started. The blockade was one reason for the low volume of cotton imports. Of greater importance, cotton factors in Mobile urged planters not to ship any cotton to the city. The *Advertiser and Register*, supporting the factors, asserted that the blockade prevented it from being shipped and that stockpiles of cotton would prove "a strong temptation to the enemy to organize land and naval armaments for attacking" Mobile.[8]

At the beginning of 1862 blockade runners began attempting to sneak in and out of Mobile Bay. Most of these vessels successfully eluded the few blockaders stationed near the bay. A few, however, were not so fortunate. On January 20 the *Andrieta* tried to get into Mobile, but the USS *R.R. Cuyler* sighted her. The captain of the *Andrieta* raised the British colors, ran his ship ashore east of Fort Morgan, and ordered his men to abandon her. Federal boarding parties reached the *Andrieta* and secured ropes to her. Shortly afterward Captain William Cottrill's company of mounted scouts reached the beach and opened a heavy fire on the Federals, driving them away from the beached vessel. The enemy boarders had done their job, however, and when the tide rose they hauled the ship off as a prize. The British consul at Mobile attempted fruitlessly to persuade the commander of the Federal squadron that the *Andrieta* had not intended to run the blockade.[9]

Official Confederate policy on blockade running out of Mobile began taking shape in the spring of 1862. Three or four businessmen in Mobile approached General Sam Jones and his successor in command at Mobile, General Butler, about taking cotton to Havana so they could use the proceeds to purchase military supplies for the Confederacy. Both Jones and Butler expressed reluctance to grant them permission. Jones did allow a few small cargoes to go out but under restrictions "requiring that the parties interested, the Captain and Crew, shall be loyal and indentified [sic] in interest with the Confederate States and that the return cargoes shall as far as practicable be composed of munitions of war."[10] The Confederate Navy Department signed contracts with two or three individuals to supply munitions to the government after taking cotton out of Mobile. Secretary of War Randolph encouraged Jones to allow blockade running on the grounds that it was "good policy to exchange produce for arms and munitions of war" even though "the practice is liable to great abuse and should not be allowed indiscriminately."[11]

The dash of the Confederate raider *Florida* into the bay provided one of the most dramatic incidents of the blockade of Mobile. She had only recently entered Confederate service when her captain, John Newland Maffitt, ran her into the bay on the afternoon of September 4, 1862. Maffitt intended to sail his ship from Havana to Mobile so that he could enlist a full crew and procure complete equipment to fire her guns. Both he and his undersized crew suffered from yellow fever. When the *Florida* received her cannons from the British at Nassau, she had not gotten the rammers, sights, sponges, and other items necessary to work the guns. Maffitt had no pilot familiar with the waters of Mobile Bay, and all channel markers had been removed, so he had to attempt to get into the bay during daylight hours. To get by the four Union blockaders guarding the entrances to the harbor, he decided to fly the British colors and depend on the *Florida*'s resemblance to a British warship to deceive the enemy. It seemed a desperate gamble but one Maffitt had to take.[12]

Three Union blockaders guarded the main ship channel into Mobile Bay. Commander George H. Preble of the ten-gun steam sloop *Oneida* did not know that Maffitt's cruiser was nearby. After successfully bluffing his way past the two other enemy vessels, Maffitt steamed directly for the *Oneida*. As the *Florida* began to steam past the latter ship, Preble fired a shot across her bow. When the *Florida* did not slow down, he ordered a full broadside. Soon the two other Federal gunboats opened fire on the *Florida*. Maffitt's ruse had paid off, however. His vessel ran successfully past her enemies, and her superior speed kept her ahead of her pursuers. Despite her lead, however, a hail of shell and shrapnel struck the *Florida*. The chase lasted for two hours. Maffitt, so ill that he had to be lashed to the rail, finally took his battered vessel under the guns of Fort Morgan, where he received a greeting of a twenty-one-gun salute and the cheers of the garrison. Preble received no cheers. Secretary of the Navy Gideon Welles relieved him of command and dismissed him from the service. The Navy Department later restored his rank and returned him to duty, but not until 1872 did a court of inquiry clear Preble of blame for the escape of the *Florida*.[13]

After entering the bay, the *Florida* remained in quarantine for two weeks. She then steamed up toward the city to undergo repairs. Maffitt began to recruit his new crew and to equip his vessel for service. By early January 1863, Maffitt and the *Florida* appeared ready to go to sea.

The weather did not favor the ship's exit until January 15. On that day a gale began blowing from the north. The *Florida* started out about 2:30 on the morning of the sixteenth. Seven Federal warships waited for her to come out. Under cover of a heavy mist, the *Florida* succeeded in passing five of the enemy vessels before they discovered her. When Maffitt realized that they had seen his ship, he ordered all sails raised. The gale winds drove her forward at fourteen knots. Only one Federal vessel possessed speed enough to try to catch the *Florida*, and she chased the Confederate cruiser for three hours before the Federals lost sight of their prey and returned to the blockading squadron. Maffitt once again had eluded the Federals, and he embarked on a notable career of destroying enemy commerce vessels. After the war, Admiral David D. Porter wrote of the incident: "His being permitted to escape into Mobile Bay, and then out again, was the greatest example of blundering committed throughout the war." [14]

The success of the *Florida* in running the blockade at Mobile demonstrates the inefficiency of the blockade there during 1862. An Englishman who visited the city in the fall of that year reported: "The people of Mobile seem to drive a thriving trade with Havannah by running the blockade—their swift, well-handled steamers going in and out just when they please." [15] Some of the blockaders recognized the weakness of their efforts to guard the bay. A frustrated sailor aboard the steamer *Susquehanna* implied in a letter to a northern newspaper that many blockade runners were being allowed to escape: "If there be a case for judicial and executive investigation it is here at this post of the Gulf squadron, and it should be inquired into." [16] Although no conspiracy existed, it is easy to understand this Federal's feelings. Reports on arrivals at and departures from Mobile during the year 1862 show that 83 percent of all attempts to run the blockade succeeded. [17] The situation at Mobile typified the blockade elsewhere along the Southern coast. In his study of blockade running, Frank L. Owsley concluded that "for the first year and a half the blockade was nothing more than the plundering of neutral commerce en route to the Confederacy under the cover of a nominal blockade." [18]

Opposition to running the blockade began to surface in Mobile in early 1863. Because of the potential profits in blockade running, owners of various types of vessels prepared to take their ships out with loads of cotton. The Committee of Safety wrote to Governor Shorter to express concern about the owners of six river and bay steamers fitting out their vessels to run the blockade. These citizens felt that the vessels were essential to the transportation of supplies to the city from the interior and possibly to furnish engines and machinery for the construction of gunboats. If they were captured, their loss would be a severe blow to the city and state. The committee asked Shorter to use his influence in Richmond to prevent these ships from going out. Shorter did forward the committee's letter to Secretary of War Seddon and added his protest to theirs. Seddon replied that the Confederate government could not interfere with "such legal use of the river steamboats as the owners deem judicious." In answer to Shorter's expressed and the committee's veiled opposition to exporting cotton, Seddon stated that the Confederate Congress had sanctioned blockade running and that the War Department agreed with that policy.[19]

One Mobilian complained that the value of goods exported through the blockade far exceeded that of goods imported and that ships coming in brought too few munitions and staple goods. On the basis of statistics from the customhouse, John E. Murrell informed the War Department that from May 1862 to April 1863 cotton worth $1,823,000 had gone out of Mobile while the value of imported goods stood at only $208,168. This represented a balance of $1,614,832 against the Confederacy. Murrell, who had participated in blockade running himself, expressed concern that runners brought too much liquor into Mobile. He suggested that the blockade trade as then conducted should end or be regulated to benefit the war effort. To this end he recommended that the government order half of the space on all outgoing vessels reserved for government cotton and the same space on returning ships for government supplies. Finally, Murrell urged that the government prohibit or severely limit importation of liquor. At that time the authorities did not want to enact the policies suggested by Murrell, but in March 1864 they did establish several blockade-running regulations similar to Murrell's recommendations. These new regulations derived from a plan submitted by Murrell's friend Colin J. McRae of Mobile.[20]

The Confederate government did begin taking steps to ensure a more reliable flow of needed supplies. In early April 1863 Secretary of War Seddon authorized General Buckner to seize the iron side-wheel steamer *Alabama* as a blockade runner for the government. Once Buckner impressed the vessel, Seddon expected him to charter her to a party owning munitions in Havana to bring these supplies back to Mobile. Seddon advised that if there were sufficient room on the *Alabama* on the return trip, food supplies might be included in her cargo. The government already successfully employed blockade runners at Wilmington, North Carolina. Seddon believed that running the *Alabama* under government control would prove more successful and economical than if she remained under private auspices because "the Government can command more reliable officers, the best pilots and secure facilities."[21] The *Alabama* became a successful blockade runner, making at least five trips during the summer of 1863.

Buckner's successor at Mobile, General Maury, attempted to continue and even strengthen Buckner's policy on blockade running. He contracted at least two other steamers, the *Fanny* and the *Crescent*, to bring in goods for the Confederate armies. The War Department authorized Maury to make similar arrangements with as many ship owners as possible.[22] Maury's efforts did not always succeed, however. Some shipping firms did not honor the contracts they signed, and Maury urged the War Department to annul the contracts. He also reported: "I believe that the people concerned in running the blockade will run their ships on Government account only on compulsion or in consideration of extraordinary benefits from the Government, and it is probable that owners will sell their ships in Havana, and that future voyages will be made under a foreign flag." The solution, as Maury saw it, was for the government to have its agents in Havana buy suitable vessels and "take the business into its own hands."[23]

Both the *Alabama* and the *Fanny* ran out of luck on September 12, 1863. On that day three Federal gunboats chased the *Fanny* as she tried to enter Mobile Bay. She attempted to escape into Pascagoula Bay, but her crew set her afire to prevent her capture and thus destroyed her cargo. The *Alabama*, too, attempted to get into the bay, but Federal blockaders discovered and chased her. They finally captured her near the Chandeleur Islands and took her to New Orleans. Maury informed Joe Johnston that blockade running seemed temporarily at an end at Mobile because of the loss of these two vessels:

"They may be regarded as the last of the blockade runners, as they were the best of them."[24] Indeed, blockade running at Mobile practically came to an end for the year. Slightly more than one hundred violations of the blockade occurred from January to September but fewer than twenty after the capture and destruction of these two runners.[25]

During 1864, British side-wheel steamers dominated and revived the blockade-running business at Mobile. The most prominent of these ships were the *Denbigh, Donegal,* and *Mary.* A description of the *Denbigh* fits almost any of these vessels, which had been specifically designed to run the blockade:

> She was a side-wheeler, schooner-rigged. . . . She was built of iron, and had a marked draft of seven feet, fore and aft. She had artificial quarter galleries, an elliptic stern, and a straight stem. Boats painted white swung from iron davits on her port quarter and abreast of her mainmast. A house with a binnacle on top was athwartships, between her paddle boxes. Her funnel was painted black, and there was a bright, copper steam pipe at the after part of it. She had side houses and a hurricane deck, with her foremast through it. Her masts were bright. Mast-heads, tops, caps, crosstrees, bow-sprit, and gaff were painted white.[26]

Only the presence of large numbers of Federal warships off Mobile Bay in February and March 1864 and the capture of the forts at the bay entrances in August 1864 slowed and eventually ended the highly successful trade conducted by these steamers.

The British steamers did not always enjoy easy trips in and out of the bay. On the night of January 31, 1864, the *Denbigh* ran aground in the Swash Channel east of Fort Morgan while attempting to get out. Her crew, aided by troops from the fort, threw off the cotton that was her cargo. The blockading fleet discovered the *Denbigh*'s plight and opened fire on her. One shot hit the wheelhouse but did no damage. Artillery fire from Fort Morgan drove off the attackers. Several days later, the steamer *Dick Keys* succeeded in getting the *Denbigh* off and towed her into the bay.[27] The *Virgin* ran aground in the Swash Channel on July 9, 1864, while trying to get into the bay. During the daylight hours of the tenth and the eleventh, the blockaders fired at the *Virgin* but did not hit her. Confederate soldiers boarded the stranded vessel to protect her against enemy cutting-out expeditions, and finally they got the *Virgin* off and brought her into the bay.[28]

Another blockade runner did not share the good fortune of the *Denbigh* and the *Virgin*. The *Ivanhoe* ran aground in the Swash Channel on the night of July 1 during her first attempt to evade the blockade. Two companies of men moved out of Fort Morgan to protect her and to remove her cargo. Six or seven Federal gunboats opened fire on the *Ivanhoe* after sunrise. The enemy fleet continued to shell the steamer for several days; on each occasion the gunners in Fort Morgan returned their fire. Although Confederate shells struck several vessels, none damaged the Federals very seriously. On the night of July 5 an expedition of four Federal launches boarded the *Ivanhoe* and set her afire. Confederate soldiers on the beach opened up a strong rifle fire when they discovered the flames. The raid destroyed the bow and stern of the blockade runner but not her midsection. Eventually, Confederate engineers succeeded in getting the *Ivanhoe's* machinery out, but the passage of the Federal fleet into the bay in August ended plans to refloat her.[29]

The last steamer to run the blockade at Mobile, the *Denbigh*, went out on the night of July 27, 1864. When the Federal fleet concentrated off Mobile Bay before it ran past the forts, vessels still at Mobile were trapped. Maury gave some thought, however, to allowing one steamer to attempt to run out after the Federals had gotten into the bay. The War Department gave its permission for the *Heroine* to make the attempt if she could do so safely, but conditions prevented the attempt. Three other vessels—the *Virgin*, *Red Gauntlet*, and *Mary*— were also trapped at Mobile. Maury ordered all four seized for use by the military. The steamers served as dispatch and transport boats and did good work during the sieges of Spanish Fort and Blakely. When the army evacuated Mobile, the blockade runners carried men and supplies up the inland rivers of Alabama. The Confederate naval commander surrendered them with his other vessels at the end of the war.[30]

Blockade running had proven a highly successful and profitable business at Mobile and other Southern ports. Frank Vandiver has concluded that running the blockade "was perhaps the most successful, large-scale campaign attempted by the South."[31] He argues that the supplies brought into the Confederacy through the blockade enabled her to wage war longer than she could have without them and that with enough time, blockade running would have eliminated supply shortages. The most recent study of Confederate blockade-running activities reinforces Vandiver's conclusions: "Without blockade running, the Confederacy could not have properly armed, clothed, or fed its soldiers. As long as there were ports that the steamers could utilize, the Confederacy survived; but once the seaports were captured, the nation was destined to die."[32]

Mobile certainly played an important role in the business. Attempted violations of the blockade at Mobile numbered between 208 and 220. Slightly more than 80 percent of these attempts succeeded. The number of attempts was exceeded only at Wilmington, Charleston, and New Orleans, and the percentage of successful attempts stood as high or perhaps slightly higher at Mobile than at those three ports. Had the Confederate government better used the port, Mobile might have played a significantly more important role in supplying the armies and civilians. The government allowed operators of blockade runners to choose their port so most of them selected Wilmington or Charleston. Stephen R. Wise has suggested one way in which greater emphasis on Mobile might have aided the war effort: "The wear on the railroads and other logistical problems so encumbered the Confederate supply system that bottlenecks occurred all along the line, with the greatest strain falling on Wilmington. Mobile was in a position to relieve the transportation problems. By using its railroad and steamship lines, Mobile could have become the major supply center for the Western armies."[33]

Though strategic decisions by the Union high command delayed an attack on Mobile until the summer of 1864, a few minor engagements occurred near the mouth of the bay as early as 1861. Many of these actions resulted from the desire of the Federal naval officers commanding the blockade to test the Confederate defenses. Only on a couple of occasions did any land actions pose any potential threat to the Gulf city.

CHAPTER 10

Naval and Military Engagements at Mobile

The first fighting at Mobile Bay was a naval engagement that occurred on the morning of December 24, 1861. The gunboat *Florida* steamed out from its station near Fort Morgan to a point near Sand Island and opened fire on the Federal steamer *Huntsville*. At first the blockader replied with two guns, but her commander ordered his men to cease firing with one because its shots fell short. For at least three-quarters of an hour the two vessels exchanged shots. The troops in Fort Morgan and Fort Gaines crowded their walls, and sailors on nearby Federal blockaders also watched the duel. One Confederate soldier wrote later in the day, "Oh! it was a glorious sight, and the music of the guns was a grand accompaniment."[1] Because they stood one and a half to two miles apart, the gunboats had difficulty hitting each other. Neither side acknowledged being hit, though admitting some near misses, and each side claimed to have caused slight damage to its antagonist. The two vessels drew off with each crew thinking it had won a victory.[2]

When Captain Randolph assumed command of the Confederate naval forces at Mobile, he had received instructions to try to break the blockade whenever the gunboats *Morgan* and *Gaines* were ready.

He chose the morning of April 3, 1862, to make a foray. The little squadron sailed past Fort Morgan until it encountered the enemy. At the time, the Federal blockading force had only two vessels, and available records do not indicate whether one or both of the gunboats became involved in the action that followed. Randolph ordered his men to open fire, and the Federals soon replied. A newspaper account of the skirmish relates that the two sides exchanged only a dozen shots before the Confederate gunboats returned to their station near Fort Morgan. Neither side suffered any damage or casualties. One source states that at least one Federal gunboat pursued the Confederate vessels as they drew back into the bay but turned back when the gunners in Fort Morgan opened fire on it. Some question exists as to how serious Randolph was in making an attack on the blockaders. One of his subordinates called him an "old coward" for not making a vigorous attempt, but one postwar source described the foray as only a reconnaissance.[3]

It seems likely that Randolph did not press an attack because he had little confidence in his wooden gunboats. Even some of his subordinates expressed concern about the vessels' weaknesses. Two men complained about the lack of protection for the engines and boilers of the *Morgan* and *Gaines* as well as the location of vulnerable steam pipes on their decks. Randolph wrote to Mallory two days after the abortive attack on the blockaders and requested that construction money spent in the future at Mobile be applied only to ironclads. On April 7 Randolph again criticized wooden gunboats like the *Morgan* and *Gaines*, saying that "nothing but ironclad vessels can be relied on to protect Mobile against an attack."[4] An ironclad ram joined Randolph's squadron when on May 27 the state of Alabama turned the *Baltic* over to him. The state legislature had purchased the former lighter in December 1861 with funds appropriated the month before for construction of an ironclad. Workmen carried out the conversion in Mobile. When completed, the *Baltic* had iron plating covering most of her sides, but several areas were protected only by cotton bales. Her armament consisted of four heavy and two light guns. Though slow and hard to manage, she served as Mobile's only ironclad until early 1864.[5]

The Confederates had constructed Fort Grant at Grant's Pass in

December 1862. They moved artillery pieces in, and Captain J. M. Cary's Company C, First Alabama Artillery Battalion, transferred from Fort Morgan to man the guns. On December 14, two Union side-wheel steamer gunboats sailed to within about two miles of the battery to see what the Confederates had done. The gunboats stopped and opened fire on the battery and the Confederate gunboat *Selma* stationed nearby, but the shells fell short of their marks. The *Selma* replied to this fire, but her shots fell short also. Cary's Alabamians opened fire on the enemy gunboats. One of their shells burst before it reached the vessels, and another passed over them. With this the two side-wheelers withdrew. Though it was hardly a decisive engagement, one Mobile paper saw cause to brag about the defense of the fort: "[It] will prove an obstacle in the way of our 'particular friends,' which they may find more exciting than agreeable whenever their anticipated attack is made upon our city."[6]

The Confederates attempted to conduct another offensive operation in early February 1863. Mobile's naval officers hoped to make a night attack on the blockading squadron and capture by boarding at least one of the vessels. On the night of February 5, between sixty and one hundred men from other vessels transferred to the *Selma* for the attack. Armed with cutlasses and pistols, they wore white handkerchiefs around their caps so that they could distinguish one another from the enemy during the boarding. The *Selma* left Mobile in a dense fog, which should have aided the operation. Near the Dog River bar, however, the gunboat struck a snag or piling and began to sink rapidly. The crew got her pumps going and kept her afloat until she could be steered into shallow water. There the *Selma* ran aground. Ship carpenters came down from the city to patch the hole, and the Confederates used a steam fire engine to get the *Selma* afloat. She then sailed to the dry dock for repairs. One naval officer summarized the operation: "Now we are once more afloat, not having boarded the blockaders and 'nobody hurt.'"[7]

On April 18, 1863, the Confederates experienced success in an offensive move against the enemy. Union blockading vessels were accustomed to lying in as close to Mobile Point east of Fort Morgan as possible to try to catch blockade runners going out or coming in through the Swash Channel. In this operation, the objective of the

Confederates was to discourage the blockaders from coming in so close to land. Major James T. Gee left Fort Morgan with two lieutenants and forty-two enlisted men of his First Alabama Artillery Battalion and two rifled fieldpieces on the night of April 17. The troops marched nine miles along the point until they saw a blockader lying about one mile from the beach. At daylight the Confederates opened fire with their cannon. After being struck several times, the Union vessel withdrew from range. Two other gunboats came up, and all three fired at the Confederate position. The Union fire did no damage except to hit and destroy a stack of muskets. After two and a half hours the Union vessels sailed off, and Gee's men returned to Fort Morgan. From this time on the blockaders stayed farther out from land.[8]

The Federals made a small attack on Grant's Pass on August 24, 1863. The gunboats *J. P. Jackson* and *Genesee* steamed through Mississippi Sound toward Fort Grant and opened a long-range fire on the work. Of the approximately sixty-nine shells thrown by the Union gunners at the fort, only six or eight hit the island. None of the shells caused any damage or casualties although some Confederates narrowly escaped injury. The fort's only casualty resulted from the explosion of one of its own guns. A cannon served by men of the First Alabama Artillery Battalion burst and slightly wounded one of the cannoneers. Since this was the fort's only long-range cannon, the Confederates made no more replies to the bombardment but remained under cover "untill [sic] the Yanks were tired of the sport."[9] The enemy gunboats sailed off having sustained no damage or casualties.

Fort Grant again became the site of an engagement with Federal gunboats on September 13, 1863. About ten o'clock in the morning the gunboats *Genesee, Jackson,* and *Calhoun* sailed up toward the earthwork to test its strength and opened fire after anchoring. A Confederate gunboat and transport stationed near Fort Grant changed their positions to avoid being struck. The Confederate gunners opened up with their own guns in reply to the enemy fire, but the range was so great that none of their shots struck the vessels. This exchange continued almost without interruption until almost four o'clock in the afternoon, when the Federal vessels disengaged and steamed back toward Ship Island. Although the gunboats had thrown approximately

175 shells at the little fort, only 15 hit the island, and none did any damage. A soldier stationed at Fort Grant wrote, "The only loss on our side was a poor innocent rat that got killed in trying to make its escape out of the magazine."[10]

The most serious threat to and fighting near Mobile came in the early months of 1864. To attract attention away from his foray toward Meridian and to keep the Confederates from shifting large numbers of troops against him, Sherman requested that Banks conduct a demonstration or feign an attack against Fort Powell. Such a move would reinforce the idea that the Federals were planning an attack on Mobile. Sherman asked Banks to have naval vessels keep up the mock assault for about a week so that he could make the most of his stay in Meridian tearing up the Mobile and Ohio Railroad in that vicinity. Banks discussed Sherman's request with Farragut at New Orleans and urged him to cooperate. Farragut eagerly agreed, probably hoping that the army would send him some troops for a full-fledged attack on the forts at the entrance to Mobile Bay. He ordered six mortar boats at Pensacola readied for the attack on Fort Powell in cooperation with gunboats already in Mississippi Sound. Farragut informed the Navy Department of his intentions: "I shall therefore amuse myself in that way for the next month, unless the [Confederate] ironclads should come out."[11]

Sherman's Union army left Vicksburg February 3 on its march toward Meridian. The troops captured Jackson on February 5 and crossed Pearl River two days later. Polk's Confederates opposing Sherman lacked enough numerical strength to make a stand and fell back in front of the Federal advance. Polk requested that Maury send him two brigades from Mobile if he could spare them and promised to return them if the enemy attacked Mobile. The brigades of Quarles, Cockrell, and Baldwin left the city on Feburary 7 to join Polk. In return for these forces, Polk ordered to Maury the recently organized Twenty-second Louisiana Consolidated Infantry and three companies of the First Alabama Infantry. The men of both units had experience as heavy artillerists, and Maury had requested their services earlier.[12] Maury also relieved Shoup of his duties at Mobile and ordered him to Polk temporarily as a brigade commander. To protect his eastern division against a possible Federal raid from Pensacola, Maury sent Brigadier General James Cantey's brigade to Pollard.[13]

The troops from Mobile had barely begun arriving at Meridian when Polk decided to order them back. In addition to the three brigades mentioned above, Polk sent Maury two other brigades and the men in a camp for exchanged prisoners at Enterprise. The movements of the enemy prompted this action. Sherman reached Morton on February 8 and began marching toward Meridian the next day. Fearing that Sherman's force was part of a combined attack by land and sea on Mobile, Polk wished to strengthen its garrison, which numbered about twenty-five hundred men. He had visited Mobile several days before and expressed confidence that the defenses looked complete enough to resist an assault. Supplies at the city appeared sufficient to sustain a large garrison for six months, but Polk promised Maury he would try to send additional meat and corn. In reporting his actions to Richmond, Polk urged Davis to supply Maury's requisitions for heavy artillery ammunition. Polk encouraged Maury to ask the noncombatants in the city to leave.[14]

Maury followed up quickly on Polk's request. He informed the people through the newspapers that Mobile might be attacked and asked everyone who could not participate in the defense of the city to leave for the interior. An editorial in the *Advertiser and Register* ventured the opinion that Sherman was unlikely to move against the city but recommended that women, children, and other noncombatants leave so as not to be "in the way—an obstacle to the General commanding, and a drawback to the success of the defence." Several days later, Maury, in a letter to Mayor Slough, noted that few people had left Mobile and urged him to use his authority to make them go. He offered to furnish transportation for them. Slough appealed to the people's patriotism, pointing out that if they left, more food would be available for the soldiers defending Mobile. Governor Watts made arrangements with planters and townsmen in the interior to house the refugees. Hundreds of people finally left the city, and many of them found a welcome in Montgomery, where some of their fellow townsmen had gone earlier in the war.[15]

Confederate authorities in Richmond did not ignore the possible threat to Mobile. Davis seemed particularly anxious that Sherman's column be stopped before it could reach the Gulf. He urged Joe Johnston at Dalton to send troops to Polk to attack the Federals. The capture of Mobile would not only mean the loss of its port and rail facilities but also would give the enemy a good base for operations into the interior of Alabama. Johnston replied to the president's entreaties by saying that his army was too weak to aid Polk and hold the approaches to Atlanta at the same time. He then suggested that Polk assemble his cavalry and use it to harass Sherman's line of march. Seddon telegraphed Beauregard at Charleston to ask if he could go and assume command of the defenses of Mobile. The answer was that Charleston remained threatened and he did not think it proper for him to take over at Mobile at such a late hour because he did not know the situation there. Beauregard offered only to inspect the defenses and confer with Maury. The War Department then ordered General Rains back to Mobile from Charleston to work once more with subterranean shells. [16]

On February 13, Maury learned of Farragut's planned attack on Grant's Pass, though he apparently did not know the attack was only a feint. He asked the War Department for six thousand more men to hold the lines in the event of a siege. Though he thought he had a sufficient supply of commissary stores, Maury requested more ordnance for his heavy artillery. In response to Maury's request for experienced engineers, the Engineer Bureau made application to Seddon for several officers. [17] Maury's report to Seddon on the condition of his outer line was not optimistic. He found Fort Powell weak and difficult to strengthen properly. A determined enemy assault would probably get through Grant's Pass. The defensive posture near the main channel was not much better: "The line between Forts Morgan and Gaines is also very liable from the same causes to be forced. The channel is too wide and deep to defend or obstruct effectually. The battery to have been placed in the channel is not yet quite ready, nor has the admiral yet been able to move the *Tennessee* into the lower bay. The enemy will probably, therefore, be able to occupy the lower bay with his fleet of war ships, and will do so preliminary to the siege." [18]

The anticipated attack on Fort Powell began on February 16, 1864. Six mortar schooners and four gunboats opened fire on the fort at about nine o'clock that morning. The Confederates manning the guns in Powell replied infrequently to the enemy bombardment. None of their shells struck the Federal vessels. Most of the shells hurled at the fort also fell short. A Confederate officer wrote later to his girlfriend: "The damage to the Fort was very trifling." At least five Federal shells exploded in the officers' quarters and destroyed them. Two men in the fort, one of them Lieutenant Colonel James M. Williams, commanding the post, were wounded during the attack. A shell fragment knocked Williams down and stunned him. According to a newspaper report, he barely escaped being killed: "The shell grazed the front of his arm and body, entirely tearing away the sleeve and breast of his coat." At least one Confederate concluded from the results of the bombardment that naval fire alone would not reduce the fort.[19]

Heavy winds from the north prevented the Federal vessels from renewing their attack for a week. Maury used the lull to continue his defensive preparations. He asked the War Department for additional artillery shells, powder, and rifle ammunition. To inquiries from Beauregard, Maury and von Sheliha replied that the engineers had placed a heavy sand glacis, or cover, around the walls of Fort Morgan and Fort Gaines to protect the masonry from the fire of rifled cannons. Maury continued to collect food supplies from Polk to provide subsistence in the event of a siege. To assist von Sheliha in constructing fortifications near the city and in strengthening the outer defensive line, Maury requested the War Department to assign Major General Jeremy F. Gilmer, chief of the Engineer Bureau, to Mobile temporarily. Finally, to guard against a possible landing on the coast, Maury organized a force of sharpshooters from his infantry brigades and sent them with the Fifteenth Confederate Cavalry and two fieldpieces to Bayou LaBatre.[20]

Admiral Buchanan hoped to do his part in defending Fort Powell and the lower bay. He commissioned the *Tennessee* on February 16 and prepared to take her down the bay. Work on the ironclad had been completed in early December, and Buchanan's crew had placed all her guns aboard her by January 26. In the *Tennessee* the admiral had what many contemporaries and historians, "including Alfred T. Mahan, [considered] to be the most powerful ironclad built from the keel up within the Confederacy." She carried two 7-inch and four

6.4-inch Brooke rifled cannon. Six inches of iron plating covered the forward part of her casemate, while four inches of plating covered her sides and stern. Yet the *Tennessee* had weaknesses: poor engines making her slow, faulty gun port shutters, and exposed steering chains. Though she was ready for combat, the ironclad's deep draft prevented her from getting over the Dog River bar. Buchanan would have to wait until workmen could construct camels (wooden caissons) which he could use to raise her and float her over the bar.[21]

The Confederate high command and Maury divided their attention between defense of the city and Sherman's movements in Mississippi. Seddon advised Maury to concentrate his efforts against Sherman in the field rather than preparing to defend Mobile itself. The Federals had reached Meridian on February 14 and sent detachments south along the Mobile and Ohio Railroad to Enterprise. Maury apparently agreed with Seddon's strategy because he registered no protest and ordered Cantey's brigade up the railroad to prevent any further southward movement by the enemy. Polk granted one of Maury's requests and sent the remainder of the First Alabama Infantry to Mobile. This unit took charge of the heavy artillery in seven redoubts on the city's outer defense line. Polk also promised to send the First Mississippi Artillery to Mobile as soon as he could. Von Sheliha had gathered additional entrenching tools from Montgomery and put them to use with the force of slave laborers then coming in from the interior. By February 20 Maury had almost 9,300 men under his command ready to defend the city. Although it was not a large army, it probably was sufficient to meet the enemy forces threatening Mobile.[22]

Farragut's mortar schooners and gunboats renewed their attack on Fort Powell on February 23 and continued the bombardment the two days following. On the twenty-third, the Federal gunners fired slightly more than 300 shells at the fort but caused no damage and no casualties. During the attack on the following day, the Federal vessels threw nearly 375 shells toward Fort Powell. Again, few of the shells struck the target, and those that did had no serious effects. The Confederate artillerymen in Fort Powell initiated the action of February 25 by firing on the Federal squadron. Despite the 470 shells fired in reply by the enemy, the fort sustained less damage than it had the previous day, although the garrison lost one man killed and two wounded.[23] A frustrated Union naval officer wrote to a comrade about these fruitless attacks: "We are hammering away at the fort here, which minds us about as much as if we did not fire—that is, the fort—for the men skedaddle as soon as the fire is at all brisk, although they will keep up anything like a fair fight, as they did with me for two hours yesterday in the *Orvetta,* and until the others commenced action, when they retired."[24]

Heavy northerly winds, low tides, and bad weather prevented Farragut's vessels from renewing their attack on Fort Powell until February 29, but on that day they carried out the fiercest bombardment the fort had to sustain. They fired some 567 shells that day, but the attack again had only negligible results: "only 20 [shells] struck the island and 3, the bombproof, killing or wounding no one and damaging the Fort so slightly that ten men in ten minutes restored it to its former condition." The Confederate gunners fired slightly more effectively than before. Although one of their cannons burst, the men kept up a steady barrage. Five shells struck one of the mortar schooners, forcing her out of the action. The commander of the Confederate ram *Baltic* wrote to a friend about the engagement: "I saw some beautiful line shots made . . . during the bombardment, and am satisfied at least one of the mortar schooners would have been sunk if sailors had been handling it [a cannon], but unfortunately those who were working it knew not how to sight a gun." Finally, at sunset Farragut ordered his ships to break off the engagement. The fort's flag remained flying as the Federal vessels sailed westward.[25]

The bombardment of February 29 convinced Farragut that further attacks on Fort Powell would yield no better results. He also realized that he could do nothing that would result in the capture of the forts guarding the entrances to Mobile Bay. High winds and low tides had prevented the Federal vessels from getting any closer than two miles to the fort. Several ships ran aground during the two-week demonstration and had to be towed off. The low water also made it almost impossible for small boats to land an assault force against the fort. Buchanan's small squadron of gunboats had assumed a position in rear of Fort Powell where they could take the garrison off or reinforce it. The ironclad *Tennessee* could not get over the Dog River bar, but Farragut mistook the *Baltic* or another vessel for the *Tennessee.* Thinking the ironclad ready for action, Farragut did not feel he could run into the bay without monitors or ironclads of his own. Lacking troops to cut off the land approaches to the Confederate forts, the Union admiral decided he could not attack Mobile Bay successfully and chose to end his demonstration.[26]

The possible land threat to Mobile had ended nine days earlier, when Sherman's army began its withdrawal from Meridian. Sherman had heard nothing from Sooy Smith's cavalry, he felt his men had done all the destruction they could, and he wanted to get back to Vicksburg in time to send troops to join Banks on the Red River. Unknown to Sherman, Smith's command had not left Memphis until February 11. His force reached West Point, about eighty miles north of Meridian, on the twenty-first. There Smith imagined himself confronted by a larger force under Major General Nathan Bedford Forrest and ordered a retreat. The Confederate cavalry attacked and routed the Federals at Okolona the following day. Sherman blasted Smith's conduct in the campaign, and that general resigned his commission six months later. Sherman felt that he had accomplished his goal in the raid despite Smith's failure to cooperate: "We staid at Meridian a week, and made the most complete destruction of railroads ever beheld.[27] He predicted that the devastation would deny the use of the railroads to the Confederates during the spring campaigns.

Fort Powell had come through this baptism of fire very well, although certain aspects of the defense had not satisfied the Confederate command. In each attack the Confederate guns had been silenced because the weight of metal thrown against the fort had made it impossible for the artillerymen to remain at their stations. The Confederate engineers could not strengthen the earth and sand parapets and traverses so that the men could remain safely at their guns. None of the torpedoes placed in the waters west of Grant's Pass exploded even though the Federal vessels struck many of them. Later the engineers discovered that marine worms had formed clusters on the tops of the torpedoes and prevented the firing mechanisms from working. Despite these disappointments, the Confederate military authorities were pleased with the defense of the fort. The garrison had lost only one man killed and five wounded. None of the nearly two thousand shells fired at the fort did any damage that could not be repaired overnight: "Not a single gun had been dismounted, not a single traverse had been seriously damaged, nor had the parapet and the bombproof lost any of their strength, all damage done by the exploding shells being at once repaired by throwing sandbags in the open craters. [28]

Admiral Buchanan attempted to conduct a sortie against the Federal blockading fleet in late May. His ironclad ram, the *Tennessee*, finally got across the Dog River bar on May 18, and he raised his flag on her four days later. Davis and the Navy Department had pressured Buchanan to raise the blockade even though he wished to wait until completion of the ironclad *Nashville*. Accompanied by the *Baltic*, *Gaines*, *Morgan*, and *Selma*, Buchanan took the *Tennessee* down the bay to an anchorage near Fort Morgan. On the first night chosen for the attack, bad weather hampered the squadron's movements and prevented an offensive. The *Tennessee* ran aground the next night. By the time she floated off, Buchanan had decided to cancel the attack because he considered Farragut's fleet too strong. Farragut had expected the Confederates to come out and had reinforced the blockading fleet until it numbered a dozen vessels. Although the results of Buchanan's foray down the bay were negative, at least one army officer supported his cancellation of the attack: "Everyone thinks the admiral acted most prudently. I don't think the younger portion of the gunboats [officers] fancied the expedition much." [29] A few months later, Buchanan and his men would finally meet the Federal fleet in action.

CHAPTER 11

The Battle of Mobile Bay

By late July 1864, Union forces along the Gulf Coast began making final plans for an attack on Mobile Bay. Concerned that the Confederates would continue to strengthen Fort Morgan, Farragut had urged Canby to send him some troops so that he could attack the forts before the Confederates made them too strong. Even before Canby agreed to loan the men, Farragut proceeded with his own preparations. He saw his objective only as the reduction of Fort Morgan, Fort Gaines, and Fort Powell, thus sealing off blockade running in and out of the bay. Farragut outlined his strategy to his subordinates in orders and correspondence. First, his main attack force—fourteen wooden gunboats and four monitors—would run through the main ship channel. Once inside the bay, the gunboats would try to destroy or disperse Buchanan's wooden vessels. Farragut intended that the monitors would attack and capture or sink the ram *Tennessee*. Seven gunboats in the Gulf and five or six more in Mississippi Sound would assist and protect the landing of Canby's infantry and artillery on Dauphin Island. Farragut considered the capture of Fort Gaines essential so that he could supply his vessels in the bay during further operations. Following the reduction of Gaines, the combined Union forces would capture Fort Powell and Fort Morgan in turn.[1]

Canby designated a force of approximately fifteen hundred men to operate in conjunction with the navy against the Confederate forts. He hoped to reinforce this expedition if circumstances required. Major General Gordon Granger commanded the Union forces, while Brigadier General George F. McGinnis held immediate command of the infantry. Although precise numbers cannot be ascertained, it is clear that the Confederate troops opposing Granger and Farragut numbered slightly fewer than the Union landing force. From his headquarters in Fort Morgan, Page commanded the Third Brigade, District of the Gulf, which consisted of the garrisons of the three forts. The garrison of Morgan consisted of five companies of the First Alabama Artillery Battalion, two companies of the First Tennessee Heavy Artillery, and one company of the Twenty-first Alabama Infantry: in all about 500 men. Colonel Charles D. Anderson, Twenty-first Alabama, commanded Fort Gaines. Six companies of Anderson's regiment and two companies of the First Alabama Artillery Battalion, some 400 men, made up that garrison. At Fort Powell, Lieutenant Colonel Williams still held command with a force consisting of two companies of the Twenty-first Alabama and a portion of Captain James F. Culpeper's South Carolina Battery, a total force of about 140 men.[2]

At daylight on August 5, 1864, lookouts at Fort Morgan saw Farragut's vessels approaching the main ship channel. The admiral used the same tactics he had employed in an unsuccessful attack on the Confederate batteries at Port Hudson in March 1863: his vessels steamed up in pairs, lashed together, with the more powerful ships on the side facing Fort Morgan. The monitors were stationed between the gunboats and the fort, where Farragut hoped they would silence both the water battery and the fort's parapet guns. In approaching Fort Morgan, the lead monitor, the *Tecumseh,* fired a few shots to test the range of the fort. Shortly after 7 A.M., when the Union vessels had come within a mile of the fort, Page ordered his gunners to open fire. The Federal squadron took approximately forty-five minutes to pass the fort. Page's men fired 491 shot and shell at the enemy from the fourteen heavy and several lighter guns that bore on the channel. Heavy smoke from the guns on both sides obscured the gunners' vision, and their fire had very little effect on the gunboats or monitors and caused few casualties. One shell did disable the *Oneida* when it struck her boiler, but the *Oneida*'s consort, the *Galena*, took her into the bay with the other vessels.[3]

The Confederates did destroy two Union vessels during Farragut's run into the bay, but neither of them fell victim to the fire of Fort Morgan's guns. Farragut's four monitors steamed between the wooden gunboats and the fort with the ultimate intention of attacking the *Tennessee*. The leading monitor, the *Tecumseh*, proceeded as ordered through the gap between the Confederate torpedoes and Fort Morgan. Her commander, T. A. Craven, directed her into the torpedo field so that he could engage the Confederate ironclad, but the *Tecumseh* struck a mine and sank almost immediately. Only twenty-one of her crew members managed to escape before she went down. One historian has termed the sinking of the *Tecumseh* "the most completely disabling blow struck by torpedoes during the entire war." The side-wheel steamer *Philippi* became the second victim of the Confederates. She attempted to follow the main attack force into the bay but struck the shoal on the western edge of the channel. The Confederate gunners at Morgan directed a heavy, effective fire into her, and her commander ordered her abandoned. A party of men from the Confederate gunboat *Morgan* soon boarded the *Philippi* and burned her.[4]

Buchanan's small squadron added what firepower it could to oppose Farragut's vessels as they steamed into the bay. The gunners delivered a raking fire into the Federal gunboats, which the latter could not return. When the Federal gunboats finally did open on the Confederate squadron, their fire was heavy and accurate. The *Gaines* received several hits below the waterline and began sinking. Lieutenant John W. Bennett steered his ship toward Fort Morgan and about five hundred yards from the fort ran her onto the beach, where he ordered his men to abandon her. The commanders of the *Morgan* and *Selma* attempted to get their gunboats into shallow water after they witnessed the disabling of the *Gaines*. Lieutenant Peter U. Murphey took his *Selma* toward the northeast. The Union gunboat *Metacomet*, which had cast off from the flagship *Hartford*, gave chase. After the *Metacomet* disabled one of his guns and caused a dozen casualties with her heavy guns, Murphey surrendered the *Selma* rather than risk sinking and more casualties. Commander George W. Harrison managed to get the *Morgan* safely under the guns of Fort Morgan. That night Harrison ran past the Federal fleet and reached the safety of the upper bay batteries. The officers and crew of the *Gaines* also escaped to Mobile during the night in six boats from the *Gaines* and the *Tennessee*.[5]

The dispersal of the Confederate wooden gunboats left only the *Tennessee* to face Farragut's squadron. Buchanan had attempted to ram the *Hartford* and *Brooklyn* as they steamed past into the bay, but the ironclad's inferior speed prevented her from coming close enough to do anything other than fire her guns into the enemy. Once inside the bay, Farragut's vessels gathered about four miles from Fort Morgan and began to anchor. Buchanan determined to renew the battle and try to sink one or more of the enemy gunboats. The latter all raised their anchors and joined in the fray. Three gunboats rammed the *Tennessee* but caused little damage, though Buchanan suffered a broken leg when an enemy shell knocked loose the after port cover and it struck him. The Federal fire cut the *Tennessee*'s steering chains and made it impossible for her crew to change her position. When the ram's smokestack was shot away, she filled with smoke, and her crew could not answer the increasing hail of enemy shells. Commander Johnston finally surrendered the ironclad after an engagement of about an hour's duration, a fight Farragut called "one of the fiercest naval contests on record."[6] Casualties in the small Confederate squadron numbered 12 men killed and 20 wounded. In Fort Morgan, Page lost 1 man killed and 3 wounded. Farragut's force suffered 52 men killed and 170 wounded, not counting the drownings aboard the *Tecumseh*.[7]

Farragut's squadron got safely into Mobile Bay despite the Confederates' efforts. In analyzing the Battle of Mobile Bay in later years, von Sheliha concluded: "The Federal attack would not have succeeded—, nay, it would even have resulted in disaster to Admiral Farragut's fleet—had it been possible to obstruct the channel between Fort Morgan and the eastern bank." The shifting sand of the channel bottom combined with the tidal flow and strong winds over the bay prevented the Confederate engineers from either placing piles in the channel or securing a floating battery there. All the Confederates could do was to place torpedoes across the western portion of the channel. Maury ordered a gap of four to five hundred yards left between the easternmost torpedoes and Fort Morgan so that either Buchanan's squadron or blockade runners could pass in and out. He felt safe in doing so because of the more than twenty guns that bore on the channel from Fort Morgan: "No vessel yet built could pass through that channel in daylight."[8]

The Federals knew about the torpedoes and the gap left in the channel. In his orders outlining the plan of attack, Farragut directed his ships to sail well to the east of the buoy he knew marked the eastern end of the torpedo field. To protect his wooden vessels as much as possible against the heavy Cconfederate fire they would face, Farragut ordered sheet chains draped over the ships' sides and sandbags or chains placed on deck over the ships' engines. The sinking of the *Tecumseh* caused Farragut to alter his plans. He directed his flagship to the head of the line and into the torpedo field. By steaming further to the west, Farragut avoided the heavy fire from Fort Morgan. When some of Farragut's officers had inspected the torpedo line the night before the battle, they found no torpedoes. Farragut thus theorized that the mines had floated in the water so long that they had become ineffective, and he was willing to risk going through them. Events proved the admiral correct because none of the mines exploded. Officers on several gunboats reported after the battle that they had heard numerous torpedo primers snapping as the vessels passed through the field.[9]

There is no good answer as to what went wrong with the Confederate torpedoes. Many of them had been placed only three weeks before the Federal attack. Milton Perry wrote, "No one knows why the mines did not explode." He speculates that overlong submersion had made the powder damp and frozen the trigger springs. Following the demonstration against Fort Powell in February 1864, the Confederate engineers discovered that some of the torpedoes there had failed to explode. Marine worms had clustered on them and prevented the firing pins from functioning. Yet there is no evidence that the Confederate engineers ever again inspected the torpedoes near Fort Morgan. They may have simply accepted examining board reports earlier in the war that the torpedoes were "not liable at any time to be out of order." Although one Confederate torpedo officer felt that few of the Federal vessels could have gotten into the bay if the gap had not been left in the torpedo line, what actually occurred when the Federals passed through the field supports von Sheliha's later assessment: "Had the gap been closed by torpedoes alone, we have our very serious doubts if it would have made any material difference."[10]

Buchanan's small squadron had little more success in stopping Farragut's ships than did the torpedoes. The Confederate tars did their best work and caused the most damage to the Federal vessels when they passed Fort Morgan and thus were unable to return the fire of the Confederate gunboats. Farragut reported that most of his casualties resulted from shells fired by Buchanan's ships. For example, one shell killed ten men and wounded five others aboard the *Hartford.* Once the Federal squadron got into the bay, the unprotected wooden Confederate gunboats did not stand a chance of success against the superior enemy force. Only luck allowed the *Morgan* to escape capture or destruction. The loss of his gunboats left Buchanan in a difficult position. His ironclad was one of the most powerful ever built, but she lacked speed and had lost her smokestack during the passage of the Federal fleet. Buchanan felt that he had two options: to continue the battle and do as much damage to the enemy as possible before retiring under the guns of Fort Morgan or to sit back and await the inevitable destruction of his vessel. His move clearly surprised Farragut and the other Federal commanders. The destruction of the *Tennessee*'s rudder chains foiled Buchanan's plans to return to Fort Morgan and resulted in the surrender of the ironclad. The Confederate admiral might be criticized for risking his vessel when it could have proven more effective as a floating battery at Fort Morgan, but he was a fighting sailor and pursued the course he thought correct. His actions characterized the man: "He embodied the values of the Jones and Decatur era as a man of action willing to challenge long odds. Making single-ship charges like a knight of old in the *Merrimac* and the *Tennessee* was in keeping with the romantic warrior ideal that seemed to drive him."[11]

The evacuation and destruction of Fort Powell by the Confederates gave Farragut the route he needed to supply his vessels in Mobile Bay. While Farragut's squadron ran past Fort Morgan, five Federal gunboats in Mississippi Sound opened fired on Fort Powell. Lieutenant Colonel Williams's garrison replied with the four guns that faced the sound.

Only five Federal shells struck the fort, and none of them did any damage. The Confederates failed to hit any of the enemy gunboats. This action lasted about two hours before the Federals broke off the engagement. They renewed their fire about 11:45 A.M. but ceased firing when they received no reply from the fort. In midafternoon, the monitor *Chickasaw* approached Fort Powell from the east and captured the barge *Ingomar*, which the engineers had used in working on the fort. Williams ordered his men to open on the monitor with a rifled gun on the fort's south face. He had two guns on the east face, but they were exposed because the engineers had not completed the parapet. Only one shell struck the monitor, knocking away its smokestack. The Federal gunners fired twenty-five shells in reply, and their fire had more effect. Williams reported the damage his fort sustained: "A shell entered one of the sally ports, which are not traversed in the rear, passed entirely through the bombproof, and buried itself in the opposite wall. Fortunately it did not explode. The shells exploding in the face of the work displaced the sand so rapidly that I was convinced unless the ironclad was driven off it would explode my magazine and make the bombproof chambers untenable in two days at the furthest." [12]

Williams found himself in a difficult position and turned to Colonel Anderson at Fort Gaines for advice. Anderson told him to evacuate his men if he could not hold the fort. Convinced that he could not defend the work against additional attacks by the *Chickasaw*, Williams marched his garrison out of Fort Powell and blew up the magazine. Maury, von Sheliha, and the Mobile press criticized Williams's failure to hold Fort Powell, and Maury relieved him of command pending an investigation of his conduct. [13] The military tribunal that looked into the case acquitted Williams and determined that he acted correctly in saving his garrison from an indefensible position. Although restored to duty, Williams did not receive Maury's permission to take command of his regiment until December. Fort Powell fell because its eastern face had no protection against the fire of the *Chickasaw* or any of the other monitors. After the war, Williams expressed his opinion on the reason for the weakness of the fort: "The bay side of Fort Powell had been left unprotected while our engineers were engaged in many absurd works, and some which deserve a worse name—such as the construction of batteries near Fort Morgan for no other purpose than the protection of blockade runners in the swash channel."[14] Available evidence indicates that Williams had sufficient supplies and labor to enable him to throw up at least a temporary parapet so that he could have defended the fort for several days. The surrender of Fort Gaines on August 6, however, would have negated any advantage gained by Fort Powell holding out.[15]

The Confederates began making preparations for the defense of Fort Gaines following the landing of Granger's Federals late on the afternoon of August 3, 1864. Maury was away in Meridian temporarily commanding the Department of Alabama, Mississippi, and East Louisiana, and Higgins acted in his place at Mobile. When Page learned that the Federals had landed, he requested reinforcements so he could attack the enemy force on Dauphin Island. Higgins had no real force to send Page but did order two hundred reserves, local defense troops, and marines from the city to Gaines. He also ordered the Twenty-second Louisiana to proceed from Pollard to Gaines.[16] The initial two-hundred-man reinforcement from Mobile arrived at the fort on the fourth. Although subjected to the fire of a Federal monitor, they successfully disembarked. The gunners in Gaines replied briefly to the monitor's fire. Unfortunately for the Confederates, their heaviest gun facing the Federal fleet outside the bay became dismounted during this skirmish.[17] Page did not have enough men to conduct an attack, but Anderson's men burned their outbuildings and prepared for siege operations. Problems with its transport vessel prevented the Twenty-second Louisiana from leaving Tensas Landing on schedule, and consequently it did not reach Fort Gaines before Farragut's fleet got into the Mobile Bay. The unit did, however, escape being taken prisoner when the fort fell.[18]

Granger's men edged in close to Fort Gaines during August 4 and by midnight had gotten their light artillery within twelve hundred yards of the fort. During Farragut's passage of Fort Morgan, the Federals opened with these guns on Fort Gaines. Granger reported that his fire took the fort's water battery in reverse and silenced the guns, but it is unlikely that the Confederates would have attempted to fire on the enemy fleet because they had no guns which would fire that far. Anderson's men did open on the Federal batteries but caused no damage. When the *Tennessee* attacked Farragut's fleet, the Confederates fired a few shots at the Federals with ten-inch columbiads which faced in that direction. Anderson signaled Page asking what he should do. He stated that his fort would offer little protection to his men if fired on from Dauphin Island and the enemy fleet. Page advised Anderson to do his best and to keep up the men's morale. On the fourth Anderson had assured Page that he would resist the enemy for as long as possible, and he repeated that assurance on the afternoon of the fifth: "'We will emulate our glorious old admiral and do our very best.'"[19]

On the afternoon of August 6, the monitor *Chickasaw* steamed to within several thousand yards of Gaines and opened fire. Most of the monitor's shells struck the fort but did not cause any serious damage, but they did kill several men who lay sick in the post hospital. Anderson again requested guidance from Page, who sent two of his staff officers, Captains Clifton H. Smith and R. T. Thom, to consult with Anderson. These officers left Gaines with the impression that Anderson would defend the fort to the last. Shortly after the captains left, however, Anderson received a letter signed by all but two of the officers in the garrison asking him to surrender the fort, which they felt would soon be torn apart by the enemy's fire, rather than risk further loss of life in a hopeless situation. Anderson acceded to his officers' wishes and asked Farragut for surrender terms early on August 7. Page attempted to learn the purpose of the flag of truce he observed and signaled for Anderson to hold the fort. Ignoring Page's signals, Anderson visited Farragut and Granger aboard the *Hartford* that evening and agreed to their terms. While he was away, Page visited Gaines in an attempt to stop the proceedings but had no success. At eight o'clock on the morning of the eighth Anderson surrendered to the Federal navy. His garrison numbered 46 officers and 818 enlisted men. Twenty-six guns, a large supply of ordnance stores, and food supplies for twelve months fell into Federal hands.[20]

Anderson's surrender of Fort Gaines brought no less controversy or condemnation than Williams's evacuation of Fort Powell. Page dubbed the surrender a "deed of dishonor and disgrace to its commander and garrison." Maury echoed Page's sentiments and said that the men should have defended the fort. In a confidential letter to

Braxton Bragg, Maury posited one theory to explain the conduct of both Anderson and Williams: "I think constant croaking and discussion of the weakness of that line had greatly prepared the minds of the commanders to give it up, and when the tremendous fleet placed itself between them and the city, the Garrisons were overwhelmed by dismay."[21] Maury's assessment seems to apply more to Fort Gaines than to Fort Powell. The men at Gaines had served in the Mobile Bay defenses for nearly two years without seeing combat. They had no heart for a fight. Colonel Anderson wrote his wife that he was sure the garrison would have mutinied had he tried to continue the fight. The troops at Fort Jackson and Fort St. Philip below New Orleans had done just that in April 1862 under similar circumstances.

Officers stationed at Fort Morgan were shocked by the surrender of Gaines. One lieutenant confided his feelings to his diary. "Humiliation and sorrow were in our hearts, but indignation soon expelled from our hearts all other feelings."[22] An officer at Gaines who had not signed the letter asking Anderson to surrender later defended the colonel's actions even though he felt Anderson should have waited until the Federals demanded a capitulation: "Col. Anderson may have acted injudiciously in yielding to its [the letter by the officers] request by making the overture to Admiral Farragut, but as we are in honor bound to tell the whole truth, we shall here state that from the moment that the Federal fleet succeeded in running the gauntlet of Fort Morgan and the famous Tennessee had surrendered, from that moment the men of Fort Gaines lost heart."[23]

With the smaller forts captured, the Federals turned on Fort Morgan on August 9. Granger's infantry, which had received reinforcements from New Orleans, landed at Navy Cove and began moving toward the fort. Page chose not to oppose the landing and turned his attention to preparing his position for a stubborn defense. Since the passage of Farragut's fleet, the Confederate garrison had worked to construct sand traverses around the guns, quarters, and sally port. Page telegraphed Jefferson Davis that he planned to hold out "to the last extremity." The Confederates burned all the buildings between the fort and Navy Cove and cleared the ground as much as possible. On the afternoon of the ninth, Farragut and Granger demanded an unconditional surrender of the fort after the fleet had bombarded it for several hours. The enemy fire had done no damage and slightly wounded one man. Page replied: "I am prepared to sacrifice life and will only surrender when I have no means of defense." By sundown, the Federal troops had moved to within two miles of Fort Morgan and completed the investment of the place.[24]

Nothing of consequence occurred at Fort Morgan during the next few days. Granger pushed skirmishers and sharpshooters to within several hundred yards of the fort's walls while his engineers and artillerymen established batteries and siege approaches. Within the fort, officers joined with the men in working on the traverses. Although everyone was tired, morale remained high. The men had provided for the siege by driving cattle and hogs into the fort to furnish fresh meat. One lieutenant wrote in his diary: "My cow and calf were browsing in the luxuriant grass in the ditch near me, happily unconscious of their impending doom." Page detailed 160 men as sharpshooters under Major Gee, First Alabama Artillery Battalion, to meet any attack. From time to time these men exchanged shots with the Federal sharpshooters. The *Tennessee,* now manned by Federal sailors, and Farragut's three monitors opened fire on the fort on August 13 and continued the bombardment sporadically through the next day. Page's gunners returned the fire but had no effect on the ironclads. When one Confederate saw the shells bouncing off her, he pronounced the *Tennessee* impregnable. The accurate Federal fire had caused several casualties, and the post adjutant wrote in his diary: "The casemates are not safe; the shells have no respect for them."[25]

Beginning on August 15, the Federal forces on the peninsula kept up a fairly steady fire on Fort Morgan with artillery as well as that of their sharpshooters. One or more of Farragut's monitors continued the fire from the fleet. The Confederate sharpshooters maintained a sporadic return fire but had to lie low because of the heavy and accurate shooting of the Federals. Except for several brief bombardments of the enemy camp, Page did not allow his artillerymen to open on the Federal land or naval forces. One of his officers reported that Page refused to fire because he did not think the Confederate artillery could retard the enemy advance and because he feared a heavy bombardment in retaliation. Many men in the garrison disagreed with Page's policy and thought it demoralized the soldiers. Several officers stated that the occasional Confederate fire did hamper Granger's advance: "It is a

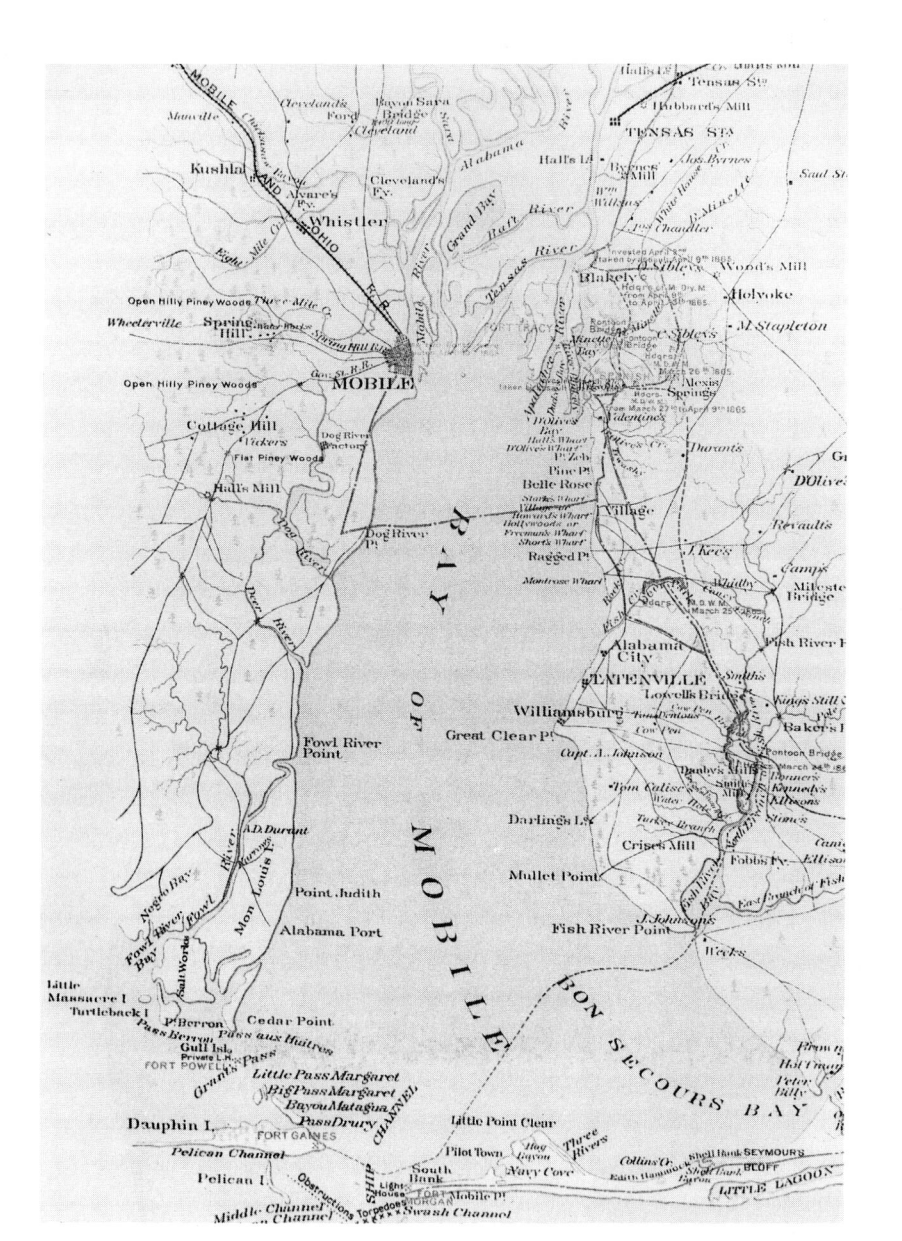

Map of Mobile Bay and its environs. From *The Official Military Atlas of the Civil War.*

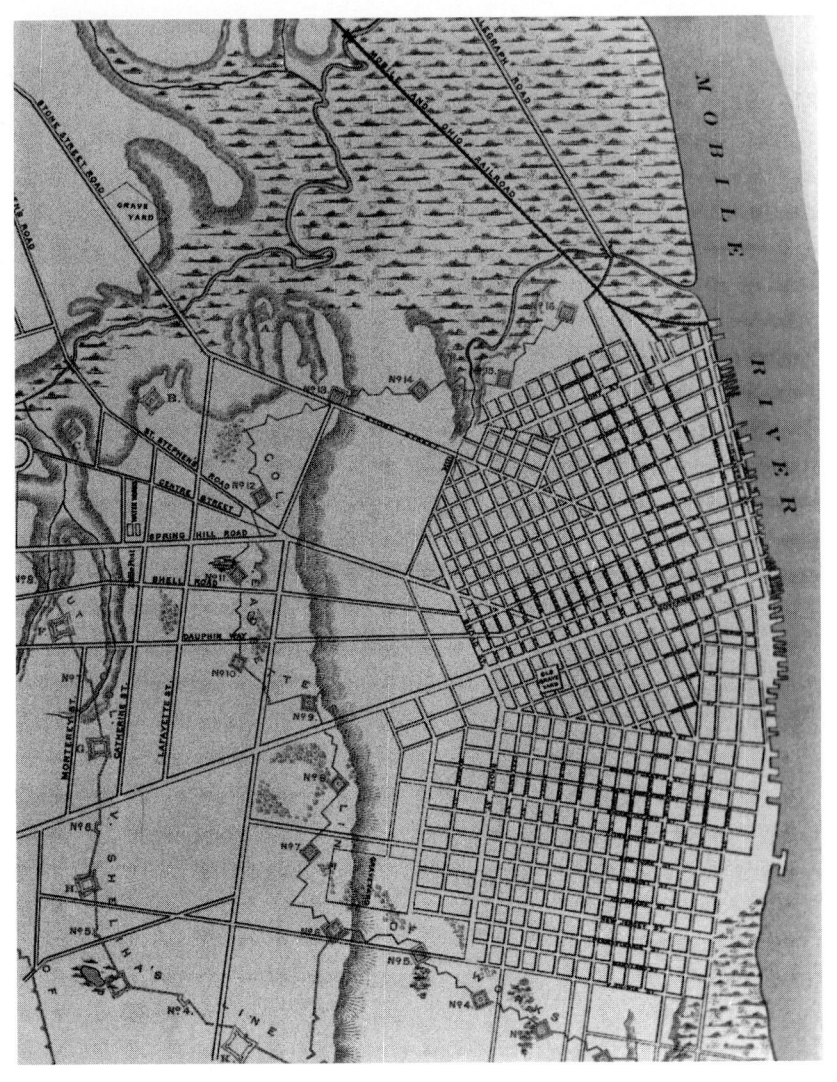

Map of Mobile as it appeared during the Civil War. From *The Official Military Atlas of the Civil War.*

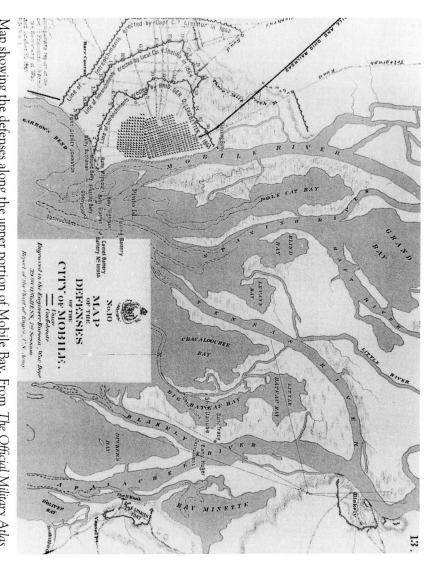

Map showing the defenses along the upper portion of Mobile Bay. From *The Official Military Atlas of the Civil War.*

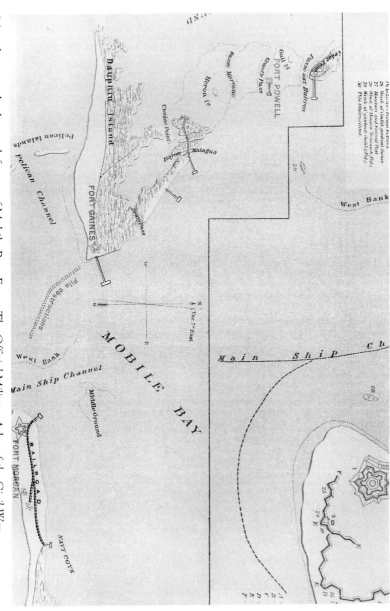

Map showing the lower defenses of Mobile Bay. From *The Official Military Atlas of the Civil War.*

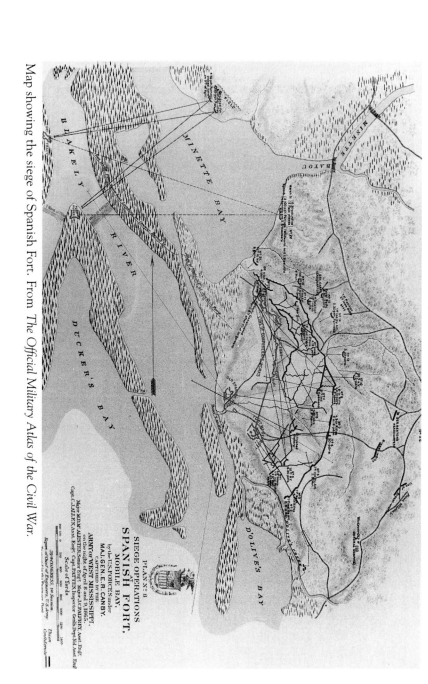

Map showing the siege of Spanish Fort. From *The Official Military Atlas of the Civil War.*

PLAN Nº 8
SIEGE OPERATIONS
AT
SPANISH FORT,
MOBILE BAY,
by the U.S. FORCES under
MAJ. GEN. E. R. CANBY,
CAPTURED BY THE
ARMY of WEST MISSISSIPPI,
on the night of April 8 and 9, 1865.
Maj.r MINE MINISTER, Senior Eng.r Major J. C. PALFREY, Asst. Eng.r
Capt. C. J. ALLEN, Asst. Eng.r Capt. PATTEN, Inspector Genl. & Dep.t Mil. Asst. Eng.r

Scale of Yards

Left: Major General Samuel Jones. Courtesy Cook Collection, Valentine Museum, Richmond, Va. *Below:* Major General Braxton Bragg. Courtesy Confederate Memorial Hall, New Orleans, La.

Left: Major General Dabney H. Maury. From the collection of Arthur W. Bergeron, Jr.

Right: Major General Simon B. Buckner. Courtesy Cook Collection, Valentine Museum, Richmond, Va.

Above: Admiral Franklin Buchanan.
Courtesy Library of Congress. *Right:*
Major General Franklin Gardner.
Courtesy Confederate Memorial Hall,
New Orleans, La.

very fine thing to stand off cooly [sic], aim the gun as if at target practice, & fire at a parcel of poor devils cooped up in a pile of bricks, when there is no danger in the way, but when both sides talk Mr Fed is rather nervous." Throughout the Federal bombardments, Page moved about the fort sending officers and men to secure places and exposing himself to enemy fire.[26]

Life became dangerous for the men of the Fort Morgan garrison, and instances of close calls from death and of heroic actions occurred frequently. On one occasion, a fifteen-inch shell from a monitor tore into a casemate used as an office and destroyed much of the furniture. The shell landed at the feet of several men standing in the office but failed to explode. On another occasion, a fifteen-inch shell entered a casemate used as sleeping quarters for forty men and exploded. The explosion miraculously killed no one and wounded only three men. Page's Confederates began holding prayer meetings every morning at the sally port. Religious services provided no protection, however, for one morning a shell fragment struck and killed a soldier on his way to the meeting. Sentries on the fort's walls tried to warn their comrades of incoming shells. In one instance, a man had barely called out to those below him when a Parrott shell tore off his head. Despite the hardships, the men kept their morale, and relatively few deserted. An officer summed up the situation: "Entirely cut off & with 350 men hemmed in by a fleet of Forty vessels besides a large land force, confined in a small circle scarce large enough to drive a cart in, with a certainty of captivity & perhaps death before us, resistance is heroism & it is our unanimous resolve to sell this Post at a costly price."[27]

By August 21, Granger had twenty-five cannons and sixteen mortars ready to bombard Fort Morgan. Joined by all the vessels in Farragut's squadron, the Federal artillerymen opened a tremendous fire on the fort. Page reported the effect of the hail of shot and shell: "This fire disabled all the heavy guns save two . . . partially breached the walls in several places, and cut up the fort to such an extent as to make the whole work a mere mass of debris."[28] The bombardment had such force that the Union soldiers as far away as Fort Gaines could feel the concussions.[29] Fearing that his magazine might be hit, Page ordered most of his powder destroyed. He also directed his men to spike the fort's artillery. The enemy shells set fire to the citadel, and the fire caused the Federals to increase their barrage, which they had reduced considerably as night fell. After consulting some of his officers and seeing his men fight a second fire at the citadel, Page decided on the morning of the twenty-third to surrender. The ceremonies occurred at 2 P.M., and a Federal officer recorded a description of the Confederate commander: "Page, in a plain suit of citizen's clothing, looked very stiff. . . . From the starched manner in which the late lord of Fort Morgan bore himself, I could well understand why our sailors had dubbed him 'Ramrod Page.'"[30]

Page surrendered Fort Morgan because, as he put it, he "had no means left of defense."[31] The enemy's fire, both from artillery and sharpshooters, and the smoke and flames from the burning citadel made it impossible for the Confederates to man their guns or make any effective reply to the bombardment. With all the casemates at least partially breached, the men had little protection from the Federal shells. After the war, von Sheliha wrote: "A bombardment of another twenty-four hours would have changed the place into a shapeless pile of rubbish." Some six hundred men and forty-six artillery pieces fell into Union hands when the fort's garrison capitulated. Page had lost only about three men killed and sixteen wounded during the siege, but the loss of life would have mounted if the enemy bombardment had continued. On the eve of the Battle of Mobile Bay, Maury had seemed disposed to replace Page: "General Page is too despondent. He seems to see only the weak points of these forts. We need a buoyant man there." Following the siege of Fort Morgan, however, Maury could not fault Page's actions: "From all that is known of the conduct of this officer and the garrison under his orders, it is believed that they nobly strove to redeem the disgrace upon their arms inflicted by the hasty and unsoldierlike surrender of Fort Powell and Gaines."[32]

Farragut's relatively easy victory came primarily because of weaknesses in several elements of the Confederacy's coastal defense system at Mobile. Perhaps most prominent was the lack of a strong naval force to support the forts and to battle enemy vessels. Although the *Tennessee* was strongly armored and well manned, her slow speed prevented her from doing more damage. Also, the *Tennessee* stood virtually alone because the wooden gunboats could offer no effective opposition to the Federal squadron. If Buchanan had had the ironclad *Nashville* and floating batteries *Huntsville* and *Tuscaloosa* ready for action in the lower bay, he might have severely damaged or turned back

Farragut's vessels. The presence of these additional ironclads might even have deterred Farragut from attempting to run into the bay. The successful defense of Fort Sumter demonstrated that if properly supported by a strong navy and other defensive fortifications a masonry fort could hold out against enemy attack even when virtually reduced to rubble. Mobile Bay's forts could lend each other no support. Weak garrisons in Fort Gaines and Fort Morgan could not prevent the small Federal land force from establishing footholds and siege lines on their land faces. Maury had no available troops in Mobile for a relief force nor could he get men from other theaters because enemy forces threatened almost all of them. The Confederate troops on the lower bay thus found themselves isolated and facing the enemy alone. Surrender of the forts was almost inevitable.

The operations in Mobile Bay resulted primarily in the termination of blockade running at the port. It is impossible in the absence of accurate importation statistics for the entire Confederacy to access the exact impact of the cessation of the flow of supplies into Mobile, but the Confederate war effort obviously suffered. Canby did not have a sufficient infantry force for a land campaign against the city itself, and Farragut's fleet could do nothing without land support. Both Sherman and Farragut opposed a direct attack on Mobile. The general preferred to have a Confederate garrison tied up there rather than a Union garrison, while the admiral believed "it would be used by our own people to flood rebeldom with all their supplies."[33] The conduct of the Confederate army and navy commanders involved in the various actions is also difficult to analyze. Buchanan did what any fighting admiral would have done. He might, however, have provided more assistance in defending the forts if he had attempted to keep his squadron, particularly the *Tennessee,* under the guns of Fort Morgan. Maury probably made a correct assessment when he wrote that the commanders and officers of the forts had been psychologically prepared for a surrender by constant talk of the weakness of the forts. If Fort Powell and Fort Gaines had held out longer, their capture might have been delayed or Farragut might have been forced to take his squadron back out of the bay for supplies. Of course, the forts' commanders would have risked sacrificing lives in a gamble that might not have paid off.

CHAPTER 12

Preparing for the End

In anticipation of Farragut's attack on the lower bay forts, Maury and his subordinates had made hasty preparations to defend Mobile. The need for experienced troops occupied a prominent place in Maury's plans. Since all of his regular veterans except the Twenty-second Louisiana had rushed into Fort Gaines in time to be captured there, the need was particularly acute. Colonel Patton's Twenty-second Louisiana occupied half a dozen works upon its arrival in the city. Maury requested Bragg to order the return of the First Louisiana and First Mississippi artillery regiments to Mobile. The former reached Mobile from Montgomery on August 6 and took positions along the city line. Bragg directed the First Mississippi Artillery to move from Atlanta back to Mobile. En route the regiment's train ran into a landslide between Pollard and Tensas Landing, and the accident resulted in the deaths of or injuries to eighty-seven men. Instead of keeping the Mississippians in Mobile, Maury ordered them on picket duty below Blakely on the eastern shore. Even the former officers and crew of the *Gaines* found themselves assigned to a bay battery because of the destruction of their vessel. These men helped fill gaps the local defense troops and convalescents could not cover, but Maury still desired further reinforcements: "Veteran troops should be sent here as soon as they can be spared elsewhere and they should be troops not connected by any ties with Mobile."[1]

Maury appealed to the men in Mobile to organize to defend the city. He ordered Andrew S. Herron and Thomas J. Judge, both colonels and judges in the military court, to supervise the organization of these men. Herron was responsible for the Louisiana refugees and government employees, while Judge had all remaining men. Maury asked those who had arms and ammunition to furnish them and promised that unarmed men would find weapons available. The newspapers urged the city's men to comply with Maury's request: "All men within the city capable of bearing arms, are bound, and will be obliged, to shoulder them."[2] Maury ordered city defense troops that had not gone to Fort Gaines organized into a battalion for permanent guard duty under Lieutenant Colonel Stewart W. Cayce. Even the men of the city police department formed themselves into a military company and elected Mayor Slough as their captain. Governor Watts sent available reserves to Mobile after receiving requests from Maury and Davis. These reserves arrived in the city very slowly, however. By August 9, Maury could report only four thousand troops of all types on duty in the District of the Gulf.[3]

Captain Ebenezer Farrand assumed command of the Mobile naval squadron on August 7. A native of New York, Farrand had entered the U.S. Navy from Florida. When the Civil War began, he resigned and became a commander in the Confederate navy. His early service was in Virginia, but in 1862 Farrand was assigned to the shipyard at Selma. He selected the construction sites and negotiated contracts for the ironclads built at Selma, Montgomery, and Oven Bluff. Farrand apparently assumed command of one of the gunboats at Mobile in the spring of 1864. Buchanan spoke of him as "respected," but at least some of the officers of the squadron did not hold a high opinion of him. When rumors of a change in command surfaced, one officer wrote: "The present incumbent is not thought much of. Most anything would be an improvement in that respect."[4] The cooperation between the services that had existed while Buchanan exercised command deteriorated under Farrand.

The loss of the *Tennessee*, *Gaines*, and *Selma* left Farrand with only the ironclads *Nashville, Huntsville,* and *Tuscaloosa* and the wooden gunboat *Morgan.* The side-wheel ram *Nashville* had finally gone into commission in July but did not have adequate iron plating. Buchanan had decommissioned the *Baltic* and ordered its armor removed for placement on the *Nashville.* Even then the ram had only two inches of plating on the aft section of her casemate and none around her paddle wheels. Because of an iron shortage in the Confederacy not only would the *Nashville* never have enough armor but also the vessels under construction on the Tombigbee River would never be completed to join the Mobile squadron. Federal control of most of Mobile Bay limited Farrand's gunboats to the river systems at the upper end of the bay. The squadron could still lend powerful support to the upper bay and Apalachee batteries.[5]

Because he was exercising temporary departmental command, Maury needed a capable subordinate to fill in for him at Mobile. He had little confidence in Higgins, the only other general officer in the district: "While he is well qualified to fight ships, he is possessed of such an infirmity of temper as sets the whole community, including the officers under him, against him." On August 12, Major General Franklin Gardner arrived in Mobile, and Maury asked the War Department to allow him to retain Gardner for temporary duty. In a letter to Bragg, Maury explained his request: "He will be very useful, and has the confidence of the people and Troops."[6] Gardner's previous experience at Mobile and his outstanding defense of Port Hudson certainly qualified him for duty under Maury. The War Department approved the request, and on August 17 Maury assigned Gardner to temporary command of the District of the Gulf.[7] In addition to a temporary district commander, Maury wanted two brigade commanders and recommended Colonel Henry Maury and Major Bryan M. Thomas, the latter then serving in the Alabama State Reserve. Thomas received a promotion to brigadier general and orders to report to Maury. Instead of promoting Henry Maury, the War Department directed Brigadier General St. John R. Liddell to Mobile. Liddell had recently crossed the Mississippi River from western Louisiana, where he had served under Major General Richard Taylor.[8]

Von Sheliha and his engineers concentrated on preparing the eastern shore and bay batteries for a possible attack once they knew Farragut had passed the lower bay line. Because the bay batteries had received so much attention in the past, the Confederates put most of their energy into work on the eastern shore. Von Sheliha admitted that the defenses there had been neglected and were unreliable. He ordered all gaps in the obstructions in the Apalachee and Blakely rivers closed and the obstructions themselves strengthened. At Battery Huger, von Sheliha mounted five additional heavy guns and thickened the fort's walls. He also began preparing Battery Tracy for new guns. To support these two works, von Sheliha recommended that the navy move either the *Huntsville* and *Tuscaloosa* or three blockade runners mounted with heavy guns into position near the forts. He also initiated construction of works on the heights east of the two batteries to protect their land approaches. Batteries at Blakely would stand too far north to provide effective protection by themselves so on the recommendation of Colonel John H. Gindrat, von Sheliha chose the site of an old Spanish fort as the position for another permanent work: "I propose to countersink our guns commanding the river, and to protect the battery by a bastion line in rear. Time is everything to us now, and we have to make the best use of the short respite the enemy seems willing to grant."[9]

Maury and von Sheliha disagreed on the best means of defending the direct water approaches to the city. The former wished to place the ironclad floating batteries *Huntsville* and *Tuscaloosa* near Choctaw Spit to guard the lower line of obstructions. Von Sheliha thought the Confederates' firepower should be concentrated at the upper obstructions. He saw the Choctaw Spit position as too isolated and weak to resist a strong enemy attack. He persuaded Gilmer to intercede with Maury in support of his ideas, but Maury maintained his position, and the Prussian had to accede.[10] Along the city works and bay batteries the engineers strengthened and put in order all existing works. They placed torpedoes in Garrow's Bend and in the main channel below the obstructions. The only operations of note in this area involved the clearing of land in front of the outer city line. Higgins ordered all persons living within one thousand yards of the line to evacuate their homes. Then von Sheliha put nearly two hundred men to work cutting down the trees in this zone. By mid-August von Sheliha expressed confidence that the works could resist any water attack on the city.[11]

Two small military operations briefly interrupted the operations

conducted by Maury's men. The first of these involved an attempt by
Maury to relieve Fort Morgan. He ordered the First Mississippi Artillery, then stationed at Tensas Landing, to begin moving down the
eastern shore with the idea of creating a diversion in the rear of Granger's land forces besieging Fort Morgan. He hoped to force the Federals to break off the land siege or at least delay its progress. On August
13, Brigadier General Alexander Asboth left Pensacola with fourteen
hundred Federal infantry, cavalry, and artillery on a march toward the
Perdido River. Maury feared the Federal move might threaten Blakely
and ordered the Mississippians back to a point just south of that place.
Asboth's Federals returned to Pensacola without having crossed the
Perdido. Even so, Maury abandoned the idea of trying to relieve Page's
men at Fort Morgan because he did not have enough men both to
dispatch there and to defend the approaches to Mobile.[12]

On August 15, Farragut conducted a reconnaissance of the obstructions below the bay batteries. Granger accompanied the admiral, and
the two planned to study both the land and naval defenses of Mobile.
Four gunboats, one of them the former Confederate vessel *Selma*, and
two monitors moved to within three and a half miles of the city. At
two o'clock that afternoon, the Federal gunners opened fire on the bay
batteries and the gunboat *Morgan*, which was anchored behind the
line of obstructions. This bombardment continued for two hours although the Federals did not put out a heavy fire. The Confederate
batteries did not reply to the Federals, but the crew of the *Morgan* did
send an occasional shell toward the enemy. None of the Federal shots
did any damage to the Confederate defenses. At sunset Farragut ordered his force back down the bay. He had found the channel into
Mobile completely obstructed. The Confederates had sunk the unfinished ironclad *Phoenix* in the only gap that had remained in the line
of piles. In his report to the Navy Department, Farragut said that
unless his men could remove these obstructions there seemed no possibility of even his light-draft gunboats getting close to Mobile. A
Vermont native living in Mobile witnessed the brief action and pronounced his verdict: "So effective was this water line, protected as it
was by water batteries, that Farragut's fleet might as well have attempted to sail through the Green Mountain range."[13]

Von Sheliha and his engineers continued their operations through the end of August. He received some opposition in his attempt to clear the land in front of the city defenses. Various military headquarters issued orders preventing the ax parties from cutting down some of the trees. He requested that subordinate commanders inform him of any further exemptions. The engineers built two new batteries on the bay shore, where they could assist in guarding the obstructions. Each of these works contained heavy rifled guns or columbiads. The former crew of the gunboat *Gaines* assisted in mounting the guns. Even though these fortifications and the other bay batteries appeared in good shape for defensive fighting, some of the garrisons found themselves in a less than ideal situation. An officer at Battery McIntosh described his fort: "The quarters are not very good and very much crowded. The water is very bad and unhealthy. Most of the garrison are suffering from diarrhea." Von Sheliha did not like the construction or location of Battery Huger and Battery Tracy but strengthened their walls and placed heavier guns in them. He hoped these improvements would enable the works to put up stiff resistance to any attack.[14]

The problems von Sheliha faced, particularly the shortage of slave labor, weighed heavily on him and undoubtedly caused him to become somewhat pessimistic. His letters to Gilmer indicated that he felt that Governor Watts was helpless to aid him and that Maury could not impress the needed labor. In one communication he wrote: "If not sustained by my Government, I will resign unconditionally and immediately."[15] Obviously spurred by von Sheliha's attitude, Maury asked Gilmer to send another engineer officer to his district. Because the man Maury requested was ill, Gilmer recommended that the War Department order Lieutenant Colonel Samuel H. Lockett to Mobile. Lockett held the position of chief engineer for the Department of Alabama, Mississippi, and East Louisiana and had served at Mobile early in the war. Von Sheliha outranked Lockett so Gilmer got Lockett a promotion to full colonel. Gilmer possibly did not intend for Lockett to supersede von Sheliha completely because the former's orders called for him to continue his duties with the Department of Alabama, Mississippi, and East Louisiana. When von Sheliha learned of Lockett's assignment, he submitted his resignation but offered to remain in Mobile until the threat to the city had ended. The War Department turned down his resignation request.[16]

As August ended and September began, Maury continued to look
for troops to defend the city. Although Governor Watts urged him to
leave Mobile "a heap of ashes" if he could not hold it, Maury remained confident that with enough troops he could conduct a successful defense. The War Department tried to aid Maury by requesting
that Watts call out as many state militiamen as possible and send them
to Mobile. State troops alone would not suffice for Maury's needs,
however. One problem was that these units arrived very slowly from
their scattered mustering places. More seriously, many of the men fell
ill once they reached the city. Maury requested some veteran infantrymen from General John Bell Hood, who had replaced Johnston in
command of the Army of Tennessee in Georgia. Hood responded with
a brigade of four Alabama regiments (some seven hundred men) commanded by Brigadier General Alpheus Baker. When they arrived at
Mobile on August 28, Gardner ordered these troops to Spanish Fort
to defend that position and to picket the eastern shore. One of Baker's
regiments took up its station at Pollard so it could guard the railroad.[17]

At the same time that he asked Hood for men, Maury requested
Major General Nathan Bedford Forrest to come south from northern
Mississippi with some of his cavalrymen if his situation there permitted it. Forrest ordered two thousand men to Mobile even though he
undoubtedly did not favor such a move. Before these troops could
move southward, Davis telegraphed Maury that he could best use Forrest's men in a raid on Sherman's line of communications in Tennessee
and that state reserves would do as well in the trenches as dismounted
cavalrymen. Maury acceded to the president's wishes and suspended
the movement of Forrest's men. Lieutenant General Richard Taylor,
new commander of the Department of Alabama, Mississippi, and East
Louisiana, reached Meridian and assumed command on September 6.
He decided to send Forrest's cavalry into Tennessee to operate against
Sherman's supply lines: "It is better to risk the fall of Mobile than to
leave any reasonable efforts and means untried to defeat Sherman."
To give Maury some support, Taylor agreed to send one of Forrest's
brigades to Mobile. Colonel Robert McCulloch and his brigade,
nearly one thousand strong, moved southward from Meridian to the
Gulf city.[18]

Despite these additions, the troop strength in the District of the

Gulf did not satisfy Maury. Sickness, still prevalent among the new troops at Mobile, had reduced the force by about two thousand men. Toward the end of September, Maury received through Taylor a request by Hood for the return of Baker's brigade to the Army of Tennessee. Maury explained his situation to Taylor and stated that he did not feel justified in reducing his army by detaching Baker's men. He pointed out that the unit was his sole veteran infantry force and held the important works on the eastern shore. Taylor supported Maury and passed on word that he could not spare Baker's brigade. Maury did agree to send one of his Alabama cavalry regiments to northern Mississippi to help guard that region in the absence of Forrest's cavalry. By the end of September, the effective force in the District of the Gulf numbered only sixty-six hundred.[19]

By the end of September the engineers at Mobile had made good progress in preparing the various defensive works for active service. They did not have a great deal of construction to do along the city line because they had completed most of the redoubts and redans along it. Their primary concern here consisted of dressing up the forts, strengthening their magazines, and connecting them with trenches. Redoubt "N" received the attention of most of von Sheliha's work force. This position, also known as Fort Sidney Johnston, anchored von Sheliha's line to Garrow's Bend and, with Battery Missouri, Mound Battery, and Battery Buchanan, covered the water obstructions from the west. Von Sheliha felt the completion of this redoubt was so important that he employed a force of five hundred slaves on it day and night. A citizen who made a brief excursion along the Shell Road described what he witnessed: "It would be a novel sight to one unaccustomed to the presence of the sable race, to witness the crowds of darkies employed in building the fortifications. They are in such numbers that they look like ants on the side of an ant hill. Just as we passed, the signal to 'knock off' work was given, & they obeyed the summons with alacrity, forming at once into companies, to march into the city, where they are quartered."[20]

Battery Gladden and Battery McIntosh received minor repairs and several new guns. The engineers placed one seven-inch Brooke rifle in the latter. They also prepared a platform in McIntosh for a ten-inch columbiad. This fort seemed susceptible to an attack by enemy launches so the engineers used a pile driver to place obstructions in front of the work while they strung a boom out along the western face. An officer in the garrison at Battery McIntosh wrote in his diary that the men there could not make much of a defense at the battery unless they received strong reinforcements. The men suffered from chills and fever: "Thirty six men out of three companies are all we have for duty today." To strengthen these two batteries further, the engineers moved two floating batteries to the vicinity. They transferred one of the ironclad floating batteries up from the lower obstructions and placed it in the channel between McIntosh and Gladden. In the rear of McIntosh, the engineers anchored a wooden battery (called Camel Battery) that mounted two forty-two-pounder rifles.[21]

Lockett placed Colonel Gindrat in charge of all engineer operations east of the Tensas River, and Gindrat made good progress there. His men did little on Battery Tracy and Battery Huger except place more earth over their magazines and keep them clean. The engineers had almost completed the main work at Spanish Fort by the end of September and mounted two guns in it. They finished the largest of the four redoubts (No. 2) on the line in rear (east) of Spanish Fort but did not have it ready for guns. They had nearly completed practically all of Redoubt No. 3 and Redoubt No. 4 by the end of the month. The laborers dug more than 250 yards of rifle pits and cleared the timber for about 300 yards in front of the entire line. To aid in an evacuation of the works if it became necessary, Gindrat's men began construction of a road through Bay Minette swamp to a point across the Apalachee River from Battery Tracy. At von Sheliha's suggestion, a portion of Gindrat's force erected a battery at Blakely and began clearing land for a supporting line similar to that at Spanish Fort. In the Blakely and Apalachee rivers, the engineers placed additional piles and constructed rafts to block the streams.[22] These operations in the eastern division completed the basic framework of the Mobile defenses, and most subsequent work would only complete or strengthen what the engineers had already begun.

From October 1864 until the commencement of the final Federal campaign against Mobile in March 1865, the Confederate command in the city concentrated on strengthening its defenses and preparing to meet an enemy attack. Maury remained concerned about obtaining a sufficient military force to man his numerous works in the event of a siege. The small force at his disposal suffered from various illnesses, primarily chills and fever, which reduced its effective strength. In early October, out of nine hundred men present, Colonel Patton could count only one hundred fit for duty in his brigade. Maury reported in mid-November that he had only about seven hundred men to defend the land lines around Mobile. By the latter part of that month, his entire effective force in the District of the Gulf numbered slightly less than three thousand men. He asked the War Department for four or five thousand veteran troops, preferably from states other than Alabama: "A few Virginia regiments would be particularly well suited for a tour of service here." Taylor echoed Maury's request but recognized that few such units existed. He was sure Mobile would fall if attacked in its weakened condition. As Taylor anticipated, the War Department could then find no troops to send to Maury. Seddon wrote: "Re-enforcements cannot under more pressing exigencies elsewhere be spared for the doubtful contingency of an unreported attack."[23] Confederate armies in Virginia and Georgia had their hands full contending with the armies of Grant and Sherman.

The only source from which Maury could draw reinforcements was the Alabama State Troops. Practically all of these men then in service had already moved to Mobile. Taylor urged Maury to allow portions of the militia and reserves to return home for short periods of time when he could spare them. These furloughs, Taylor felt, might encourage the men to turn out more readily when an attack became imminent.[24] Maury requested four thousand more men from Governor Watts and pointed out that necessities elsewhere made it impossible for regular Confederate units to come to Mobile. Taylor also addressed an appeal to Watts. He asked the governor to urge the state legislature to pass laws that would make possible the raising of an adequate force for Mobile's defense. Taylor pointed out that the Gulf Coast presented the only threat of invasion of the state. Sherman's March to the Sea had ended any threat from the East, and Hood's invasion of Tennessee had secured the state's northern border. Until Watts and the Alabama legislature could act, Taylor searched his department for men to send to Maury. The only unit he could find consisted of "galvanized Yankees"—foreigners who had deserted the Union army—and this unit numbered only 450 men of dubious reliability.[25]

In the waning months of 1864, several changes among the general officers occurred at Mobile. In September Taylor had requested that Gardner be assigned to command southwestern Mississippi and eastern Louisiana, where Taylor hoped he would succeed in correcting a chaotic situation. The War Department acceded to Taylor's request and in October ordered Gardner to Meridian and to report to Taylor for orders.[26] Maury also lost the services of Higgins in October but did so willingly. Higgins had left his command without orders in September when he thought the enemy would attack Mobile, and Maury removed him from duty. When Higgins applied to Taylor for reinstatement, Maury informed the latter of Higgins's conduct and asked that he not be allowed to return to Mobile. Taylor supported Maury.[27] In late November General Beauregard, now in charge of all western armies, ordered Major General Martin L. Smith to report to Maury for temporary duty commanding the Mobile defenses. Maury wrote to Beauregard explaining that he would assign Smith as temporary commander of the District of the Gulf while he acted as department commander during Taylor's absence in Georgia. When Smith arrived at Mobile, however, Maury decided to make him chief engineer of the Mobile defenses and to turn the district over to Smith only when he himself had to go outside of its boundaries.[28]

Von Sheliha and his engineers did a considerable amount of work on the line of city defenses during the last months of 1864. For the most part, they made repairs and added earth to strengthen walls and magazines during October and November. The largest portion of the labor force of the city works still concentrated on Redoubt "N" (Fort Sidney Johnston) to ready it for service against the enemy's gunboats. Heavy rains, cold weather, a shortage of workers, limited transportation, and a shortage of construction materials prevented von Sheliha from making the progress he desired. To help alleviate the shortage of slave laborers, Taylor authorized Maury to employ his soldiers in completing the fortifications at Mobile.[29] In early December von Sheliha shifted most of his work force to the redans located between the redoubts on the city line. He wanted to put them in good condition so that they could give the necessary support to the larger earthworks in the event of an attack. The engineers had all of the redans in fighting condition by the end of the month. General Smith ordered von Sheliha to prepare *chevaux-de-frise* for placement in front of the lines to protect them against infantry assault. By the end of 1864, the city line seemed ready for active defense.[30]

The bay batteries required less work than the city works. At Battery Gladden the engineers replaced an eight-inch gun with a ten-inch one, made repairs necessitated by heavy rains, constructed a new wharf, and drove obstructions in the waters in front of the work to stop boat attacks. Von Sheliha's men constructed gun pits and mounted two new ten-inch columbiads at Battery McIntosh. They also brought in additional earth to strengthen the walls and traverses of the fort. As was the case at Gladden, severe storms had eroded some of the sand and earth at McIntosh and made repairs necessary. To protect Gladden's left flank, von Sheliha ordered an octagonal floating battery placed five hundred yards northeast of the fort. This battery would mount two guns when completed. The engineers also employed the *Huntsville* and *Tuscaloosa* and a wooden battery constructed on camels (wooden caissons)—each mounting several heavy guns—in support of Gladden, McIntosh, and the bay obstructions. Because the bay batteries and eastern shore works had to share a steamboat for transporting supplies, von Sheliha could not do as much strengthening and repair work as he had hoped, but by the end of December he had all the bay batteries in fair fighting order.[31]

Of the works on the eastern shore, Battery Huger and Battery Tracy received less attention than Blakely and Spanish Fort because the engineers had practically completed the two former forts. Tracy required only minor repairs and additional sodding. Von Sheliha began erection of a new, stronger magazine at Battery Huger. After the engineers covered it with about eight feet of earth, von Sheliha mounted a gun atop it. Because Huger lay closer to the enemy's fleet, making it more vulnerable in case of an attack, von Sheliha wanted to make its walls as strong as possible. He ordered his men to raise and thicken the parapet, especially on the work's south face. He also instructed his engineers to place additional sand on various parts of Huger's interior. Whenever possible, von Sheliha had his labor force place sod on the walls to cut down on erosion. Likewise, he had them drive piles in front of Huger to reduce damage by tidal action. Some limited work remained to be done on Battery Tracy and Battery Huger, but von Sheliha and Lockett both felt that the forts could put up a satisfactory defense.[32]

For practically all of October and much of November, the Confederate engineers accomplished little construction at Blakely. Maury had ordered them to cease work on the water battery there to make all supplies available for use at Spanish Fort. During October, the small labor force at Blakely divided its time between clearing land for the line of redoubts and trenches in the rear of the water battery and loading barges with earth and sod for use at Battery Huger and Battery Tracy. In mid-November, fifty laborers had to be diverted to make repairs on the Mobile and Great Northern Railroad. The engineers began more intensive work on the fortifications in December, although some of their men still had to provide sod and earth for Huger and Tracy. By mid-month Lieutenant E. A. Ford, engineer in charge of the Eastern Division, could report that he had completed two redoubts on the land line. This progress did not please Lockett, however, because he expected Ford to have all of the redoubts in fighting order before any of them reached completion. By Christmas Ford got two more redoubts ready for cannon platforms and fifty yards of infantry rifle pits dug. The engineers would have to do considerable work in the new year to have Blakely ready for troops and all its guns.[33]

Lieutenant John T. Elmore, in charge of engineer operations at Spanish Fort, had plenty of work to keep his men busy. They mounted the guns von Sheliha planned for the main water battery (called No. 1 or Spanish Fort) and completed the work's main magazine. They also strengthened the face of the fort on the land side and began erecting traverses around the guns. Redoubt No. 2 (later called Fort McDermott) received almost as much attention as Spanish Fort because it was the largest fort on the land line. Elmore's laborers strengthened the fort's walls, placed a thick cover over its magazine, and made the ditch deeper and wider. By mid-December they had completed embrasures for six guns. Work slackened in late December because of a shortage of slave labor. Along the entire land line, the engineers began erecting a line of abatis (felled trees with sharpened branches facing the enemy) to protect the works against an infantry assault. Smith still saw a need for much work on the various fortifications as the year ended. He recommended light artillery positions at various points to cover the approaches to the main redoubts. He also recognized the need for safe communication routes between the redoubts and from the land line to a source of fresh water. As at the city works, Maury authorized the engineers to use the soldiers stationed at Spanish Fort to do needed construction.[34]

Maury faced no serious enemy attacks in his district in late 1864, although the Federals did conduct several raids or feint attacks. One of these raids occurred in mid-December and had Pollard as its objective. A force of about eight hundred Negro troops moved from Barrancas, Florida, with orders to break up the railroad at Pollard. They brushed aside the weak Confederate force under Brigadier General James H. Clanton and reached the village on December 16. After destroying part of the tracks and burning several government buildings, the Federals began marching back to Barrancas. The Confederates gathered troops to oppose the raid. Liddell took a mixed force of infantry and cavalry from Baker's and Colonel Charles G. Armistead's brigades, respectively, at Blakely and caught the enemy about six miles below Pollard, where a running fight began. The pursuit continued for about thirty miles, ending only because the Confederates' horses became too exhausted to go farther. The Federals admitted losing eighty-one men killed and wounded, but one Confederate newspaper report placed the enemy casualties at two hundred. Liddell's men captured ten enemy wagons and much of their supplies. The Federals had done little damage to the railroad, and by December 24 repair crews had it back in operation.[35]

Union troops made two other forays on the western side of Mobile Bay. On November 27, Brigadier General John W. Davidson rode out of Baton Rouge, Louisiana, with a force of about four thousand cavalrymen, headed for southern Mississippi. Davidson hoped to strike the Mobile and Ohio Railroad northwest of Mobile and tear up as much of the track as possible. A brigade of Louisiana Confederate cavalrymen pursued the Federal column but lacked the strength to risk an engagement. Maury ordered Colonel McCulloch to deploy his brigade and the Fifteenth Confederate Cavalry to oppose the enemy, and he scraped together a small infantry force at Meridian to serve under General Thomas. Rain turned the roads into quagmires, and the streams and rivers overflowed their banks, impeding Davidson's movements. Only a small Federal detachment threatened the rail line, but McCulloch's men repulsed it in a skirmish on December 10. Unable to cross the Pascagoula River and fearing the Confederate forces gathering against him, Davidson decided to take his men to West Pascagoula, where they could get transports to East Pascagoula and be available to make further threats against the railroad.[36]

General Granger, commanding Union forces around Mobile Bay, proposed a demonstration against Mobile from East Pascagoula to force the Confederates to keep their troops in the city instead of sending them against Davidson or the troops moving against Pollard. After landing at East Pascagoula on December 15 with three thousand infantrymen, Granger began his march toward Mobile. He asked Canby to allow him to use Davidson's cavalrymen, who had just arrived at West Pascagoula, so that he could try to destroy part of the Mobile and Ohio Railroad. Canby ordered only two regiments to Granger because he intended to use the rest of Davidson's men in a raid from Memphis against Hood's Confederate army's communications in Tennessee. The Federal advance halted at Franklin Creek, about twelve miles from East Pascagoula, without encountering any opposition. At Franklin Creek, the Federals threw up some light entrenchments and began stripping sawmills in the area of their lumber. Granger gave up any plans for a strong push against the railroad and contented himself with keeping the Confederates' attention on him and his men.[37]

To oppose the Federals at Franklin Creek, Maury ordered a small infantry force and three cavalry regiments to the area. Taylor wanted Gardner to concentrate all available men from southern and central Mississippi and eastern Louisiana and to station them between Meridian and Mobile so they could cooperate with Maury. One of Taylor's dispatches contained an evaluation of the city's status at this stage of the war. He regarded "the lines of communication with Mobile and the safety of the city as of vital importance, not only to this department, but to the maintenance of General Hood in Tennessee."[38] Several skirmishes between the opposing forces at Franklin Creek convinced Maury that Granger would not advance any farther and that he could not successfully attack the Federals, who were protected by their trenches. He then advised Taylor that he did not need to send any more men from Gardner's command toward Mobile. By Christmas, Maury no longer thought Granger's force was a real threat to the city, an opinion that was confirmed when the Federals retreated on December 26 because of a lack of supplies. Taylor asked Governor Watts and Governor Charles Clark of Mississippi to send available reserves to Maury in case another threat occurred.[39]

The news that reached Taylor from Tennessee certainly seemed to forebode a threat to Mobile. A Union army had smashed the Army of Tennessee in a two-day battle just south of Nashville. Informing Maury that he had become "satisfied that Genl. Hood has suffered a severe reverse," Taylor predicted, "for the first time, that Mobile will be seriously threatened—not immediately, but so soon as the enemy, having pressed his pursuit of our army as far south of the Tennessee [River] as the condition of the roads will permit, shall be in a position to return the force—some 20,000 men—which he obtained from Canby." Taylor urged Maury "to make steady and energetic preparations for the anticipated movement." He stressed the importance of completing Mobile's defenses and setting up enough mills to supply the garrison with cornmeal. Maury replied that Smith found the works defensible and close to completion. He had six mills with a total capacity of 2,200 bushels of meal per day, but most of the corn in the city did not seem fit for issue. Maury hoped Taylor would send proper supplies in time to meet the demands of a siege. Maury also emphasized that the troops then in the city could not make a successful defense against an attack. Only men from field armies would constitute "a good and proper garrison."[40]

The new year found the Confederacy in a precarious position. In the East, Union armies under Grant had defeated a Confederate army in the Shenandoah Valley and kept Robert E. Lee's army closely confined to its lines around Richmond and Petersburg. Grant sent part of his force to attack Wilmington, North Carolina. In the West, Sherman's March to the Sea had devastated Georgia, and his men had captured Savannah in late December. He planned a new campaign into the Carolinas to cut off all supplies to Lee's army. Hood's attempt to reconquer middle Tennessee met with disaster at Nashville. His

Army of Tennessee no longer constituted an effective fighting force. In the Trans-Mississippi area, a Confederate army had failed in an invasion of Missouri, effectively ending the Trans-Mississippi as a battleground. The reelection of Lincoln signaled the determination of the North to prosecute the war. Thousands of Confederate soldiers deserted the armies. A recent study has concluded that by early 1865 "the Confederates had exhausted their morale and will to win."[41]

In view of the possible threat to Mobile, Taylor began in January 1865 shifting troops from Hood's army, recently arrived at Corinth, to the District of the Gulf. Brigadier General James T. Holtzclaw received orders to take his Alabama brigade of Major General Henry D. Clayton's division to Mobile to relieve Baker's brigade, which would replace Holtzclaw's in the division. Maury preferred to have a brigade of troops from another state because he felt they would be less likely to desert and would not be distracted by being so near their homes. Still, he did not adamantly oppose the assignment of Holtzclaw's men to his district. When the Alabamians reached the city, he ordered them to the eastern shore to garrison Spanish Fort and Blakely.[42] Another of Clayton's brigades—Brigadier General Randall L. Gibson's Louisianians—also received orders for Mobile. Gibson's men arrived in early February and camped in the city suburbs.[43] Initially Taylor had received permission to retain Lieutenant General Alexander P. Stewart's corps of Hood's army for use in his department, but he thought the men should go to the Carolinas to fight Sherman's armies. Taylor did retain Major General Samuel G. French's division (now under Brigadier General Francis M. Cockrell) for duty at Mobile but ordered the rest of Stewart's corps eastward. Cockrell's three brigades occupied a camp on the Shell Road about five miles below the city. In all, some three thousand veteran infantrymen had augmented Maury's force at Mobile.[44]

In addition to these infantry units, Taylor ordered approximately fifteen hundred artillerists to Mobile. These men had manned light batteries in Hood's army but had lost their cannon during the disastrous Tennessee campaign. Taylor intended Maury to use these men as infantry until he could find cannon for them. Maury planned, however, to place the men in the works on the city line to handle the siege guns. Most of the men did receive infantry weapons, however.

They had to be trained and drilled in handling heavy artillery and mortars. The captain of one battery wrote to his wife that his men drilled four times a day and worked around the fort the rest of the day. The men of Lumsden's Alabama Battery practiced with their coehorn mortars by firing at targets set out in the marsh in front of their redoubt. These new duties did not satisfy all of the men involved. The officers of the Fifth Company, Washington Artillery, of Louisiana, for example, wrote to Joe Johnston asking for a transfer to his command in the Carolinas. Even the batteries fortunate enough to get field guns did not have enough animals to pull their cannon. Attempts to find additional horses and mules failed. [45]

In January the Confederates used yet another new weapon in defense of Mobile: a torpedo boat. The vessel, the *St. Patrick*, was designed by John P. Halligan, who obtained a contract from the government to build the boat and supervised its construction at Selma. Only one description of the *St. Patrick* survives. She was similar to the "Davids" in appearance: a slender cylindrical body fifty feet long, tapering nearly to a point at each end, with a copper torpedo attached to a twelve-foot spar extending from her bow. The commandant at Selma thought she would prove a "very formidable" vessel: "It is to be propelled by steam (the engine is very compact), though underwater by hand. There are also arrangements for raising and descending at will, for attaching the torpedo to the bottom of vessels, etc." [46]

Shortly after Farragut's squadron entered Mobile Bay, Maury attempted to get the torpedo boat to Mobile so it could attack the enemy vessels. The *St. Patrick* was not yet completed and apparently did not reach the city until September. Halligan was commissioned as a lieutenant in the Confederate navy so he could command his boat, but he refused to take her out against the Federals. Maury complained to the secretary of war in December that he doubted Halligan would ever act and asked permission to place someone else in command. Later in the month, Taylor reported that Farrand refused to order the *St. Patrick* into action or to allow the army to use her. Finally, Maury wrote to Davis about the matter, and the president told Mallory to order Farrand to turn the boat over to Maury. [47]

The flag officer transferred the *St. Patrick* to Maury, who assigned Lieutenant John T. Walker of the navy to command her. Walker be-

gan making preparations to attack the Federal squadron but discovered
that Halligan had taken off some of the boat's machinery. Walker
succeeded in recovering the missing parts and steamed into the bay on
the night of January 27. About 1 A.M., the *St. Patrick* attacked the
side-wheel gunboat *Octorara*. The torpedo grazed the gunboat just behind the wheelhouse but failed to fire. A sailor aboard the *Octorara*
grabbed the torpedo boat's smokestack but had to release it when
someone on the *St. Patrick* shot at him. Although the Federals poured
artillery and musket fire at the *St. Patrick*, she escaped uninjured and
returned to Mobile. There the engineers hauled her up to repair machinery that had broken down during the foray. The *St. Patrick* never
again went into action, and the Confederates probably destroyed her
at the end of the war.[48]

The rift between the army and navy, which began over the use of
the torpedo boat, intensified late in January. Maury complained to
Taylor that the navy had not provided enough assistance in perform-
ing picket duty. He said Farrand kept all but one of his vessels near
the city rather than supporting the bay batteries and obstructions.
Farrand also refused to use his launches for picket duty at the obstructions, claiming "it is too severe on his men." This forced the artillerymen stationed in the bay batteries to do most of that work. The only
other group helping with picket duty was the former blockade runners,
now operated by the Quartermaster Department and manned by soldiers. Maury stated: "Under these circumstances, I am unable to prevent the enemy's boats from taking soundings or removing the obstructions. If there be any more important service for the naval forces
here to engage in, than this, I am unaware of it." He told Taylor that
he would continue asking Farrand to allow "the use of his men and
boats."[49]

Taylor, in turn, wrote to Jefferson Davis concerning Farrand's failure to cooperate with Maury. Because the gunboats always remained
at the Mobile wharf, Taylor pronounced Farrand's squadron "a farce"
and stated, "The payment of its expenses is a waste of money."[50] Davis
may have taken up the matter with Mallory, but there is no evidence
that he did. Some behind-the-scenes diplomacy obviously occurred
during the month of February because in March Maury reported that
relations with the navy had improved. Farrand had "responded, by

very cordial expressions, of his desire and purpose" to cooperate with the army: "He says he will place his vessels in any position I may desire—and do all in his power to aid me." Farrand sent Maury a report of the armament and crew strength of his vessels, and the squadron did lend important support to the eastern shore defenses later in the month.[51]

In anticipation of an enemy campaign against Mobile, Taylor and Maury concentrated their efforts on preparing the city and its defenses for a protracted siege. Taylor urged Maury to have on hand rations to feed ten thousand men for four months. Maury replied that the quartermasters had failed to accumulate a sufficient amount of corn and reminded him that he had no control over supply agents or means of transporting supplies. Taylor pointed out that Pemberton at Vicksburg had been deceived by his commissaries and quartermasters about the quantity of supplies in that beleaguered city. He ordered Maury to have one of his staff officers inspect his supplies daily and make a report to Taylor. He promised to aid Maury in removing any obstacle to the accumulation of fuel, forage, and other supplies. Maury employed the former blockade runner *Virgin* to bring foodstuffs down the Tombigbee River. Once subsistence supplies reached Mobile, they were stored in five warehouses located in areas of the city least likely to come under enemy fire.[52]

Maury did not think he had an adequate supply of ordnance stores or small arms ammunition, but a report by Lieutenant Colonel J. R. Waddy indicated the contrary. Waddy found a small armory in the city employing six men. These workers could repair between seventy-five and one hundred small arms a week. Maury's chief of ordnance had accumulated enough percussion caps, powder, paper, and other material to make 1 million cartridges. He lacked only a sufficient supply of lead for bullets. To make up for the shortage of lead, Maury had arranged with the city government to take up the pipes of the city's waterworks. Waddy stated that there was an average of 115 cartridges per man on hand in Mobile. Some of the troops, however, did not receive ammunition until early March. A soldier of the Forty-sixth Mississippi Infantry wrote in his diary that although his brigade had gotten new Austrian rifles on its arrival in Mobile, the men did picket duty with empty weapons.[53] Except for three types of guns,

Waddy reported that most of the 209 heavy artillery pieces in the District of the Gulf had an ample supply of ammunition, and "in many instances the number of rounds per gun is too great, or rather, greater than our present limited resources would authorize."[54]

In early March 1865, as it became increasingly clear that the enemy would soon move against Mobile, Maury issued orders and circulars outlining actions for soldiers and civilians to take when the attack came. He instructed the artillery commanders along the city line to destroy or remove any buildings, trees, or other obstacles to the effective fire of their guns. He advised anyone living within range of these guns outside the works to move their belongings to a safe place. Because a siege would expose the city to heavy enemy fire and cause a shortage of provisions, Maury urged all noncombatants to leave and asked them at least to send their slaves to the interior. In compliance with instructions from Taylor, Maury took steps to send out all government Negroes not necessary for siege operations and prepared to burn all state-owned cotton within the city limits as soon as a siege began.[55] He expressed confidence that the city could be defended: "Our fortifications are strong—our stores are abundant and good—our troops are veterans—and with the cordial support of the people in all measures required for the public safety, and, with the blessing of Almighty God, are confident of victory."[56]

CHAPTER 13

The Last Days

The Union high command had begun making plans for a serious attack on Mobile in January 1865. Neither Grant nor Halleck saw the city as the chief objective of a campaign by Canby's forces. Grant expected Canby to capture Mobile if he could do so without an extensive siege and then move against Selma or Montgomery in conjuction with a cavalry force under Major General James H. Wilson, which was riding south from Tennessee. Mobile would serve only as a base for these subsequent movements. If Canby encountered much delay at the city, he could bypass it and go on to his real objective: the industrial area around Selma and Montgomery. Not only would his men destroy the industries and railroads in central Alabama, but they would prevent the planting of crops in the area. Canby's movement would coincide with Sherman's armies' raid into the Carolinas from Savannah and continue the war of exhaustion Grant had begun the previous spring.[1]

Grant agreed to send eighteen thousand infantry and five thousand cavalry troops from Tennessee to reinforce Canby, who concentrated approximately twenty-six thousand men under his command at Barrancas, Florida, and on Dauphin Island. Because the fortifications around Mobile seemed so strong and might stand up to a lengthy siege, Canby decided to capture the works on the eastern shore and then either move against the city by the Tensas and Alabama rivers or cut it off from above. He could not bypass Spanish Fort and Blakely because the troops there would pose a threat to his supply line between Pensacola and Montgomery. Bad weather had delayed his movements past the January starting date Grant had ordered, and the troops were not ready to move until March. This delay angered Grant because it was too late for them to assist in Sherman's march into the Carolinas. Canby ordered the force at Barrancas, under Major General Frederick Steele, to march against Pollard to cut the railroad there and create the impression of a march toward Montgomery. Steele began his movement on March 20. The remainder of Canby's army congregated near Fish River and began its march toward Spanish Fort and Blakely on March 25.[2]

Maury had only about nine thousand men in the District of the Gulf for the defense of Mobile in early March.[3] Despite the heavy disparity in numbers between his force and that of the enemy, he and Taylor were determined to hold Mobile. General Robert E. Lee advised Taylor to evacuate the city if the enemy army was too strong to defeat in the field. Nevertheless, he told Taylor, "The defence of your Department must be left entirely to your own judgment."[4] Davis agreed with Taylor on the importance of holding Mobile and wrote Lee that he thought the garrison there strong enough to defend against any attack from the Gulf. When Canby's campaign began to develop, Taylor reported to Lee: "I am ready to receive any attack he may make at Mobile." Taylor planned to use Forrest's cavalry to defeat enemy raids into northern Alabama and then send the cavalrymen south to aid in the defense of Mobile. By the time the cavalrymen disengaged themselves in central Alabama, however, Canby had already invested the eastern shore defenses so Taylor kept Forrest's forces near Meridian. Maury had to do the best he could against adverse odds.[5]

Once Taylor and Maury learned that Canby's army had begun active operations, the Confederate authorities issued additional orders to assist in the defense of the city. The post commander, Colonel Thomas H. Taylor, issued circulars directing all able-bodied men to join local defense units or face expulsion from Mobile. At this time, at least one company of free Negroes formed to defend the city. Maury forbade persons from going to or from the enemy's lines at the lower bay without special permission. Mayor Slough ordered the registration of all male slaves between eighteen and forty-five years old so that he or the army could locate them if needed for labor around the city.[6]

Liddell, commanding on the eastern shore, informed Maury on March 20 of the Union landing at Fish River. He requested reinforcements to hold the works at Blakely and Spanish Fort. To contest the enemy's advance, Maury sent his entire infantry force across the bay to Liddell. The latter general stationed his men south and east of Spanish Fort along D'Olive's Creek and planned to give battle on March 26. He thought that only a small portion of Canby's army had gathered in front of him, and he hoped to attack and defeat this detachment before reinforcements could reach it. The Federals had a much stronger force than Liddell anticipated, however. In addition, instead of advancing directly toward Spanish Fort, Canby's men began outflanking Liddell in the direction of Blakely. Liddell withdrew most of his force toward Blakely and ordered General Gibson to assume command of Spanish Fort. To hold the lines at the latter place, Gibson had 500 men of his own Louisiana brigade, 950 men of Thomas's brigade of Alabama Reserves, and 360 artillerymen, a total force of approximately 1,810 men. Gibson found six heavy guns, fourteen fieldpieces, and twelve coehorn mortars in the various redoubts at Spanish Fort.[7]

Soon after the occupation of the works, Gibson conducted an inspection of the lines. He reported later: "It was apparent that an immense work with the spade, pick, and ax was before us." Gibson ordered his men to dig rifle pits and strengthen existing works. The men constructed bombproofs behind the works to use as magazines, temporary hospitals, and living quarters: "We cut down great trees, rolled the trunks over the mouth, then put a layer of brush and dirt; then came another layer of heavy logs crosswise, then a layer of brush and dirt, until the roof was six to eight feet thick."[8] To delay the enemy advance and give his men extra time to dig in, Gibson ordered an attack on the enemy's pickets on the morning of March 27. Lieutenant Colonel Robert H. Lindsay led 550 men in the attack, which broke through the Union skirmish line but fell back after observing the main Federal force forming a line of battle. The losses on both sides in this skirmish were light, but Gibson's tactics succeeded in slowing the enemy's advance for several hours.[9]

The Federals began easing their lines forward on the afternoon of the twenty-seventh. Those of Gibson's skirmishers who had entrenching tools held their positions by digging in, but men who did not have tools had to fall back within the main trench line. Despite their cautious advance, the Federals completed the investment of Spanish Fort by nightfall. Gibson reported his losses for the day as five men killed and forty-four wounded.[10] Thomas's Alabama Reserves, most of them young boys, performed well in opposing the Union advance. One veteran, however, felt they did not protect themselves as well as they might have: "They thought it was 'not soldierly,' and they stood up and were shot down like sheep."[11] During the night Gibson sent off all of his horses and wagons. He asked Maury and the district ordnance officer for rifle and cannon ammunition as well as whiskey and tobacco. To Liddell he sent a request for more entrenching tools. Gibson expressed a desire to keep Thomas's brigade, which Liddell wanted to move to Blakely, because he did not know whether the enemy would assault his lines the next morning. Liddell allowed Gibson to retain the men temporarily.[12]

During March 28 and 29 the Federals contented themselves with erecting batteries and advancing their skirmish line. A Confederate officer wrote in his diary that the enemy siege lines lay about 1,000 to 1,200 yards from the trenches, but the Union skirmishers had worked their way to points from 250 to 300 yards of the Confederate lines. The Confederate artillery fire was superior during these two days. To protect the gunners from enemy sharpshooters, the engineers constructed screens over each embrasure. These screens consisted of steel plates two feet by three feet square and about one-half inch thick: "They were so secured to the inner faces of the embrasures that they were quickly lowered and raised as the gun ran into battery or recoiled."[13] Maury visited Spanish Fort on the twenty-eighth and decided to strengthen the garrison with troops from Blakely. Under orders from Maury, Liddell directed one regiment from Holtzclaw's brigade to move to Spanish Fort and relieve one of the Alabama Reserve regiments. Liddell also ordered a detachment of sharpshooters armed with Whitworth rifles to Gibson.[14]

March 30 saw only desultory firing by sharpshooters and a few artillery pieces. The Federals did succeed in pushing some of their pickets to points within fifty yards of the Confederate pickets. Much of the artillery fire centered on Battery Huger and Battery Tracy, which had added their firepower to that of the redoubts around Spanish Fort from the start of the siege. The Federals began erecting a heavy battery on the north shore of Bay Minette to bombard the two forts and succeeded in virtually ending steamship communication between Huger and Tracy and Mobile.[15] Maury visited Spanish Fort again on the thirtieth and recognized the need to reinforce Gibson. The garrison had lost approximately 320 men as casualties through that day. Maury ordered Holtzclaw's and Colonel Julius A. Andrews's brigades from Blakely to Spanish Fort to relieve the remaining Alabama Reserves. Two steamers transferred the men during the night. Gibson assigned Holtzclaw to command the two brigades, which then made up his left wing.[16]

The Federal sharpshooters became particularly obnoxious on March 31. Their fire struck down several men, including Maury's chief of artillery, Colonel William E. Burnett, who was conducting a reconnaissance of the enemy's lines with Gibson. The latter requested four hundred "Beauregard screens" to protect his own sharpshooters. These screens were wooden embrasures covered by sandbags and had been devised by Beauregard at Charleston. Maury reported that the screens provided "great security to the sharpshooters."[17] Gibson decided that active measures were needed to protect his men. He ordered a bombardment of the nearest enemy force, which lay about 150 yards outside the Confederate lines, and asked for volunteers to conduct a sortie against this force that night. Captain Clement Watson, Lieutenant A. E. Newton, and fifteen volunteers from Gibson's brigade rushed the Federal rifle pits just after dark. They captured one captain and twenty-one men and drove back the rest of the enemy force without any loss to their own party. Maury formally congratulated the men for their "brilliant and successful sortie."[18]

Life for the men in the garrison at Spanish Fort became more difficult as each day passed. One soldier recalled: "Every day was full of incident, and it soon got so that we had no rest day or night." The men experienced great danger as well as discomfort: "Artillery duels became of daily occurrence, our 'head logs' were constantly knocked down upon us, bruising and crippling us; squads of sharpshooters devoted their especial attention to our port holes or embrasures and poured a steady stream of bullets through them from early morn till dewy eve."[19] Another veteran remembered that during daylight men could move about only by crawling through areas where they had dug no communication trenches.[20] The people of Mobile made liberal donations of food so the men were well fed. Their morale began to sag, however, and Gibson urged his officers to cheer and encourage their men. He also asked that they set examples to give the men confidence: "It is morale that defeats a charge—it increases as the great Napoleon said—a resisting power tenfold."[21] Gibson made frequent visits to the trenches, exposing himself to enemy fire.[22]

Gibson still did not think he had enough men, and he frequently asked for reinforcements. He told Maury that there were wider gaps between each soldier on the line than there had ever been under Johnston and Hood in the Atlanta campaign. Gibson issued orders and circulars designed to place his men in the safest positions possible while still maintaining vigilance and the ability to respond quickly in case of an assault. One order established a force of sharpshooters for each artillery piece, who were to keep up a steady fire on the enemy skirmishers to prevent them from picking off the Confederate cannoneers.[23] Gibson tried to get his men to conserve their ammunition, pointing out on April 5 that they had expended nearly fifty-four thousand rounds in two days and at that rate would soon run out.[24] Gibson and Maury encouraged the men to collect "solid shot, shell, bullets, and missiles of every description" to send to the ordance department in Mobile for recycling.[25]

Throughout much of the siege, the Confederate troops endured artillery bombardments by the enemy. One of the most severe bombardments occurred on April 4. In Mobile the people could feel the vibrations of the shells striking the earth and could hear the reports of the heavy guns: "This evening the firing is terrific, not a moment elapsing between the booming of 'heavy artillery.'"[26] The cannonading lasted for about two hours, and Gibson and his artillery officers estimated that the Federals used thirty to forty heavy guns and at least a dozen mortars. Redoubt No. 3, manned by veterans of the Fifth Company, Washington Artillery, of New Orleans, took the brunt of much of the Union fire. Two shells disabled the redoubt's heaviest gun, an eight-inch columbiad nicknamed "Lady Slocomb," and the bombardment practically leveled the parapets. When Maury offered to relieve the Louisianians with a fresh unit from the city, Captain Cuthbert H. Slocomb submitted the proposal to his men and reported back: "'General, the company, grateful for your kind intention, desire to hold this position to the end. We respectfully decline to be relieved.'"[27]

Increasing enemy activity occurred on Gibson's left flank during the last days of the siege. The marshy, densely wooded ground there made it almost impossible for the men to erect earthworks for protection. Federal batteries established on high ground north of this flat dominated the area. The enemy also began moving launches to the area so that they could operate on Bay Minette and the Apalachee River. A battery from Liddell's command at Blakely and the gunboats *Nashville* and *Morgan* provided some relief to Gibson's hard-pressed left, but increasing numbers of enemy heavy guns in the area drove these supports back. Federal Parrott guns partially disabled the *Nashville* and kept the gunboats from the area during daylight hours.[28] Gibson developed a plan to attack the enemy troops opposite his left but canceled it when he could not get an ironclad to enfilade the Federal flank. He did station additional men and two fieldpieces on his extreme left to guard against a surprise attack. Gibson finally got the assistance of several navy picket boats to help watch his flank.[29]

By April 7 the Federals had dug almost up to the main Confederate works around Spanish Fort. The enemy had concentrated so much heavy artillery and so many mortars around the position that the Confederate gunners could reply but briefly to the bombardment. To give themselves added protection, the men of the garrison threw up more traverses and bombproofs. Gibson found that the Negroes at the fort's cooking yard were not busy all day so he ordered them to the front lines to assist in erecting the new defenses and provide relief for his exhausted soldiers. Gibson also renewed his requests to Maury for hand grenades, engineer troops, subterranean shells, and more Negro laborers. He warned: "I must have the things I have asked for within the last three days, else disaster may happen." A shortage of ammunition forced Gibson to order the main line to cease rifle fire except for sharpshooters in advanced rifle pits. Gibson directed his officers to make sure these advanced pits had Beauregard screens and were safe from a sudden enemy rush.[30]

Maury sent Gibson several howitzers, some hand grenades, and an undetermined number of laborers on the night of April 7–8. Unusually heavy activity by the Federals early on the eighth prompted Gibson to order his skirmishers to keep up a steady small arms fire on the enemy work parties. He also urged his commanders to exercise vigilance and monitor all movements on their fronts: "Every precaution must be taken to prevent a surprise."[31] During the afternoon Gibson ordered the men in Fort McDermott to open artillery fire on the Federal working party on their front. In reply, the enemy poured such a concentrated fire into the fort that the Confederates soon had to cease firing. The Federal shelling disabled one gun and destroyed an ammunition chest. Gibson decided to test the enemy's strength and determine his intentions. Accordingly, he ordered his batteries to be ready to open up at sunset. His officers would watch the Federal lines closely for their reaction and prepare the defenses for whatever might occur. Gibson feared that "the moment had at length arrived when I could no longer hold the position without imminent risk of losing the garrison."[32]

Unknown to Gibson, Canby planned a bombardment of his own for sundown on the eighth. The Federals had fifty-three siege guns in position, and Canby ordered his infantry commanders to be ready to exploit any favorable situation. Gibson's gunners opened first, about 5:30 P.M. but got off only a few rounds before the Union bombardment silenced them. The enemy fire became so heavy that the men of the garrison found no safety in their bombproofs and had to find shelter wherever they could behind their works. Shells from the Federal fifteen-inch mortars caused particular destruction, penetrating six feet of solid earth or the strongest bombproof before exploding. One member of the garrison remembered that the men could see these big shells dropping into the works, but "we had to stand and take it." Few men could recall such a severe hail of shot and shell. The enemy musket fire and the dense smoke generated by firing cannons and exploding shells added to the confusion: "It was though the mouth of the pit had yawned and the uproar of the damned was about us. And it was not taking away from this infernal picture to see men, as I did, hopping about, 'raving, distracted mad,' the blood bursting from eyes and ears and mouth, driven stark crazy by concussion or some other cause."[33]

During the bombardment and as darkness fell, the Eighth Iowa Infantry advanced against the works on Gibson's left, striking Andrews's Texans and driving them from their positions. A small force under Captain James A. Howze of the Fourteenth Texas Dismounted Cavalry charged the Iowans, but when their color-bearer fell, the Texans retired with the rest of the brigade: "They were retreating in great confusion, every man pretty much his own commander."[34] The Federals captured several hundred men and overran three hundred yards of trenches. Lieutenant Alfred G. Clark led the garrison's hundred-man provost guard to the scene of action and counterattacked. Although Clark fell mortally wounded, his assault stopped the enemy advance. The Federals threw up light trenches and awaited further developments. Holtzclaw reported to Gibson that his force was not strong enough to push the enemy back, and Gibson decided, in accordance with standing orders from Maury, to abandon his works rather than risk the capture of his men. He ordered his old brigade withdrawn from the right flank, posted some of the men to watch the left, and stationed the remainder in position to cover the retreat.[35]

The men in the various redoubts spiked their guns, and the entire garrison, including the sick and wounded and Negro laborers, assembled on the beach. Maury and his engineers had prepared for an evacuation by erecting a wooden treadway from the rear of Spanish Fort across the marsh to a point on the Apalachee River opposite Battery Huger. Gibson orderd the men to remove their shoes and boots and to carry their weapons on the side away from the enemy. Filing silently down the treadway under the cover of darkness, the troops reached the end of the planks without alerting the enemy to their movement. Steamers conveyed the garrison from Battery Huger to Blakely. A few men had to travel across the marsh directly to Liddell's lines. After a short rest there, the soldiers traveled on the steamers to Mobile. The people of the city first became aware of what had happened. Many of the citizens expressed disbelief at first: "Still I had to believe the evidence of my own eyes, for our soldiers were passing by in squads, from an early hour, dirty, wet and completely worn out."[36]

Gibson reported his casualties during the siege of Spanish Fort as 73 men killed, 350 wounded, and 6 missing. In the final bombardment and assault, he lost 20 men killed, 45 wounded, and 250 missing. On April 8 as many as 325 men might have been captured. The Federal losses at Spanish Fort were 52 men killed, 575 wounded, and 30 missing. In his memoirs, Taylor praised the Confederate garrison at Spanish Fort: "Gibson's stubborn defense and skillful retreat make this one of the best achievements of the war." Maury echoed this assessment: "It is not too much to say that no position was ever held by Confederate troops with greater hardihood and tenacity, nor evacuated more skillfully after hope of further defense was gone." Gibson praised his officers and men for their "steady valor and cheerful endurance" and disavowed any personal recognition: "If any credit shall attach to the defense of Spanish Fort, it belongs to the heroes whose sleep shall no more be disturbed by the cannon's roar."[37] The defense of this position for two weeks by fewer than three thousand men against eight times as many Federals certainly should stand as one of the most heroic episodes of the war.

When Canby's army laid siege to Spanish Fort, Liddell employed his forces in preparing the lines at Blakely for an attack. He also kept scouts out on the approaches from Pollard to watch for Steele's forces, which he expected might move against Blakely. Initially, Liddell had under his command a small artillery force, Holtzclaw's brigade, and three brigades of Cockrell's division. The latter units had arrived from Mobile late on March 24. As the siege of Spanish Fort progressed, Liddell detached Holtzclaw's brigade and Matthew D. Ector's brigade (under Colonel Andrews) of Cockrell's division and sent them to Gibson. He received in exchange Thomas's brigade of Alabama Reserves. On April 1, the First Mississippi Light Artillery Regiment, armed with rifles, reported to Liddell, giving him approximately twenty-seven hundred effectives to defend his works. The position at Blakely consisted of nine lunettes connected by rifle pits, the whole line covering some three thousand yards. Advanced rifle pits, abatis, and land mines helped protect the ground in front of the works. Liddell assigned Claudius W. Sears's Mississippi brigade (Colonel Thomas N. Adaire commanding) to the left, Cockrell's brigade (Colonel James McCown commanding) to the center, and Thomas's Alabamians to the right. He did not have enough men to fill the works, and at some points on the line ten paces separated each soldier.[38]

Steele's Federals did not reach the vicinity of Blakely until April 1. Early on that morning, Steele's cavalrymen encountered one of Liddell's outposts near Wilkins's plantation on the Stockton Road, about four miles north of Blakely. This outpost consisted of one hundred men of the Forty-sixth Mississippi Infantry under Captain J. B. Hart. The Mississippians watched one regiment dismount and advance on foot while another followed closely behind on horseback and with drawn sabers. Taking advantage of fences and other obstructions, Hart's men fell back slowly for about one mile. At that point the mounted enemy troops charged and routed the Confederates. Three officers, seventy-one men, and the regimental colors became captives of the Federals. The Union pursuit continued almost up to the Confederate trenches at Blakely. Colonel McCown's Missourians had also been on outpost, and he stationed one of his regiments in a ravine across the road to stop the enemy advance. The fire of this unit, supported by artillery in the works, broke the Federal pursuit and forced them to fall back. A Missouri officer wrote: "'It must have been a downfall to their pride to know that they had been whipped and routed by less than an hundred ragged Missouri infantry.'"[39]

Liddell anticipated that Steele would attempt to storm his lines during the day. He telegraphed Maury asking for 150 rifles for distribution to the artillerymen who had none. He ordered Cockrell to put men from his Missouri brigade in the advanced skirmish pits on his front: "They are the only ones here that can be relied upon thoroughly . . . and therefore it is necessary to have the best men in those pits." Thomas received similar instructions, including directions to station six men in each pit. Liddell informed Thomas that most of Steele's men were Negro troops who would not "spare any of our men should they gain possession of our works" and urged him to "impress upon their [Thomas's men] minds the importance of holding their position to the last, and with the determination never to surrender." Steele's men did not attack on April 1, but Liddell attempted to have Ector's (Andrews's) brigade returned from Spanish Fort that night. Maury, however, decided that the Texans should remain with Gibson.[40]

The Confederate skirmishers on the Stockton Road tried to drive in the Federal cavalry pickets on the morning of April 2. Brigadier General John P. Hawkins, commander of the First Division, U.S. Colored Troops, quickly threw his men into line of battle. With a heavy force of skirmishers in front, the Negro troops advanced toward the sound of battle. Confronted by overwhelming numbers, the Confederates slowly fell back toward their main line. The Federals followed until the Confederates reached their advanced rifle pits and the protection of their artillery. At that point, about half a mile from the Confederate works, the enemy halted and began digging rifle pits. Several hours later, Steele's division of white troops took position on the left flank of Hawkins's men and began entrenching. Liddell again feared an attack on Blakely and asked Maury to send him any light artillery he could spare and some coehorn mortars to use on his flanks. Liddell also requested the services of the gunboat *Morgan* to bombard the Federals' right flank. The ironclad *Huntsville* was in the vicinity, but her men could not elevate their guns enough to fire over the bluff. The attack Liddell feared did not occur.[41]

Two divisions from the force in front of Spanish Fort joined Steele on the third, and the Federals completed the investment of Blakely. From the third to the eighth, they occupied themselves in advancing their siege approaches and erecting batteries. Liddell's men kept up a steady fire from their skirmish pits and batteries to try to slow the Union work parties. The ironclads *Nashville* and *Huntsville* and the gunboat *Morgan* all added their firepower in defense of the land lines. Steele reported that the bombardment of these vessels "was very harassing and destructive, especially to Hawkins' division" on the Federal right flank.[42] Liddell's artillery suffered little inconvenience from the Federals because it was protected by wooden screens and the enemy at first had only a few light guns. To illuminate the area in front of their works at night, the Confederate gunners employed fireballs sent up by coehorn mortars, thereby keeping up an accurate rifle and artillery fire even after sundown. Toward the end of the siege,

Liddell received three heavy guns from Mobile but barely got them mounted in time for use against the enemy.[43]

The siege of Blakely was not as intense as that at Spanish Fort. Both sides conducted occasional operations against the other's advanced rifle pits. Usually these skirmishes resulted in few casualties and no lasting tactical success. On the morning of April 7, for example, Federal troops attacked the pits held by the Alabama Reserves, but the boy soldiers succeeded in driving back the enemy. To retaliate, Liddell ordered a sortie for the next morning before daylight. About midnight the Confederate artillery opened fire on the Federal lines. After a bombardment of nearly an hour, Lieutenant Colonel Junius A. Law's Second Alabama Reserves charged the enemy pickets. They got to within forty yards of the Federal pits before they received any enemy fire. At that point, however, the enemy poured heavy musketry at them and threw them back with a loss of fifteen men killed and twenty-two wounded.[44] When not on the skirmish line, Liddell's men used spades and picks to strengthen their works. Naturally, these activities sapped their energy, and Liddell asked Maury to send him one hundred Negro laborers to relieve his soldiers from the engineer work.[45]

Conditions for the Confederate soldiers at Blakely were similar to those at Spanish Fort, but they apparently had no extensive system of bombproofs to use as quarters at Blakely. One officer wrote his mother that the soldiers lived in caves and holes and were generally exposed to both enemy fire and the elements. He asked his mother to have a servant gather up rags to send to Blakely: "We fire constantly & the men have literally nothing to wipe out their rifles with."[46] In addition to the regular rifle and artillery fire by the Federals, Blakely's garrison suffered from the fire of sharpshooters. Liddell reported that these sharpshooters could hit men at the wharf from behind the Federal lines. Captain J. L. Bradford of the First Mississippi Light Artillery related that a sharpshooter's bullet struck one of his men in the head and killed him instantly. Bradford himself had barely escaped death when a bullet hit him near the heart but was stopped by two letters folded in his pocket. In spite of the danger and privations, the men maintained high morale: "If we only had plenty of ammunition we would hold the dogs at bay forever, but we are stinted, & they will gain on us little by little I fear."[47]

The Federal artillery began a heavy fire on Blakely on the morning of April 8 in conjunction with the bombardment of Spanish Fort. Liddell had planned an artillery barrage of his own to start at 8 A.M. The enemy replied briskly, and his guns could not silence its fire. A masked battery of heavy Parrott rifled guns opened on the Confederate naval squadron, lying nearby in the Tensas River, during the afternoon. The *Morgan* received several hits, one near the waterline, and had to withdraw when her ammunition ran out. The *Nashville* also ran out of shells and fell back even though no Union shells had struck her.[48] Liddell ordered his gunners and skirmishers to fire, with the aid of fireballs, on the enemy on the night of the eighth to help cover the evacuation of Spanish Fort and to discover the intentions of the enemy on his front. On the morning of April 9, the Federals renewed their bombardment in preparation for an assault. This bombardment did little damage, however, except to dismount two cannon. Liddell issued orders for his men to remain alert for an attack.[49]

Following the evacuation and fall of Spanish Fort, Canby began shifting his forces there toward Blakely and ordered Steele to get ready to assault Liddell's lines. The attack opened at 5:30 P.M., and the four Federal divisions that had occupied the trenches since April 3 advanced simultaneously. With a shout the Federals rushed forward and drove Liddell's skirmishers back to their main line. Soon the enemy force carried the entire line of earthworks. Many Confederates surrendered at that time, while others fell back to the wharf only to become prisoners there. Some 3,700 men fell into Union hands, but between 150 and 200 men managed to escape to the naval squadron by swimming or floating on pieces of wood. All three Confederate brigadiers— Liddell, Cockrell, and Thomas—became prisoners of war.[50] The Federals lost 105 men killed and 466 wounded in the assault. Total Union casualties during the siege of Blakely numbered 116 men killed, 655 wounded, and 4 missing.[51]

Maury had planned to evacuate the Blakely garrison on the night of the ninth. He did not pull the men out on the night of April 8 with the Spanish Fort garrison because he felt they could hold their works throughout the next day. Shortly after the end of the war, Liddell wrote that he could have repulsed the Union assault if Maury had allowed him to retain the men from Spanish Fort and place them in his trenches: "The weight of volume of fire would have been sufficiently heavy and deadly to have driven back the assaulting columns." The small force under his command, the men spaced about one yard apart, simply could not put up a successful resistance. Liddell did not criticize Maury's decision but stated that the latter "did all in his power."[52] It seems unlikely that reinforcements from Gibson's command could have prevented the Union forces from overrunning the lines at Blakely because Canby's army had such an overwhelming numerical superiority.

The fall of Blakely left only the small garrisons at Battery Huger and Battery Tracy to prevent the Federals from moving through the rivers in the area toward Mobile. Two hundred men of Companies B and K, Twenty-second Louisiana Infantry, and Company C, First Mississippi Light Artillery, held Battery Huger. Major Washington Marks, commander of Huger, had eleven cannon in his work. At Tracy, 120 men of Companies G, H, and I, Twenty-second Louisiana, manned the five guns of that fort, and Captain Ambrose A. Plattsmier had charge of the garrison. Lieutenant Colonel John A. Brown had commanded both Huger and Tracy until April 3, when he reported to Maury as inspector of artillery. Major Marks then assumed direction of the two forts.[53] Both garrisons fired their guns in support of Spanish Fort in the first few days of the siege of that place, but a shortage of ammunition in the works led Maury to order the men not to fire throughout the remainder of the siege. From March 31 to April 8, the two forts endured daily bombardments from a Union Parrott gun battery on Bay Minette and occasional fire from the Federal fleet in Mobile Bay. The enemy shells did little damage to the earthen walls, and the men filled shell holes and strengthened the parapets with sandbags floated down to the forts on flatboats at night.[54]

Colonel Patton of the Twenty-second Louisiana took his four companies from the Spanish Fort garrison and assumed command of Huger and Tracy on April 9. The men in the forts had to hold those positions at first to prevent the Federal fleet from cutting off retreat from Blakely and later to prevent the enemy from interfering with the evacuation of Mobile. Maury gave Patton permission to use his cannon: "'Open all your guns upon the enemy, keep up an active fire, and hold your position until you receive orders to retire.'" The Louisianians faced the fire not only of the guns in the Bay Minette battery and the fleet but also some of the artillery abandoned at Spanish Fort and Fort McDermott. The men kept up a heavy, accurate fire against the Union land batteries from April 9 to 11. They endeavored to expend every round they had before they had to abandon their works. On the night of the eleventh, Maury sent a staff officer to Patton with orders to retire. The first steamer sent to pick up the men ran aground at Conway Bayou, but a second vessel succeeded in bringing off the men. They spiked the guns before leaving. Maury wrote later: "These garrisons fired the last cannon in the last great battle of the war for the freedom of the Southern states." A Unionist living in Mobile expressed his admiration for the defense of Huger and Tracy: "Never was a devoted garrison more bravely defended, and never was [there] a finer display of scientific gunnery." [55]

In Mobile Maury had begun preparations for a siege about the time the Federals invested Spanish Fort. On March 30 he declared the city to be in a state of siege, which enabled the military to arrest and hold suspicious persons. Taylor issued orders forbidding noncombatants from visiting the city without permission from his headquarters but removed this restriction after five days. The state of siege enabled the post commandant to close all saloons and drinking establishments in Mobile. Finally, the military began gathering up for burning all cotton in the city. Major William H. Ketchum impressed every dray he could find and hauled the bales out to a plain north of Mobile. A citizen reported: "Going home, one day, I was surprised to see bales of cotton tumbling from the attic windows of some of the best mansions in the city. . . . Almost everyone had secreted a little of that commodity in their homes to serve their wants when the Confederate money should collapse." [56]

The losses suffered at Spanish Fort and Blakely caused Maury to begin planning for the evacuation of Mobile. Not only had the casualties in the two garrisons cost him half of his effective force, but the fighting had expended a considerable amount of artillery and small arms ammunition. Forrest's defeat in central Alabama removed any real hope of relief. In a telegram to Taylor, Maury stated that he would be unable to hold Mobile for even a day if the enemy attacked the city.[57] Because so many men were tied down defending Spanish Fort and Blakely, the city had long had only a few artillerymen and home guards manning the works. An officer at Battery Gladden recognized the susceptibility of the defenses to assault: "The Federal Comr. has displayed a great want of knowledge by not landing on this side of the bay some time since. The entrance to the city has always been open."[58] Maury stated in later years that he would have been unable to hold the city for long if Canby had moved directly against it rather than operating on the eastern shore. Canby might even have bagged most of Maury's army: "The city was level and exposed throughout the whole extent to fire from any direction. There were near 40,000 non-combatants within its lines of defence, whose sufferings under a siege would soon have paralyzed the defence by a garrison so small as ours was; and the early evacuation would have been inevitable, while it would have been exceedingly difficult of accomplishment."[59]

The ringing of alarm bells broke the stillness of the city on the morning of April 10. The bells pealed to call out the local defense troops to participate in preparations for the evacuation. Maury had about eighteen steamers at the city, and the home guards and regulars began loading them with ordnance and commissary stores. The soldiers appropriated the drays that had carried cotton out of the city and used them to move the stores to the landing. The men put some supplies on the few railroad cars remaining in the city. Many of the troops departed that day, while Maury kept a small infantry and cavalry force in the city as a rear guard. Some sick and wounded soldiers who could not be evacuated were placed in the City Hospital and Marine Hospital under the care of the Sisters of Charity. Maury hoped that the enemy would not molest these men while they were under the care of this religious order. The cloudy, dismal weather reflected the feelings of many of the city's residents: "Never have I experienced such feelings as now take possession of me—perfectly miserable, as may be imagined. Every body is excited and running around, gathering what information they can." Fortunately, the feelings of depression did not spread to the soldiers. An officer wrote during the evacuation: "Amidst all the reverses, the men seem to be in good spirits."[60]

The removal of men and supplies continued on April 11, and the few remaining officers and men prepared to disable the artillery and ammunition which they could not take with them. Confusion marred the orderly conduct of these operations. The local defense troops did not surrender their weapons and seemed ill disposed to obey any orders from regular officers. Lieutenant Daniel Geary took it upon himself to disable the forts on the city lines. He requisitioned spikes and had them distributed to the various batteries for spiking the guns. He instructed the battery commanders to dump their ammunition into the water of the moats, burn the gun carriages, and set fire to the bomb-proofs.[61] The garrisons of the bay batteries evacuated their works last. At Battery Gladden the men emptied their powder into the bay, threw shells into the water, and broke all implements and tools. Rather than spiking their guns, the soldiers threw into the bay the elevating screws and wheels, which prevented the enemy from using the guns. Some delay occurred in evacuating the men because the crewmen and Negro firemen on several steamers had deserted. The soldiers had to collect wood and navigate the steamers as best they could. Finally, the last of the garrisons steamed away from the wharf: "Mobile was left with great reluctance by both officers and men. The men, though low-spirited, behaved well."[62]

Flag Officer Farrand prepared his small naval squadron for the evacuation of the city. The engines of the floating batteries *Huntsville* and *Tuscaloosa* were so weak that they could not steam upriver against the current. Farrand had no towboats to pull the vessels and ordered them scuttled in the main channel of the Mobile River. This left him with only the gunboats *Nashville, Morgan,* and *Baltic* and steamers *Black Diamond* and *Southern Republic,* the latter carrying what naval stores the seamen could load aboard her. The former blockade runners *Virgin, Red Gauntlet, Mary,* and *Heroine* accompanied Farrand's squadron. The flag officer hoped to go up the Alabama River to Selma but soon learned that the Federals had captured that town and its naval station. He then ordered his vessels up the Tombigbee River and had his men place torpedoes near its junction with the Alabama River to prevent enemy vessels from pursuing.[63]

Maury left Mobile early on the morning of April 12 with the rear guard of three hundred Louisianians commanded by Lieutenant Colonel Lindsay. Maury left behind General Gibson with Lieutenant Colonel Philip B. Spence's Twelfth Mississippi Cavalry Regiment and a section of an artillery battery. This small force departed Mobile about 11 A.M. and set fire to the cotton bales piled up north of the city. A citizen reported that when the cavalry had left the scene of the conflagration the home guards or municipal officials rang the alarm bells so that the people could rush out and try to save some of the cotton. They reportedly saved nearly 1,500 of the 3,500 bales which the military had stacked up. Maury's commissary officer had turned over to Mayor Slough some supplies for distribution to the poor of the city. A young woman described the events that occurred after Spence's cavalrymen left the city: "Each one of that class [the poor], helping herself freely [to the supplies], and endeavoring to carry off as much as possible—each one tries to be first, and consequently much scuffling and rioting ensues."[64] Eventually some home guards and armed citizens restored order.

Canby ordered two divisions under Granger to cross Mobile Bay and occupy the city. Granger's men landed at Catfish Point, about five miles below the city, at 10:30 A.M., and Granger sent a dispatch to Slough demanding the unconditional surrender of Mobile. At noon Slough and several citizens rode down the Shell Road in a carriage to near the Magnolia Racetrack. Using a large sheet as a flag of truce, Slough informed Granger that the Confederate troops had left the city, and he formally surrendered to the Federals.[65] A regiment from Granger's force occupied the town during the afternoon and raised the United States flag over the customhouse. About sundown, a small number of Confederate cavalry scouts made a quick raid on the city and captured several Federal soldiers. Granger then ordered an entire brigade into Mobile to occupy the former Confederate works. One citizen described the entry of these soldiers: "The city was resonant with every patriotic refrain, from the Star Spangled Banner to John Brown's Soul is Marching On. Every one realized for the first time, as he listened to the 'tramp, tramp' of the orderly files, that 'the boys' had come."[66]

Indeed, it was only the strains of such tunes as "Yankee Doodle" and the cheers of the Federal soldiers that made many citizens realize that Mobile had finally fallen: "I began to realize what *had* and was taking place, as before *that*, I had been so much excited that I hardly had time for thought."[67] Though late starting, Canby's campaign had proceeded fairly smoothly and quickly. His army suffered relatively few casualties in the fighting at Spanish Fort and Blakely. One study of these operations concluded: "Had the campaign occurred with the same result some two years earlier it would have been universally acclaimed as one of the most brilliant operations of the war."[68] The delay in getting started, however, had given Wilson's cavalry all the time needed to push back Forrest's outnumbered troopers and capture Selma. By the time Canby's advance guard marched into Mobile, he had learned of Wilson's success and that the cavalrymen were on their way toward Montgomery. The destruction conducted by Wilson's raid negated any last-ditch stand the Confederates in the West might have contemplated and made it unnecessary for Canby to move his army beyond Mobile.[69]

Three days after Robert E. Lee's surrender at Appomattox Courthouse, the war ended for the Gulf city. Many days, however, would elapse before life in Mobile returned to a semblance of normality and even longer before it recovered something akin to its former status. Twelve days after the surrender of Mobile, a northern newspaper correspondent described the effects of the war on the city:

> The city is a sad picture to contemplate. The stores look a thousand years old. They wear something of the appearance of the old castles to be seen in some of the countries of Europe. They are empty and forsaken, except here and there an old man seated like some faithful sentinel at his post. Shelves are forsaken of their silks, and occupied only with the flies and the dust. The people look sad and sorry. The best people of the city are poor, and poorly clad. There is no money save the scrip of the confederacy. The people are distressed. No money except coin and greenbacks will pass. They have little of the former—none of the latter. We have witnessed such sorrow over this order of things as we do not desire again to behold.[70]

Epilogue

Though Mobile was the last major Southern city to fall to Union forces, its occupation had no effect on the war. On April 2, when Steele's Federals began surrounding the lines at Blakely, Confederate forces evacuated Richmond and Petersburg. Lee surrendered the Army of Northern Virginia to Grant on April 9, the day Blakely fell. Canby's army had no reason to move into central Alabama; Federal cavalry raiders had captured Selma on April 2 and Montgomery ten days later. Joe Johnston arranged an armistice with Sherman in North Carolina on April 14. That night John Wilkes Booth sneaked into a box at Ford's Theater in Washington and assassinated Abraham Lincoln. Johnston surrendered the remnants of the Army of Tennessee and other forces in the Carolinas to Sherman on April 26. After learning about these events, Taylor met with Canby on April 30 to arrange an armistice. Taylor surrendered his command, including the remnants of Maury's Mobile army, at Cuba Station, Alabama, on May 8. The former defenders of Mobile thus became part of the last organized Confederate force east of the Mississippi River to lay down their arms.

Each of the four elements of the Confederacy's coastal defense strategy came into play at Mobile. Using the labor of thousands of slaves, soldiers, and civilians, the Confederates constructed around the city one of the most extensive complexes of earthwork fortifications in the South. The engineers strengthened Fort Morgan and Fort Gaines and partially obstructed the main ship channel into Mobile Bay with pilings and torpedoes. As the fortifications grew in size and strength, the Union high command realized that a large land and naval force would be required to assure success in an attack. Mobile's naval squadron began small and weak. In time, however, the construction of ironclads made the squadron more formidable and able to provide important support to the masonry forts and series of earthworks. The presence of Confederate ironclads in the waters near Mobile delayed a Union naval assault until Federal ironclads could participate.

After formation of the new nation, the Confederacy quickly organized a volunteer army. Elements of this army occupied the various fortifications around Mobile. The strength of the army at Mobile varied because demands in other areas drew soldiers away from the city. Alabama raised local defense and state reserve forces to augment or replace the soldiers of the regular army at Mobile. Even if not numerically strong, the army at Mobile enjoyed the advantage of protective fortifications. If an enemy attack occurred, Mobile had an excellent transportation system to the interior so that reinforcements could rush to the city. This system of railroads and river steamers also enabled the Confederates to keep the military and civilians adequately supplied. The Union high command recognized the advantages interior lines of communication gave the Confederates and waited to attack until operations by Federal armies elsewhere tied down any Confederate troops that might go to reinforce Mobile.

In at least one respect, the coastal defense system at Mobile seemed to work better there than it did at other points. The various commanders at the city responded more positively in lending assistance to defend other threatened points of the Confederacy. Several authors have pointed out an obvious weakness in Jefferson Davis's departmental system: the reluctance (and often failure) of commanders to send reinforcements to other departments. Richard McMurry describes the mind-set that has afflicted military bureaucracies throughout history: "Almost every commander believes that he holds the key position and that any reduction in his force will undermine the national security."[1] Bragg, Forney, Buckner, Maury, and others frequently stripped their command of soldiers, artillery, and supplies to aid armies in Tennessee, Mississippi, and Georgia. Leaving themselves at times with little more than a "corporal's guard," these generals admirably performed their jobs as departmental or district commanders.

The assignment of these generals to Mobile went against a general trend that saw the Confederacy's least able commanders receive orders to one of the western armies. McMurry has decried "the gross, indeed, the almost criminal incompetence of the Confederate generals who served in the West."[2] As he points out so forcefully, the generals in Lee's army usually performed more satisfactorily because they had had some military training or experience before the war. All of the long-term commanders at Mobile had either received a military education or had served in the army during the antebellum years. The same cannot be said about their subordinate commanders. This work has shown that some of them fell into the category described by McMurry, though they may not have fit the definition of "incompetent." Fortunately, their shortcomings rarely had an adverse effect on the defense of Mobile.

One might argue, however, that throughout much of the war the officers under the rank of general and many of the military units stationed in the Mobile defenses for long periods of time did not measure up to their counterparts in the Army of Tennessee, much less those in the Army of Northern Virginia. This weakness may have played a crucial part in the defense of Fort Gaines and Fort Powell in August 1864. Most of the officers and enlisted men in those garrisons seemed to have had no real stomach for a fight. Had the officers been cut from a better mold, they might have served as examples to their men and encouraged them to hold their posts longer than they did. The majority of these officers undoubtedly had had no military training or experience and lacked the crucial spark of leadership needed at the time. The Confederacy was probably fortunate that they were not tested before Farragut's attack.

Union capture of Mobile at almost any earlier time would have had a significant effect on the course of the war. Federal troops would not only have severed the vital rail link but would have been poised for a thrust into the interior. They could have followed the rivers or rail line toward Montgomery and eventually moved against Atlanta. Such a campaign would have hastened the collapse of the Confederacy. This book has demonstrated that Union land and naval forces might have captured the city at several different times during the conflict. Weaknesses in the coastal defense system of the city made it vulnerable. Strategic and diplomatic considerations on several occasions diverted Union forces that might have attacked Mobile, but the defensive system protecting the city and bay—or at least the Union perception of the strength of that system—played an equally critical role in preventing or delaying an attack. The simple threat of a Union attack did not serve the same purpose that an actual attack would have. Except when active operations against the bay occurred, the strength of the Mobile garrison remained at a low level.

After much of Tennessee fell into Union hands in 1862, Alabama and northern Georgia were the most significant portions of what Thomas L. Connelly called the Heartland of the Confederacy still in Southern hands. Denied the foodstuffs, raw materials, industries, and manufacturing establishments located there and in Mississippi, Confederate armies as far away as Virginia would soon have felt their loss. Viewed in this light, Mobile was the "soft underbelly" of the Confederacy, the back door to the Heartland. Even without an enemy thrust into the interior, the presence of a Union army in Mobile would have required a significant force of Confederate troops to keep it there. The resultant drain of men from the major Confederate field armies might have exposed those armies to defeat and precluded offensive operations such as the three invasions of the North by Lee and Bragg in 1862 and 1863. The Union high command committed a grave strategic error in not attacking Mobile before August 1864.

Conversely, Confederate retention of Mobile until almost the end of the war represented a strategic success for the South. Mobile's importance to the Confederacy lay in three main areas: her system of interior transportation lines, the importance of blockade running there, and the potential for disaster if Union forces captured the city. Though the volume of blockade running in and out of Mobile Bay never rivaled that at Wilmington or Charleston, Mobile was the only blockade-running port in the eastern Gulf of Mexico. Every shipload of supplies that came into the bay helped to keep the war effort going. Had the government put more emphasis on blockade running there, Mobile would have served the Confederacy much better than it did. The transportation lines, both rail and river, allowed for efficient distribution of supplies brought in from abroad and enabled the Confederate armies to shift troops back and forth between Mississippi and Georgia when necessary. The fall of Mobile earlier in the war would have greatly shortened the life of the Confederacy. All the time, money, and labor that went into constructing and maintaining the city's defenses certainly made the effort worthwhile.

Notes

INTRODUCTION

1. Samuel R. Bright, Jr., "Confederate Coast Defense" (Ph.D. dissertation, Duke University, 1961), 3, 13–14, 32.

2. Christopher C. Andrews, *History of the Campaign of Mobile; Including the Cooperative Operations of General Wilson's Cavalry in Alabama* (New York: D. Van Nostrand, 1867), 10.

CHAPTER I

1. Joseph Wheeler, "Alabama," in *Confederate Military History*, ed. Clement A. Evans, 12 vols. (Atlanta: Confederate Publishing Co., 1899), 7:7–12; U.S. Bureau of the Census, *Eighth Census of the United States, 1860, Population* (Washington, D.C.: U.S. Government Printing Office, 1864), 9.

2. Albert D. Richardson, *The Secret Service, the Field, the Dungeon, and the Escape* (Hartford, Conn.: American Publishing Co., 1865), 95.

3. William Rix, *Incidents of Life in a Southern City during the War* (Mobile: Iberville Historical Society Papers, 1865), [1]; FitzGerald Ross, *Cities and Camps of the Confederate States*, ed. Richard B. Harwell (Urbana: University of Illinois Press, 1958), 201.

4. U.S. Bureau of the Census, *Eighth Census, Population*, 10.

5. Thomas C. DeLeon, *Four Years in Rebel Capitals: An Inside View of Life in the Southern Confederacy, from Birth to Death*, ed. E. B. Long (New York: Collier Books, 1962), 72.

6. William Howard Russell, *My Diary North and South*, ed. Fletcher Pratt (New York: Harper & Row, 1965), 106, 108.

7. Harriet E. Amos, *Cotton City: Urban Development in Antebellum Mobile* (University, Ala.: University of Alabama Press, 1985), 216–18; Sister Esther Marie Goodrow, *Mobile during the Civil War* (Mobile: Historic Mobile Preservation Society, 1950), 11–12; "Mobile—Its Past and Present," *DeBow's Review* 28 (1860): 310–11. The Can't-Get-Away-Club was the most famous

of the city's charitable organizations. Formed in 1839, it had as its goal the aiding of victims of yellow fever epidemics. The name derived from the fact that the original members were citizens who could not get away from the city during the 1839 epidemic. Frances Annette Isbell, "A Social and Economic History of Mobile, 1865–1875" (M.A. thesis, University of Alabama, 1951), 75; Amos, Cotton City, 173; Mobile Press Register, Oct. 17, 1948.

8. Amos, Cotton City, xiv; Robert L. Robinson, "Mobile in the 1850s: A Social, Cultural and Economic History" (M.A. thesis, University of Alabama, 1955), 66; U.S. Treasury Department, Commerce and Navigation of the United States, 1860 (Washington, D.C.: George W. Bowman, Printer, 1860), 350, 522, 556, 560.

9. Weymouth T. Jordan, "Ante-Bellum Mobile: Alabama's Agricultural Emporium," Alabama Review 1 (1948): 180–81; Agriculture of the United States in 1860; Compiled from the Original Returns of the Eighth Census (Washington, D.C.: U.S. Government Printing Office, 1864), xciv; Robinson, "Mobile in the 1850s," 66–67.

10. Clarence P. Denman, The Secession Movement in Alabama (Montgomery: Alabama State Department of Archives and History, 1933), 120; Amos, Cotton City, 235.

11. Mobile Daily Advertiser, Dec. 7, 1860.

12. Ibid., Dec. 9, 1860.

13. Wheeler, "Alabama," in Confederate Military History, ed. Evans, 34; Mobile Daily Advertiser, Dec. 4, 19, 1860; William L. Barney, The Secessionist Impulse: Alabama and Mississippi in 1860 (Princeton: Princeton University Press, 1974), 253–54.

14. Mobile Daily Advertiser, Dec. 21, 1860.

15. Denman, Secession Movement in Alabama, 120; Leavy Dorman, Party Politics in Alabma from 1850 through 1860 (Wetumpka, Ala.: Wetumpka Printing Co., 1935), 194; Barney, Secessionist Impulse, 253.

16. Amos, Cotton City, xiii–xiv, 238.

17. New Orleans Daily Picayune, Jan. 13, 1861; Caldwell Delaney, The Story of Mobile (Mobile: Gill Printing Co., 1953), 111; Goodrow, Mobile during the Civil War, 16.

18. Mobile Daily Advertiser, Jan. 11, 1861.

19. U.S. War Department, War of the Rebellion: Official Records of the Union and Confederate Armies, 128 parts in 70 vols. (Washington, D.C.: U.S. Government Printing Office, 1880–1901), Ser. I, vol. 1, pp. 327–30 (hereinafter cited as OR; all references are to Series I unless otherwise noted); Thomas A. Smith, "Mobilization of the Army in Alabama, 1859–1865" (M.A. thesis, Auburn University, 1953), 13; Lee F. Irwin Memoirs, Irwin Collection, Mobile Museum Department, Mobile, Ala.;

"Report of the Engineer Bureau, Nov. 30, 1861," in *Report of the Secretary of War*, Sen. Exec. Doc. 1, 37th Cong., 2d sess., 2:103; J. Thomas Scharf, *History of the Confederate States Navy*, 2d ed. (Albany, N.Y.: Joseph McDonough, 1894), 21; Malcolm C. McMillan, "Alabama," in *The Confederate Governors*, ed. W. Buck Yearns (Athens: University of Georgia Press, 1985), 17.

20. *Mobile Daily Advertiser*, Jan. 9, 22, 1861.

21. *OR*, vol. 52, pt. 2, p. 5.

22. *New Orleans Daily Picayune*, Jan. 24, 1861.

23. Leroy P. Walker to Colonel John H. Forney, Feb. 26, 28, 1861, Telegrams Sent by the Confederate Secretary of War, 1861–65, Chap. IX, vol. 33, pp. 2, 4, Record Group 109, National Archives (hereafter RG, NA).

24. *OR*, vol. 52, pt. 2, p. 23.

25. *Mobile Daily Advertiser*, Mar. 8, 1861; *Mobile Daily Tribune*, Mar. 8, 1861.

26. *OR*, vol. 52, pt. 2, p. 27; Ezra J. Warner, *Generals in Gray: Lives of the Confederate Commanders* (Baton Rouge: Louisiana State University Press, 1959), 124.

27. *OR*, vol. 52, pt. 2, pp. 30–31, 35; DeLeon, *Four Years in Rebel Capitals*, 73.

28. *OR*, vol. 52, pt. 2, p. 48.

29. Ibid., 45–46.

30. Ibid., 52.

31. John Tyler, Jr., to Percy Walker, Apr. 16, 1861, Letters Sent by the Conference Secretary of War, 1861–65, Chap. IX, vol. 1, p. 196, RG 109, NA; General Samuel Cooper to Danville Leadbetter, Mar. 19, 1861, Letters and Telegrams Sent by the Confederate Adjutant and Inspector General, 1861–65, Chap I, vol. 35, p. 8, RG 109, NA; *OR*, vol. 52, pt. 2, pp. 52, 53, 60, 61.

32. Irwin Memoirs; *Mobile Daily Advertiser*, Apr. 24, 1861; Henry Hotze, *Three Months in the Confederate Army*, ed. Richard B. Harwell (University, Ala.: University of Alabama Press, 1952), 13.

33. Hotze, *Three Months in the Confederate Army*, 13; *Mobile Daily Advertiser*, Apr. 24, 1861.

34. *Mobile Advertiser and Register*, July 17, 1861; U.S. Bureau of the Census, *Eighth Census, Population*, 2.

35. Willis Brewer, *Alabama: Her History, Resources, War Record and Public Men, from 1540 to 1872* (Montgomery: Barrett & Brown, 1872), 589–705.

36. *OR*, vol. 52, pt. 2, p. 65.

37. Ibid., 65–66.

38. Ibid., 85–87.

39. Russell, *My Diary North and South,* 109–11. Fort Morgan had a total of 107 guns mounted at this time (*OR,* Ser. IV, vol. 1, p. 227).

40. *Mobile Advertiser and Register,* June 30, 1861.

41. Ibid., July 2, 1861.

42. Ibid., July 4, Aug. 9, 20, 1861; Special Order No. 16, Headquarters Army of Alabama, Adjutant General's Office, Aug. 5, 1861, quoted in ibid., Aug. 7, 1861; Orders No. 8, Headquarters First Regiment, Alabama State Volunteers, Fire Brigade, Aug. 5, 1861, quoted in ibid., Aug. 6, 1861.

43. Robert C. Black III, *The Railroads of the Confederacy* (Chapel Hill: University of North Carolina Press, 1952), 5, 51, 74, 154–55, 158, 197–98.

44. Ibid., 75.

45. *OR,* 6:762, 766; vol. 52, pt. 2, pp. 164–65; and Ser. IV, vol. 1, p. 732; William D. Dunn to Withers, Oct. 2, 1861, Letters Received by the Confederate Secretary of War, 1861–65, RG 109, NA; Black, *Railroads of the Confederacy,* 51, 75–76.

46. Circular, Office of Chief of Bureau of Transportation, Aug. 20, 1864, quoted in *Mobile Daily Tribune,* Aug. 25, 1864.

47. Black, *Railroads of the Confederacy,* 180–81; *OR,* vol. 16, pt. 2, pp. 709, 727, and vol. 17, pt. 2, p. 626.

48. *OR,* vol. 16, pt. 2, pp. 732, 739, and vol. 17, pt. 2, pp. 656–57; *Aberdeen* (Miss.) *Examiner,* Feb. 7, 1890; Black, *Railroads of the Confederacy,* 182.

49. I am indebted to my friend and colleague Lawrence L. Hewitt, who cleared up some misconceptions about Bragg's strategy during the summer of 1862 in discussions concerning Hewitt's "Braxton Bragg and the Invasion of Kentucky: A Campaign of Maneuver" (seminar paper, Louisiana State University, 1975).

50. Black, *Railroads of the Confederacy,* 192, 271–72.

51. *Charleston Mercury,* Apr. 2, 1862; Larry J. Daniel and Riley W. Gunter, *Confederate Cannon Foundries* (Union City, Tenn.: Pioneer Press, 1977), 88–89; James C. Hazlett, Edwin Olmstead, and M. Hume Parks, *Field Artillery Weapons of the Civil War* (Newark: University of Delaware Press, 1983), 82, 150.

52. *OR,* vol. 26, pt. 2, p. 153; Daniel and Gunter, *Confederate Cannon Foundries,* 88.

CHAPTER 2

1. *OR,* 53:690.

2. Compiled Service Record of Franklin Gardner, in Compiled Service

Records of Confederate General and Staff Officers and Non-regimental Enlisted Men, RG 109, NA; *OR*, vol. 52, pt. 2, p. 110.

3. Cooper to Colonel William J. Hardee, June 17, 1861, Letters and Telegrams Sent, Adjutant and Inspector General, Chap. I, vol. 35, p. 198; *Mobile Advertiser and Register*, June 20, 1861; Warner, *Generals in Gray*, 124.

4. Colonel Henry Maury to Cooper, June 19, 1861, Telegrams Received, Secretary of War; Cooper to Hardee or "officer commanding Fort Morgan," June 20, 1861, Letters and Telegrams Sent, Adjutant and Inspector General, Chap. I, vol. 35, p. 205; *Mobile Advertiser and Register*, June 20, 1861.

5. Russell, *My Diary North and South*, 111; Dabney H. Maury, *Recollections of a Virginian* (New York: Charles Scribner's Sons, 1894), 200.

6. *OR*, vol. 52, pt. 2, p. 137, and 6:738; Cooper to Brigadier General Jones M. Withers, Sept. 5, 1861, Letters and Telegrams Sent, Adjutant and Inspector General, Chap. I, vol. 36, p. 65; *Mobile Advertiser and Register*, Sept. 13, 1861. The district consisted of the entire state of Alabama plus the portion of coastal Mississippi east of the Pascagoula River.

7. Robert H. Smith to Leroy P. Walker, Sept. 2, 1861 (with endorsement by Jefferson Davis), Telegrams Received, Secretary of War; *OR*, 6:738.

8. *OR*, 6:751–52, and vol. 52, pt. 2, p. 174.

9. Bragg to Davis, Oct. 22, 1861, in the William P. Palmer Collection of Braxton Bragg Papers, Western Reserve Historical Society, Cleveland, Ohio; *OR*, 6:756; Withers to Judah P. Benjamin, Nov. 2, 1861, Letters Received, Secretary of War.

10. Benjamin to Bragg, Oct. 8, 1861, and Bragg to "My dear Doctor," undated, Bragg Papers, Western Reserve.

11. Bragg to Thomas O. Moore, Oct. 31, Nov. 14, 1861, in Thomas O. Moore Papers, Louisiana State University, Department of Archives and Manuscripts, Baton Rouge; *OR*, 6:759; Bragg to "My dear Doctor," undated, Bragg Papers, Western Reserve. Thomas Bragg, Braxton's brother and the Confederate attorney general, later recorded in his diary that Davis had "seemed disposed" to place the Gulf Coast under Braxton's command but that Benjamin persuaded Davis to give it to Lovell (entry for Jan. 6, 1862, Thomas Bragg Diary, 1861–62, Southern Historical Collection, University of North Carolina, Chapel Hill).

12. Bragg to Elise Bragg, Oct. 14, 1861, Bragg Papers, Western Reserve.

13. *OR*, 6:757, 793, and vol. 52, pt. 2, p. 219; Compiled Service Records of Franklin Gardner; Benjamin to Davis, Nov. 24, 1861, Letters Received, Secretary of War.

14. Bragg Diary, Jan. 8, 1862; *OR*, 6:788–89, and vol. 52, pt. 2, p. 247.

15. *OR*, 6:797, 803.

16. Ibid., 815–16, and vol. 52, pt. 2, p. 265; *Mobile Advertiser and Register*, Feb. 1, 6, 1862; James S. Deas to unknown, Feb. 6, 1862, in Chestnut-Miller-Manning Collection, South Carolina Historical Society, Charleston.

17. Warner, *Generals in Gray*, 342–43.

18. Grady McWhiney, *Braxton Bragg and Confederate Defeat: Field Command* (New York: Columbia University Press, 1969), ix, 155–56, 195, 202–3; Nott to Bragg, Nov. 1, 1862, and John Forsyth to Bragg, Nov. 3, 1862, Bragg Papers, Western Reserve.

19. Warner, *Generals in Gray*, 166; Mark M. Boatner III, *The Civil War Dictionary* (New York: David McKay, 1959), 443; OR, 6:802, 820, 867.

20. *Mobile Advertiser and Register*, Mar. 2, 1862.

21. General Order No. 39, Headquarters Department of Alabama and West Florida, Mar. 3, 1862, General and Special Orders, Department of Alabama and West Florida, RG 109, NA; OR, 7:920–21.

22. Para I, Special Order No. 65, Headquarters Department of Alabama and West Florida, Mar. 4, 1862, General and Special Orders, Department of Alabama and West Florida; *Mobile Advertiser and Register*, Mar. 2, 1862; George Little and James R. Maxwell, *A History of Lumsden's Battery, C.S.A.* (Tuscaloosa: United Daughters of the Confederacy, 1905), 5.

23. OR, 6:852–53, 856; Brigadier General Samuel Jones to Cooper, Mar. 14, 1862, Letterbook, Bragg Papers, Western Reserve.

24. OR, 6:866, and vol. 52, pt. 2, pp. 290–91; *Mobile Daily Tribune*, Apr. 4, 1862.

25. Jones to Bragg, Mar. 24, 1862, Letterbook, Bragg Papers, Western Reserve; OR, vol. 52, pt. 2, p. 290; William M. Dunn to Benjamin, Mar. 25, 1862, and Governor John G. Shorter to Benjamin, Mar. 25, 1862, Telegrams Received, Secretary of War; Jones to Bragg, Mar. 26, 1862, Letterbook, Bragg Papers, Western Reserve; Jones to Major General Mansfield Lovell, Mar. 28, 1862, in Mansfield Lovell Papers, Henry E. Huntington Library, San Marino, Calif.; Para I, General Order No. 21, Headquarters Army of Mobile, Mar. 29, 1862, quoted in *Mobile Advertiser and Register*, Mar. 30, 1862; Para II, Special Order No. 24, Headquarters Second Corps, Army of Mississippi, Mar. 31, 1862, quoted in Compiled Service Record of Samuel Jones, Compiled Service Records of Confederate General and Staff Officers; Para I, General Order No. 40, Headquarters Department of Alabama and West Florida, Apr. 2, 1862, General and Special Orders, Department of Alabama and West Florida.

26. Cooper to Forney, Apr. 2, 9, 1862, Letters and Telegrams Sent, Adjutant and Inspector General, Chap. I, vol. 36, pp. 577, 566; OR, 6:880,

and vol. 52, pt. 2, p. 295; Jones to General Robert E. Lee, Apr. 12, 1862, Letterbook, Bragg Papers, Western Reserve.

27. Forney to General Pierre G. T. Beauregard, Apr. 28, 1862, and Bragg to Cooper, Mar. 12, 1862, Letterbook, Bragg Papers, Western Reserve; General Order No. 4, Headquarters Troops Confederate States near Pensacola, Mar. 18, 1861, quoted in *Mobile Daily Advertiser,* Mar. 20, 1861; OR, 5:493, 1058, and vol. 52, pt. 2, pp. 13, 17; Boatner, *Civil War Dictionary,* 288.

28. OR, 15:746, 766, 770.

29. Ibid., 771; *Mobile Advertiser and Register,* July 6, 1862.

30. OR, vol. 17, pt. 2, pp. 628, 659, 673, and vol. 52, pt. 2, p. 332.

31. Nott to Bragg, Nov. 1, 1862, and Forsyth to Bragg, Nov. 3, 1862, Bragg Papers, Western Reserve.

32. OR, vol. 20, pt. 2, p. 403; Surgeon A. J. Foard to Bragg, Jan. 31, 1862, Bragg Papers, Western Reserve.

33. OR, vol. 20, pt. 2, pp. 389, 403, 405; Special Order No. —, Headquarters Department No. 2, Nov. 17, 1862, in Compiled Service Record of William W. Mackall, Compiled Service Records of Confederate General and Staff Officers.

34. Para II, Special Order No. 57, Headquarters Department No. 2, Dec. 8, 1862, in Compiled Service Record of John H. Forney, Compiled Service Records of Confederate General and Staff Officers; OR, 15:899, and vol. 20, pt. 2, p. 423; William W. Mackall, *A Son's Recollections of His Father* (New York: E. P. Dutton, 1930), 174–75.

35. Nathaniel C. Hughes, ed., *Liddell's Record* (Dayton, Ohio: Morningside House, 1985), 103; OR, 15:899–900; vol. 20, pt. 2, pp. 449, 508–9, and vol. 52, pt. 2, p. 396; Leonidas Polk to wife, Dec. 25, 1862, in Leonidas Polk Papers, Southern Historical Collection, University of North Carolina, Chapel Hill.

36. Boatner, *Civil War Dictionary,* 95–96; Thomas Lawrence Connelly, *Army of the Heartland: The Army of Tennessee, 1861–1862* (Baton Rouge: Louisiana State University Press, 1967), 66.

37. OR, 15:905; *Mobile Advertiser and Register,* Dec. 27, 1862; *Montgomery Daily Mail,* Dec. 30, 1862. Shortly after Buckner's arrival, the District of the Gulf was renamed Department of the Gulf but remained under Bragg's Department No. 2. Some authorities in Richmond apparently never officially recognized the new status (OR, vol. 23, pt. 2, p. 833).

38. OR, 15:1055–56; Thomas Lawrence Connelly, *Autumn of Glory: The Army of Tennessee, 1862–1865* (Baton Rouge: Louisiana State University Press, 1971), 107.

39. Admiral Franklin Buchanan to Stephen R. Mallory, Apr. 28, 1863, Telegrams Received, Secretary of War; Committee of Safety of Mobile to James A. Seddon, Apr. 30, 1863, in Compiled Service Record of William W. Mackall; Mackall, *Son's Recollections*, 175.

40. *OR*, 15:1077, 1080; Buckner to Seddon, May 9, 1863, Telegrams Received, Secretary of War; Seddon to Brigadier General James E. Slaughter, May 13, 1863, Telegrams Sent, Secretary of War, p. 36.

41. General Order No. 192, Headquarters Department of the Gulf, May 19, 1863, quoted in *Mobile Daily Tribune*, May 23, 1863.

42. Warner, *Generals in Gray*, 215; Boatner, *Civil War Dictionary*, 519; *OR*, vol. 24, pt. 3, pp. 729, 743.

43. Cooper to Major General Dabney H. Maury, Apr. 29, 1863, Letters and Telegrams Sent, Adjutant and Inspector General, Chap. I, vol. 38, p. 219; *OR*, vol. 26, pt. 2, p. 222, and vol. 30, pt. 4, pp. 573, 653.

44. Maury, *Recollections of a Virginian*, 190.

45. *OR*, vol. 23, pt. 2, p. 822.

46. Richard Taylor, *Destruction and Reconstruction: Personal Experiences of the Late War*, ed. Richard B. Harwell (New York: Longmans Green, 1955), 247; P. D. Stephenson, "Defence of Spanish Fort," *Southern Historical Society Papers* 39 (1914): 119.

47. *OR*, vol. 26, pt. 2, p. 40, vol. 23, pt. 2, pp. 833–34, and vol. 52, pt. 2, p. 471.

48. Thomas Lawrence Connelly and Archer Jones, *The Politics of Command: Factions and Ideas in Confederate Strategy* (Baton Rouge: Louisiana State University Press, 1973), 88–92.

49. *OR*, vol. 32, pt. 2, pp. 582, 627, 692, 586, vol. 26, pt. 2, pp. 390, 678, vol. 31, pt. 4, pp. 511, 512, and vol. 32, pt. 3, p. 752; Cooper to Buckner, Feb. 20, 1863, Letters and Telegrams Sent, Adjutant and Inspector General, Chap. I, vol. 38, p. 92; Ewell to Garner, Nov. 3, 1863, Telegram Book, July 4, 1863–May 6, 1864, p. 174, Joseph E. Johnston Papers, College of William and Mary Library, Williamsburg, Va.

50. *OR*, vol. 52, pt. 2, p. 231, and 6:802; Scharf, *History of the Confederate States Navy*, 21, 24, 534–35; William N. Still, Jr., *Iron Afloat: The Story of the Confederate Armorclads* (Nashville: Vanderbilt University Press, 1971), 188.

51. U.S. Navy Department, *War of the Rebellion: Official Records of the Union and Confederate Navies*, 30 vols. (Washington, D.C.: U.S. Government Printing Office, 1894–1922), Ser. I, vol. 17, p. 17 (hereafter cited as *ORN*; all references are to Series I unless otherwise noted).

52. *OR*, 6:780, 787, 790; *ORN*, 17:14–15; Stephen R. Wise, *Lifeline of*

the Confederacy: Blockade Running during the Civil War (Columbia: University of South Carolina Press, 1988), 81–82.

53. *OR*, 6:795–96 (emphasis added); *ORN*, 18:17.

54. Still, *Iron Afloat*, 188; U.S. Navy Department, *Officers in the Confederate States Navy, 1861–1865* (Washington, D.C.: U.S. Government Printing Office, 1898), 113; *Mobile Advertiser and Register*, Feb. 13, 14, Mar. 9, 1862; *ORN*, 18:831, 835.

55. Quoted in Still, *Iron Afloat*, 190.

56. Charles M. Todorich, "Franklin Buchanan: Symbol for Two Navies," in *Captains of the Old Steam Navy: Makers of the American Naval Tradition, 1840–1880*, ed. James C. Bradford (Annapolis, Md.: Naval Institute Press, 1986), 87–88; Arthur W. Bergeron, Jr., "Franklin Buchanan," in Roger J. Spiller, ed., *Dictionary of American Military Biography*, 3 vols. (Westport, Conn.: Greenwood Press, 1984), 1:121–24.

57. Bergeron, "Franklin Buchanan," in *Dictionary of American Military Biography*, ed. Spiller, 1:121–24.

58. Still, *Iron Afloat*, 227–28.

59. Richard E. Beringer, Herman Hattaway, Archer Jones, and William N. Still, Jr., *Why the South Lost the Civil War* (Athens: University of Georgia Press, 1986), 57.

CHAPTER 3

1. Herman Hattaway and Archer Jones, *How the North Won: A Military History of the Civil War* (Urbana: University of Illinois Press, 1983), 35, 127; James M. McPherson, *Battle Cry of Freedom: The Civil War Era* (New York: Oxford University Press, 1988), 333–34.

2. Hattaway and Jones, *How the North Won*, 57, 82; Charles L. Dufour, *The Night the War Was Lost* (New York: Doubleday, 1960), 126, 135, 138; Richard S. West, Jr., *Gideon Welles: Lincoln's Navy Department* (Indianapolis: Bobbs-Merrill, 1943), 163; McPherson, *Battle Cry of Freedom*, 418.

3. *OR*, 6:465, 683, 694–95; Beringer, et al., *Why the South Lost the Civil War*, 138.

4. Dufour, *The Night the War Was Lost*, chaps. 16–21.

5. *ORN*, 18:147–48, 470, 502, 506; William N. Still, Jr., "David Glasgow Farragut: The Union's Nelson," in *Captains of the Old Steam Navy*, ed. Bradford, 171; Fox to Farragut, May 12, 1862, in Robert M. Thompson and Richard Wainwright, eds., *Confidential Correspondence of Gustavus Vasa Fox*, 2 vols. (New York: Printed for the Naval History Society, 1918–19), 1:313; Still, "Farragut," 173.

6. *ORN*, 18:147–48, 478–79; Major General Benjamin Butler to Edwin

M. Stanton, Apr. 29, 1862, quoted in Jessie Ames Marshall, ed., *Private and Official Correspondence of Gen. Benjamin F. Butler during the Period of the Civil War*, 5 vols. (Norwood, Mass.: Plimpton Press, 1917), 1:428; Forney to Beauregard, May 8, 1862, William P. Palmer Collection of Civil War Manuscripts; Western Reserve Historical Society; Cleveland, Ohio; David D. Porter, *Incidents and Anecdotes of the Civil War* (New York: D. Appleton, 1885), 38–39.

7. ORN, 18:594–95, 670, 675; Edwin C. Bearss, *Rebel Victory at Vicksburg* (Little Rock, Ark.: Pioneer Press, 1963), 27, 76, 130, 163.

8. ORN, 19:146–47, 161–62, 185; Bearss, *Rebel Victory*, 271, 274.

9. ORN, 242, 302, 306, 313, 346, 386, 390; Still, "Farragut," 176.

10. OR, 15:590, 613–14, 1096–97; Lawrence L. Hewitt, *Port Hudson: Confederate Bastion on the Mississippi* (Baton Rouge: Louisiana State University Press, 1987), 30–31; ORN, 19:409.

11. Samuel Carter III, *The Final Fortress: The Campaign for Vicksburg, 1862–1863* (New York: St. Martin's Press, 1980); Hewitt, *Port Hudson*.

12. OR, vol. 24, pt. 2, p. 523, and pt. 3, pp. 528, 530, 542.

13. OR, vol. 26, pt. 1, pp. 651–52, 659, 661–62, 666, 672; James A. Padgett, ed., "Some Letters of George Stanton Denison, 1854–1866: Observations of a Yankee on Conditions in Louisiana and Texas," *Louisiana Historical Quarterly* 23 (1940): 77–79.

14. Hattaway and Jones, *How the North Won*, 689–90, 431, 436; OR, vol. 30, pt. 4, pp. 518, 540–41; Connelly and Jones, *Politics of Command*, 134–35. Lieutenant General James Longstreet reinforced Bragg's army with two divisions from his corps of the Army of Northern Virginia, but only about half of Longstreet's men and none of his artillery reached the field in time to participate in the battle.

15. OR, vol. 24, pt. 3, p. 569, vol. 30, pt. 3, pp. 758, 773, pt. 4, p. 356, and vol. 34, pt. 1, p. 194, pt. 2, pp. 15, 55–56, 145; Hattaway and Jones, *How the North Won*, 436, 510–11.

16. OR, vol. 32, pt. 1, pp. 173–74, and pt. 2, pp. 114, 260; Hattaway and Jones, *How the North Won*, 506–9.

17. OR, vol. 32, pt. 3, pp. 245–46, vol. 34, pt. 1, p. 11, pt. 2, pp. 610–11, and pt. 3, pp. 190–92, 331–32; Hattaway and Jones, *How the North Won*, 512, 518–19.

18. Ludwell H. Johnson, *Red River Campaign: Politics and Cotton in the Civil War* (Baltimore: Johns Hopkins Press, 1958); Hattaway and Jones, *How the North Won*, 519, 552.

19. OR, vol. 34, pt. 4, pp. 185, 212, 240, 438–39, 528; vol. 39, pt. 2, pp. 79, 115, and vol. 41, pt. 2, pp. 3–4, 21–22.

CHAPTER 4

1. *OR*, vol. 53, pt. 2, pp. 125–26; *ORN*, 16:582.
2. *OR*, vol. 52, pt. 2, pp. 125–26.
3. Ibid., 130–31.
4. Ibid., 133; Compiled Service Record of Samuel H. Lockett, Compiled Service Records of Confederate General and Staff Officers.
5. *OR*, vol. 52, pt. 2, pp. 131–33.
6. *Mobile Advertiser and Register*, Aug. 29, 30, 1861.
7. *OR*, 6:726–29, 740, vol. 52, pt. 2, p. 131, and 6:729, 750.
8. Roll for Aug. 31–Oct. 31, 1861, Record of Events Cards, Company A, First Battalion Alabama Artillery, Compiled Service Records of Confederate Soldiers Who Served in Organizations from Alabama, RG 109, NA.
9. *OR*, 6:743; *Mobile Advertiser and Register*, Sept. 14, 28, 1861.
10. Bragg to Davis, Oct. 22, 1861, Bragg Papers, Western Reserve; *OR*, 6:755–57.
11. *OR*, 6:757, 761; General Order No. 6, Headquarters Department of Alabama and West Florida, Oct. 31, 1861, General and Special Orders, Department of Alabama and West Florida, Oct. 15, 1861–Feb. 28, 1862.
12. *OR*, 6:758, 761, 764–65, 772, and vol. 52, pt. 2, pp. 198, 202–3.
13. Little and Maxwell, *History of Lumsden's Battery*, 5; Rowena Reed, *Combined Operations in the Civil War* (Annapolis, Md.: Naval Institute Press, 1978), 25, 29.
14. *OR*, 6:774, 779, 780, 785; Bragg Diary, Dec. 31, 1861.
15. Caldwell Delaney, *Confederate Mobile: A Pictorial History* (Mobile: Haunted Book Shop, 1971), 120; Malcolm C. McMillan, *The Disintegration of a Confederate State: Three Governors and Alabama's Wartime Home Front, 1861–1865* (Macon, Ga.: Mercer University Press, 1986), 19; *ORN*, 17:163. In September 1862 the *Florida* was renamed *Selma*.
16. *OR*, 6:793, 802, 810; Dr. Josiah C. Nott to Dr. Samuel H. Stout, Dec. 29, 1861, in Samuel H. Stout Papers, Southern Historical Collection, University of North Carolina, Chapel Hill.
17. *OR*, 6:819; Deas to unknown, Feb. 6, 1862, Chestnut-Miller-Manning Collection; Para I, Special Order No. 51, Headquarters Department of Alabama and West Florida, Feb. 11, 1862, General and Special Orders, Department of Alabama and West Florida; Para II, Special Order No. 52, Headquarters Department of Alabama and West Florida, Feb. 12, 1862, ibid.; Para III, Special Order No. 39, Headquarters Army of Pensacola, Feb. 13, 1862, in A. C. Van Benthuysen Papers, Special Collections Division, Tulane University, Howard-Tilton Memorial Library, New Orleans.
18. *Mobile Advertiser and Register*, Feb. 13, 14, 1862; *OR*, 6:825.

19. *OR*, 6:823–25, 894; Para I, Special Order No. 54, Headquarters Department of Alabama and West Florida, Feb. 14, 1862, General and Special Orders, Department of Alabama and West Florida; Bragg Diary, Feb. 19, 1862.

20. Bright, "Confederate Coast Defense," 47, 89, 110.

21. *OR*, 6:826.

22. Ibid., 828, 834–37; Benjamin Franklin Cooling, *Forts Henry and Donelson: The Key to the Confederate Heartland* (Knoxville: University of Tennessee Press, 1987), 126–27, 233–44; Bragg Diary, Feb. 19, 1862; Paras II and III, General Order No. 37, Headquarters Department of Alabama and West Florida, Feb. 27, 1862, General Orders, Department of Alabama and West Florida, Oct. 15, 1861–Feb. 28, 1862; Para I, General Order No. 38, Headquarters Department of Alabama and West Florida, Feb. 28, 1862, General and Special Orders, Department of Alabama and West Florida.

23. Warren to Lockett, Feb. 27, 1862, in William P. Palmer Collection of Civil War Manuscripts; Roll dated Apr. 23, 1862, Record of Events Cards, Company D, First Alabama Battalion Artillery, Compiled Service Records; John Kent Folmar, ed., *From That Terrible Field: Civil War Letters of James M. Williams, Twenty-First Alabama Infantry Volunteers* (University, Ala.: University of Alabama Press, 1981), 37.

24. *OR*, 6:875–76, 879–80; Para I, Special Order No. 79, Headquarters Department of Alabama and West Florida, Apr. 13, 1862, and Para V, Special Order No. 80, Headquarters Department of Alabama and West Florida, Apr. 14, 1862, General and Special Orders, Department of Alabama and West Florida.

25. James R. Vickers to Miss Morell Vickers, Apr. 26, 1862, in Fort Gaines Collection, Mobile Museum Department, Mobile, Ala.

26. Forney to Beauregard, Apr. 28, 1862, Palmer Civil War Collection; General Order No. 50, Headquarters Department of Alabama and West Florida, Apr. 30, 1862, General and Special Orders, Department of Alabama and West Florida.

27. General Order No. 50, Headquarters Department of Alabama and West Florida, Apr. 30, 1862, General and Special Orders, Department of Alabama and West Florida.

28. Para VIII, Special Order No. 95, Headquarters Department of Alabama and West Florida, Apr. 30, 1862, General and Special Orders, Department of Alabama and West Florida; *Aberdeen* (Miss.) *Examiner*, Feb. 7, 1890; Forney to Beauregard, May 8, 10, 1862, Palmer Civil War Collection.

29. Para II, Special Order No. 81, Headquarters Department of Alabama and West Florida, Apr. 15, 1862, and Para VIII, Special Order No. 95,

Headquarters Department of Alabama and West Florida, Apr. 30, 1862, General and Special Orders, Department of Alabama and West Florida.

30. *Index* (London, Eng.), June 12, 1862.

31. Forney to Randolph, May 5, 1862, Telegrams Received, Secretary of War; *ORN*, 18:847–48; Edwards to his mother, May 11, 1862, E. H. Edwards Letters, South Caroliniana Library, University of South Carolina, Columbia.

32. Captain Charles F. Liernur to Superintendent, Mobile and Spring Hill Railroad, May 4, 1862, in Letters Sent, Engineer Office, Department of Alabama and West Florida, Apr.–May 1862, Chap. III, vol. 15, p. 62, RG 109, NA; Orders, Headquarters Department of Alabama and West Florida, May 3, 1862, quoted in *Mobile Advertiser and Register*, May 6, 1862.

33. Para XIII, Special Order No. 98, Headquarters Department of Alabama and West Florida, May 3, 1862, General and Special Orders, Department of Alabama and West Florida; *Mobile Advertiser and Register*, May 6, 1862; Harden P. Cochrane to Sophie Sarah Louisa Perkins Cochrane, May 7, 1862, quoted in Harriet Fitts Ryan, arr., "The Letters of Harden Perkins Cochrane, 1862–1864," *Alabama Review* 7 (1954): 283.

34. Liernur to Major H. O. Humphries, May 5, 1862, Letters Sent, Engineer Office, Chap. III, vol. 15, p. 63; General Order No. 51, Headquarters Department of Alabama and West Florida, May 6, 1862, General and Special Orders, Department of Alabama and West Florida.

35. Liernur to Captain William R. Neville, May 4, 1862, Letters Sent, Engineer Office, Chap. III, vol. 15, pp. 61–62.

36. Liernur to Firnan (?) Hurtel, May 5, 1862, ibid., 66; Para XII, Special Order No. 103, Headquarters Department of Alabama and West Florida, May 8, 1862, General and Special Orders, Department of Alabama and West Florida.

37. *Mobile Advertiser and Register*, May 7, 1862.

38. "Joint Resolutions by President Forsyth, Relating to the Defence of Mobile," May 14, 1862, quoted in ibid., May 15, 1862.

39. McMillan, "Alabama," in *Confederate Governors*, ed. Yearns, 23; McMillan, *Disintegration of a Confederate State*, 36–37; OR, 6:660.

40. Paras V and VI, Special Order No. 107, Headquarters Department of Alabama and West Florida, May 12, 1862, and Para III, Special Order No. 124, Headquarters Department of Alabama and West Florida, May 29, 1862, General and Special Orders, Department of Alabama and West Florida.

41. *Mobile Advertiser and Register*, May 25, 27, 1862.

42. Para III, Special Order No. 146, Headquarters Department of Ala-

bama and West Florida, June 23, 1862, General and Special Orders, Department of Alabama and West Florida; U.S. Navy Department, *Civil War Naval Chronology, 1861–1865*, 6 parts (Washington, D.C.: U.S. Government Printing Office, 1961–66), pt. 6, p. 218.

43. *OR*, vol. 17, pt. 2, p. 656.

44. *Aberdeen* (Miss.) *Examiner*, Feb. 7, 1890; *OR*, vol. 17, pt. 2, pp. 657, 659; Kate Cumming, *Kate: The Journal of a Confederate Nurse*, ed. Richard B. Harwell (Baton Rouge: Louisiana State University Press, 1959), 57.

45. Lieutenant Colonel Charles S. Stewart to Julia Stewart, Oct. 16, 20, 1862, in Charles S. Stewart Letters, Fort Morgan Museum, Gulf Shores, Ala.; Folmar, ed., *From That Terrible Field*, 101–7.

46. *OR*, 15:833–34, 842, vol. 52, pt. 2, p. 377–78, and vol. 16, pt. 2, p. 968.

47. *OR*, vol. 52, pt. 2, pp. 379–80.

48. *OR*, 15:848.

49. *History of Company B, 40th Alabama Regiment, Confederate States Army, 1862 to 1865* ([Anniston, Ala.]: Colonial Press, 1963), 12; *OR*, 15:848, 850; Cooper to Forney, Oct. 27, 1862, Letters and Telegrams Sent, Adjutant and Inspector General, Chap. I, vol. 37, p. 331.

50. *OR*, 15:874–76; Notice, District of the Gulf, Nov. 13, 1862, quoted in *Mobile Advertiser and Register*, Nov. 16, 1862.

51. *Mobile Advertiser and Register*, Nov. 11, 1862.

52. *OR*, 15:867, and vol. 16, pt. 2, p. 968; Cooper to Brigadier General Danville Leadbetter, Nov. 7, 1862, in Danville Leadbetter Papers, Dr. Thomas M. McMillan Collection, Mobile Museum Department, Mobile, Ala.; Colonel Jeremy F. Gilmer to Captain George E. Walker, Nov. 14, 1862, Letters and Telegrams Sent by the Engineer Bureau of the Confederate War Department, 1861–64, Chap. III, vol. 2, p. 51, RG 109, N.A.

53. *OR*, 15:867.

54. First Lieutenant John W. Glenn to Leadbetter, Nov. 24, 1862, Captain William R. Neville to Liernur, Nov. 25, 1862, and Forney to Leadbetter, Nov. 24, 1862, Leadbetter Papers.

55. Shorter to Leadbetter, Nov. 24, 30, 1862, Sam Tate to Liernur, Dec. 10, 1862, ibid.; *OR*, 15:888–90; Gilmer to Leadbetter, Dec. 10, 11, 1862, Jan. 5, 1863, Endorsement of Gilmer on letter from Leadbetter, Dec. 10, 1862, Letters and Telegrams Sent, Engineer Bureau, Chap. III, vol. 2, pp. 119, 121, 124, 181.

56. Brewer, *Alabama*, 644; Circular by Gov. John Gill Shorter, Nov. 21, 1862, Shorter to Leadbetter, Feb. 10, 1863, McMillan Collection; *OR*, 15:1019, 1029, vol. 26, pt. 2, pp. 27–28, vol. 32, pt. 2, pp. 600–601, and

vol. 49, pt. 2, pp. 1241, 1250; General Order No. 207, Headquarters Department of the Gulf, June 17, 1863, quoted in *Mobile Advertiser and Register,* June 20, 1863; Leadbetter to Col. J. W. Robertson, June 24, 1863, and Leadbetter to Gilmer, June 24, 1863, Letters and Telegrams Sent, Engineer Office at Mobile, June–July 1863, Chap. III, vol. 10, pp. 9–11; Warren Ripley, *Artillery and Ammunition of the Civil War,* 4th rev. ed. (Charleston, S.C.: Battery Press, 1984), 131.

57. Thomas H. Millington to Liernur, Dec. 12, 19, 1862, and Major Daniel Trueheart to Leadbetter, Nov. 24, 1862, Leadbetter Papers; *ORN,* 19:296–97, 401.

CHAPTER 5

1. Order No. 3, Headquarters Batteries Huger and Tracy, Dec. 28, 1862, and Order No. 9, Headquarters Batteries Huger and Tracy, Dec. 28, 1862, Records of the Department of the Gulf, 1861–65, Louisiana Historical Association Collection, Special Collections Division, Tulane University, Howard-Tilton Memorial Library.

2. Buckner to Colonel Abraham C. Myers, Dec. 29, 1862, in Compiled Service Record of Simon B. Buckner, Compiled Service Records of Confederate General and Staff Officers; Endorsement by Gilmer, Dec. 30, 1862, on Buckner to [Myers?], Dec. 29, 1862, and Gilmer to Leadbetter, Jan. 2, 1863, Letters and Telegrams Sent, Engineer Bureau, Chap. III, vol. 2, pp. 168, 173; Glenn to Leadbetter, Jan. 6, 1863, Leadbetter Papers.

3. Captain William Y. C. Humes to Trueheart, Jan. 16, 1863, Leadbetter Papers.

4. Thomas M. Owen, *History of Alabama and Dictionary of Alabama Biography,* 4 vols. (Chicago: S. J. Clarke, 1921), 2:1006; Glenn to Leadbetter, Feb. 1, 1863, Leadbetter Papers; *ORN,* 19:599.

5. Captain J. M. Cary to Colonel William L. Powell, Feb. 6, 1863, Trueheart to Leadbetter (with endorsement by Leadbetter to Glenn), Feb. 2, 1863, and Glenn to Leadbetter, Feb. 1863, Leadbetter Papers.

6. Leadbetter to Liernur, Jan. 3, 1863, ibid.; *OR,* 15:1010–11.

7. *OR,* 15:1011.

8. Ibid., 1012.

9. Owen, *History of Alabama,* 2:1066; Glenn to Leadbetter, Feb. 24, 1863, Leadbetter Papers.

10. *OR,* 15:1014–15.

11. Ibid., 1012, 1015; Humes to Captain L. G. Aldrich, Feb. 20, 1863, Leadbetter Papers; Moore to Cousin Blannie, Mar. 7, 1863, Southall and Bowen Papers, Southern Historical Collection, University of North Caro-

lina, Chapel Hill; *ORN*, 19:627; Lieutenant George Gift to unknown, June 13, 1863, quoted in Harriet Gift Castlen, *Hope Bids Me Onward* (Savannah, Ga.: Chatham Publishing Co., 1945), 128.

12. Leadbetter to Pillans, Feb. 26, 1863, Leadbetter Papers.

13. Leadbetter to Gilmer, Apr. 24, 1863, Letters Sent, Engineer Office, Department of the Gulf, Jan. 1863–Apr. 1864, Chap. III, vol. 12, p. 162, RG 109, NA.

14. Buckner to Cooper, Mar. 20, 1863, in Simon B. Buckner Papers, Henry E. Huntington Library, San Marino, Calif.

15. *OR*, 15:1035–36.

16. *OR*, vol. 24, pt. 3, pp. 679, 687, 691, 803; Para I, Special Order No. 32, Headquarters 1st District, Department of Mississippi and East Louisiana, Apr. 8, 1863, and Special Order No. 37, Headquarters First District, Department of Mississippi and East Louisiana, Apr. 18, 1863, Special Order Book, 1862–64, p. 51, Daniel Ruggles Papers, Fredericksburg-Spotsylvania National Military Park Library, Fredericksburg, Va.

17. Davis to Buckner, Apr. 7, 1863, in Dunbar Rowland, ed., *Jefferson Davis, Constitutionalist: His Letters, Papers and Speeches*, 10 vols. (Jackson, Miss.: Department of Archives and History, 1923), 5:469; *OR*, vol. 24, pt. 3, p. 724, and vol. 23, pt. 2, p. 750; "Diary of Captain Edward Crenshaw of the Confederate States Army," *Alabama Historical Quarterly* 1 (1930): 441.

18. *OR*, 15:1048, and vol. 23, pt. 2, p. 777; Para XIX, Special Order No. 102, Adjutant and Inspector General's Office, Apr. 27, 1863, quoted in Compiled Service Record of James E. Slaughter, Compiled Service Records of Confederate General and Staff Officers.

19. *Montgomery Daily Mail*, May 7, 1863; *OR*, vol. 23, pt. 2, p. 833.

20. Davis to Shorter, May 23, 1863, in Rowland, ed., *Jefferson Davis*, 5:494–95.

21. *OR*, vol. 26, pt. 2, pp. 26–27.

22. Ibid., 27; Leadbetter to Buchanan, May 22, 1863, Letters Sent, Engineer Office, Gulf, Chap. III, vol. 12, pp. 222–23; *ORN*, 20:828.

23. Milton F. Perry, *Infernal Machines: The Story of Confederate Submarine and Mine Warfare* (Baton Rouge: Louisiana State University Press, 1965), 200–201.

24. Still, *Iron Afloat*, 190–97.

25. General Order No. 207, Headquarters Department of the Gulf, June 17, 1864, quoted in *Mobile Advertiser and Register*, June 20, 1863; Warner, *Generals in Gray*, 107, 201, 306, 309; Delaney, *Confederate Mobile*, 99–100.

26. Circular, Headquarters Department of the Gulf, July 8, 1863, quoted

in *Index* (London, Eng.), Aug. 27, 1863; Para I, General Order No. —, Engineer Office, July 13, 1863, Letters and Telegrams Sent, Engineer Office at Mobile, June–July 1863, Chap. III, vol. 10, p. 33; Leadbetter to Captain Charles de Vaux, July 20, 1863, and Leadbetter to Robertson, July 20, 1863, Letters Sent, Engineer Office, Gulf, Chap. III, vol. 12, p. 277; General Order No. 221, Headquarters Department of the Gulf, July 23, 1864, quoted in *Index* (London, Eng.), Aug. 27, 1863.

27. *OR*, vol. 26, pt. 2, pp. 111–12.

28. Ibid., 43, 56, 130, 219; Cooper to Maury, July 7, 1863, and Cooper to Slaughter, July 17, 1863, Letters and Telegrams Sent, Adjutant and Inspector General, Chap. I, vol. 38, pp. 324, 333.

29. *OR*, vol. 26, pt. 2, pp. 130, 136, 139; Colonel H. L. Clay to Maury, Aug. 19, 1863, Letters and Telegrams Sent, Adjutant and Inspector General, Chap. I, vol. 38, p. 380.

30. *OR*, vol. 26, pt. 2, pp. 153, 160–61, 163–64; Leadbetter to Robertson, Aug. 5, 1863, Letters Sent, Engineer Office, Gulf, Chap. III, vol. 12, p. 296.

31. *OR*, vol. 26, pt. 2, pp. 136, 179–80, and vol. 28, pt. 2, p. 297; Folmar, ed., *From That Terrible Field*, 117.

32. *OR*, vol. 26, pt. 2, pp. 179, 190, 191, vol. 30, pt. 4, p. 572, and vol. 52, pt. 2, p. 519; First Lieutenant Elisha Orear to Carrie Orear, Aug. 29, 1863, in Eldridge Virgil Weaver III Collection, Special Collections Division, Tulane University, Howard-Tilton Memorial Library, New Orleans; F. Jay Taylor, ed., *Reluctant Rebel: The Secret Diary of Robert Patrick, 1861–1865* (Baton Rouge: Louisiana State University Press, 1959), 126.

33. *OR*, vol. 26, pt. 2, pp. 201–2, 211; Maury to Cooper, Sept. 5, 1863, Telegrams Received, Secretary of War; Maury to Lieutenant General William J. Hardee, Sept. 24, 1863, Letters and Telegrams Received, Department of Alabama, Mississippi, and East Louisiana; Ewell to Maury, Sept. 30, 1863, in Telegram Book, July 4, 1863–May 6, 1864, p. 138, Joseph E. Johnston Papers.

34. *OR*, vol. 26, pt. 2, pp. 274–75; Para I, General Order No. 235, Headquarters Department of the Gulf, Sept. 8, 1863, quoted in *Mobile Daily Tribune*, Sept. 8, 1863; unsigned report dated "Alabama, September 1863," in Jefferson Davis Papers, Duke University, William R. Perkins Library, Durham, N.C.; Leadbetter to Pillans, Sept. 1, 1863, Letters Sent, Engineer Office, Gulf, Chap. III, vol. 12, p. 342.

35. *OR*, vol. 52, pt. 2, p. 532; Maury to [Johnston], Sept. 29, 1863, Letters and Telegrams Received, Department of Alabama, Mississippi, and East Louisiana.

36. *OR*, vol. 26, pt. 2, p. 212, and vol. 31, pt. 3, pp. 851–52; Warner, *Generals in Gray*, 276; Maury to [Johnston], Sept. 29, 1863, Letters and Telegrams Received, Department of Alabama, Mississippi, and East Louisiana.

37. Para II, Special Order No. 251, Headquarters Department of the Gulf, Oct. 28, 1863, quoted in *Mobile Advertiser and Register*, Oct. 30, 1863.

38. *OR*, vol. 31, pt. 3, pp. 851–52, and vol. 52, pt. 2, p. 542; Arthur W. Bergeron, Jr., "'They Bore Themselves with Distinguished Gallantry': The Twenty-Second Louisiana Infantry," *Louisiana History* 13 (1972): 253–82; *Mobile Daily Tribune*, Oct. 25, 1863; Davis to Seddon, Oct. 29, 1863, in Rowland, ed., *Jefferson Davis*, 6:69; Special Order No. 30, Headquarters Third Brigade, Nov. 28, 1863, Orders, District of the Gulf, 1862–65, RG 109, NA.

39. *OR*, vol. 31, pt. 3, p. 581; Para VIII, Special Order No. 241, Adjutant and Inspector General's Office, Oct. 10, 1863, quoted in Compiled Service Record of Victor von Sheliha, Compiled Service Records of Confederate General and Staff Officers; Para VI, Special Order 75, Headquarters Department of the Gulf, Oct. 20, 1863, Letters Sent, Engineer Office, Gulf, Chap. III, vol. 12, p. 433; Rives to von Sheliha, Nov. 7, 1863, Letters and Telegrams Sent, Engineer Bureau, Chap. III, vol. 4, p. 89.

40. Orear to Carrie Orear, Oct. 3, 1863, Weaver Collection.

41. Rives to Leadbetter, Jan. 22, 1863, Letters and Telegrams Sent, Engineer Bureau, Chap. III, vol. 2, p. 231; Gilmer to Leadbetter, June 15, 1863, ibid., vol. 3, p. 104; Rives to Gilmer, Oct. 24, 1863, ibid., vol. 4, p. 46; Rives to Leadbetter, Oct. 16, 1863, ibid., p. 21. These engineering funds paid for the hire of mechanics, compensation for slave labor, hire of wagons and animals, and hire of vehicles.

42. Estimate of funds required for Engineer Service, Mobile, Dec. 1863, and Estimate of funds required for Engineer Service, Mobile, Jan. 1864, Letters Sent, Engineer Office, Gulf, Chap. III, vol. 12, pp. 523, 534–35.

43. *OR*, vol. 31, pt. 2, p. 431, pt. 3, pp. 723, 739, and vol. 52, pt. 2, pp. 547, 555; Field and Staff Roll for Apr. 30, 1863–May 1, 1864, Record of Events Cards, First Tennessee Heavy Artillery, Compiled Service Records of Confederate Soldiers Who Served in Organizations from Tennessee, RG 109, NA.

44. [Maury] to [Sterling Price], Nov. 29, 1863, in James W. Eldridge Collection, Henry E. Huntington Library, San Marino, Calif.

45. *OR*, vol. 26, pt. 2, pp. 499, 500–501, 510–11.

46. Ibid., 501–3; Orear to Carrie Orear, Dec. 1, 1863, Weaver Collection; Para VI, Special Order No. 121, Headquarters Department of the Gulf,

Dec. 14, 1863, Louisiana Historical Association Collection; Rives to von Sheliha, Dec. 18, 1863, Letters and Telegrams Sent, Engineer Bureau, Chap. III, vol. 4, p. 242.

CHAPTER 6

1. Davis to Maury, Jan. 9, 1864, in Rowland, ed., *Jefferson Davis*, 6:147; *OR*, vol. 32, pt. 2, pp. 542–44; 547–50, 552–55, 557.

2. *OR*, vol. 32, pt. 2, pp. 549, 565–66; *Mobile Advertiser and Register*, Jan. 17, 1864.

3. Diary of Lieutenant William T. Mumford, Jan. 16, 1864, in William T. Mumford Collection, Mobile Museum Department, Mobile, Ala.; *Mobile Daily Tribune*, Jan 19, 1864; *OR*, vol. 32, pt. 2, pp. 582, 601; William Pitt Chambers, "My Journal: The Story of a Soldier's Life Told by Himself," *Publications of the Mississippi Historical Society*, Centenary Series 5 (1925): 298.

4. *OR*, vol. 32, pt. 2, pp. 560–61, 577.

5. *OR*, vol. 35, pt. 1, p. 640; *Mobile Advertiser and Register*, Feb. 24, 1864.

6. *OR*, vol. 32, pt. 1, p. 401; Ross, *Cities and Camps*, 196–98; *Mobile Advertiser and Register*, Feb. 26, 1864; Mumford Diary, Feb. 25, 1864; Rives to Seddon, Feb. 26, 1864, Rives to Gilmer, Feb. 26, Mar. 2, 1864, and Rives to Maury, Mar. 3, 1864, Letters and Telegrams Sent, Engineer Bureau, Chap. III, vol. 4, pp. 473, 474, 482, 485.

7. *OR*, vol. 32, pt. 3, pp. 577–78, and vol. 52, pt. 2, pp. 631, 637.

8. *Mobile Advertiser and Register*, Feb. 18, 1864; *OR*, vol. 32, pt. 1, p. 403.

9. Davis to Captain Richard L. Page, Mar. 3, 1864, and Davis to Maury, Mar. 3, 5, 1864, quoted in Rowland, ed., *Jefferson Davis*, 6:197, 199; Cooper to Maury, Mar. 7, 1864, Letters and Telegrams Sent, Adjutant and Inspector General, Chap. I, vol. 40, p. 100; Warner, *Generals in Gray*, 227; Scharf, *History of the Confederate States Navy*, 143, 553–54, n. 1.

10. Robert Tarleton to Sallie Lightfoot, Mar. 11, 28, 1864, Sallie L. Tarleton Letters, in possession of Grace DuValle, Mobile, Ala.

11. Von Sheliha to Fremaux, Mar. 7, 12, 1864, and von Sheliha to Shoup, Mar. 15, 1864, Letters and Telegrams Sent, Engineer Office, Gulf, Chap. III, vol. 12, pp. 604, 610; Rives to Seddon, Mar. 26, 1864, and Rives to von Sheliha, Mar. 26, 1864, Letters and Telegrams Sent, Engineer Bureau, Chap. III, vol. 4, pp. 590, 595.

12. *ORN*, 21:884, 886.

13. Von Sheliha to Major E. H. Cummins, Apr. 1, 1864, von Sheliha to Gilmer, Apr. 2, 12, 1864, and von Sheliha to Rives, Apr. 2, 8, 1864, Letters Sent, Engineer Office, Gulf, Chap. III, vol. 12, pp. 629, 631, 640, 638; *OR*, vol. 32, pt. 3, pp. 779–80.

14. *OR*, vol. 32, pt. 3, p. 787; von Sheliha to Rives, Apr. 22, 1864, von Sheliha to Colonel F. S. Blount, Apr. 23, 1864, and von Sheliha to S. H. Linderberger, Apr. 26, 1864, Letters Sent, Engineer Office, Gulf, Apr.–Sept. 1864, Chap. III, vol. 16, pp. 2, 3–4, 11; Rives to von Sheliha, Apr. 29, 1864, Letters and Telegrams Sent, Engineer Bureau, Chap. III, vol. 5, p. 125.

15. "Monthly report of operations for the defence of Mobile, Ala., for the month of April, 1864," May 7, 1864, Letters Sent, Engineer Office, Gulf, Chap. III, vol. 16, pp. 30–31; *OR*, vol. 32, pt. 3, pp. 779, 810; *ORN*, 21:894.

16. *Mobile Advertiser and Register*, Apr. 5, 1864; Mumford Diary, Apr. 4, 1864; *OR*, vol. 32, pt. 3, p. 778.

17. *OR*, vol. 32, pt. 3, pp. 778, 771, 776–777, 816, 839–42, 860; Chambers, "My Journal," 313; Taylor, ed., *Reluctant Rebel*, 153–54, 156, 159; Johnston to Maury, Apr. 15, 1864, and Johnston to Bragg, Apr. 17, 1864, Telegram Book, p. 278, Johnston Papers; Cooper to Maury, Apr. 18, 1864, Letters and Telegrams Sent, Adjutant and Inspector General, Chap. I, vol. 40, p. 223; Orear to Carrie Orear, Apr. 22, 1864, Weaver Collection; Joseph H. Parks, *General Leonidas Polk, C.S.A.: The Fighting Bishop* (Baton Rouge: Louisiana State University Press, 1962), 371–73.

18. *OR*, vol. 32, pt. 3, pp. 772, 779–80; Mumford Diary, Apr. 1, 1864; Daniel P. Smith, *Company K, First Alabama Regiment, or Three Years in the Confederate Service* (Prattville, Ala.: Published by the Survivors, 1885), 92; Lieutenant Samuel A. Verdery to Captain Edward Durrive, Apr. 14, 1864, Records of the Department of the Gulf, Louisiana Historical Association Collection.

19. *OR*, vol. 38, pt. 4, pp. 654, 668; Smith, *Company K*, 94; Polk to Maury, May 4, 1864, Letters and Telegrams Sent, Department of Alabama, Mississippi, and East Louisiana, Chap. II, vol. 8 3/4, p. 235; Para VII, Special Order No. 126, Headquarters District of the Gulf, May 5, 1864, and Para VII, Special Order No. 141, Headquarters District of the Gulf, May 20, 1864, Orders, District of the Gulf.

20. *OR*, vol. 38, pt. 4, p. 732, and vol. 52, pt. 2, p. 671; Samuel E. Hunter to Stella Taylor, May 24, 1864, Hunter-Taylor Family Papers, Louisiana State University, Department of Archives and Manuscripts, Hill Memorial Library, Baton Rouge; Smith, *Company K*, 95; Roll for May and June 1864, Field and Staff, Twenty-second Louisiana Consolidated Infantry, Record of Events Cards, Compiled Service Records of Confederate Soldiers Who Served in Organizations from Louisiana, RG 109, NA; Mumford Diary, May 19, 1864.

21. *OR*, vol. 32, pt. 3, p. 860, and vol. 39, pt. 2, p. 677.

22. Rives to von Sheliha, May 21, 1864, and Rives to Captain Leverette Hutchinson, May 28, 1864, Letters and Telegrams Sent, Engineer Bureau, Chap. III, vol. 5, pp. 205, 270.

23. *ORN*, 21:901, 903–4; Tarleton to Lightfoot, June 17, 19, 22, 1864, Tarleton Letters.

24. Colonel S. Crutchfield to Gorgas, June 9, 1864, in Daniel Geary Papers, Mobile Public Library, Local History Department, Mobile, Ala.; Rives to von Sheliha, June 11, 23, 1864, Letters and Telegrams Sent, Engineer Bureau, Chap. III, vol. 5, pp. 303, 362; Order No. —, Engineer Office, June 15, 1864, and von Sheliha to Gilmer, June 25, 1864, Letters Sent, Engineer Office, Gulf, Chap. III, vol. 16, pp. 67, 71.

25. *OR*, vol. 39, pt. 2, pp. 677–78; General Order No. 1, Headquarters Commandant of Mobile, June 4, 1864, quoted in *Mobile Evening News*, June 10, 1864; Mumford Diary, June 5, 6, July 1, 1864.

26. Mumford Diary, July 5, 1864.

27. *OR*, vol. 39, pt. 2, pp. 695–96, 712, 700, 702, and vol. 52, pt. 2, pp. 687, 691–93, 708.

28. Maury to Bragg, July 14, 1864, Braxton Bragg Papers, Duke University, William R. Perkins Library, Durham, N.C.; *OR*, vol. 39, pt. 2, pp. 687, 693, 697, 703.

29. Mumford Diary, July 18, 20, 1864; Para IX, Special Order No. 202, Headquarters District of the Gulf, July 20, 1864, Orders, District of the Gulf.

30. *OR*, vol. 39, pt. 2, p. 702; *Mobile Daily Tribune*, July 13, 1864; Mumford Diary, July 22, 1864.

31. Tarleton to Lightfoot, July 10, 21, 26, 1864, in William N. Still, Jr., ed., "The Civil War Letters of Robert Tarleton," *Alabama Historical Quarterly* 32 (1970): 69–70, 74, 76, 77; Ellsworth H. Hults, "Aboard the *Galena* at Mobile," *Civil War Times Illustrated* 10 (Apr. 1971): 19; Maury to Bragg, July 14, 1864, Bragg Papers, Duke.

32. *OR*, vol. 39, pt. 2, pp. 705, 739; Rives to von Sheliha, July 22, 1864, Letters and Telegrams Sent, Engineer Bureau, Chap. III, vol. 5, p. 500; Tarleton to Lightfoot, July 19, 1864, in Still, ed., "Civil War Letters of Robert Tarleton," 74.

33. *OR*, vol. 39, pt. 2, p. 705; Endorsement of Gilmer on telegram from von Sheliha, July 22, 1864, and Lieutenant J. H. Alexander to von Sheliha, July 28, 1864, Letters and Telegrams Sent, Engineer Bureau, Chap. III, vol. 5, pp. 497, 528.

34. *OR*, vol. 39, pt. 2, pp. 705, 740; *Mobile Daily Tribune*, July 27, 1864.

35. *OR*, vol. 39, pt. 2, pp. 707–8, 739; *ORN*, 31:905–6.

36. *OR*, vol. 39, pt. 2, p. 706; *American State Papers, Military Affairs*, vol. 5, 22d Cong., 2d sess., no. 551, p. 185; Victor K. R. von Scheliha, *A Treatise on Coast-Defence* (London: E. & F. N. Spon, 1868), 17.

37. *OR*, vol. 39, pt. 2, pp. 706–8; Tarleton to Lightfoot, July 12, 19, 1864, in Still, ed., "Civil War Letters of Robert Tarleton," 71, 74.

CHAPTER 7

1. [Mary E. Brooks?], "War Memoirs," typescript in Irwin Collection; Delaney, *Story of Mobile*, 115–16; Robert Tarleton to unknown, undated, in Tarleton Letters; H. E. Sterkx, *Partners in Rebellion: Alabama Women in the Civil War* (Rutherford, N.J.: Fairleigh Dickinson University Press, 1970), 162; *Montgomery Daily Mail*, Feb. 18, 1863.

2. Stephenson, "Defence of Spanish Fort," 118–19; Cumming, *Kate*, 248; Tarleton to Sallie Lightfoot, Apr. 2, 1865, in Still, "Civil War Letters of Robert Tarleton," 78.

3. Ephraim McD. Anderson, *Memoirs: Historical and Personal; Including the Campaigns of the First Missouri Brigade* (St. Louis: Times Printing Co., 1868), 257–58; *Mobile Daily Mail*, Jan. 4, 1863; Amos, *Cotton City*, 65.

4. Anderson, *Memoirs*, 255.

5. A. D. Kirwan, ed., *Johnny Green of the Orphan Brigade: The Journal of a Confederate Soldier* (Lexington: University of Kentucky Press, 1956), 48–49.

6. John P. Dyer, *From Shiloh to San Juan: The Life of "Fightin' Joe" Wheeler* (Baton Rouge: Louisiana State University Press, 1961), 25.

7. Moore to Cousin Blannie, Mar. 7, 1863, in Southall and Bowen Papers; *Mobile Advertiser and Register*, Feb. 20, 1864; Ross, *Cities and Camps*, 202.

8. Sterkx, *Partners in Rebellion*, 98, 104; Cumming, *Kate*, 55; Thad Holt, ed., *Miss Waring's Journal, 1863 and 1865* (Chicago: Wyvern Press, 1964), 11–12; Chambers, "My Journal," 301–2; McMillan, *Disintegration of a Confederate State*, 45; Bessie Martin, *Desertion of Alabama Troops from the Confederate Army* (New York: AMS Press, 1966), 163–64.

9. Sterkx, *Partners in Rebellion*, 104.

10. *Mobile Advertiser and Register*, Jan. 18, 1862, Mar. 26, 1863; McMillan, *Disintegration of a Confederate State*, 45; Martin, *Desertion of Alabama Troops*, 165.

11. Peter J. Hamilton, *Mobile of the Five Flags* (Mobile: Gill Printing Co., 1913), 302–6; Minute Book, Confederate District Court, Southern Division of Alabama, Apr. 18, 1861–Jan. 13, 1865, Federal Records Center, East

Point, Ga.; Delaney, *Story of Mobile,* 119; *Mobile Advertiser and Register,* Feb. 5, 1862; Cumming, *Kate,* 249.

12. *Mobile Advertiser and Register,* May 7, Sept. 5, 1862, Feb. 5, 1863.

13. Rix, *Incidents of Life,* [5].

14. *Mobile Advertiser and Register,* Oct. 25, 29, 1862.

15. Ibid., Mar. 25, 29, Apr. 13, 1864.

16. W. J. Donald, ed., "Alabama Confederate Hospitals," *Alabama Review* 15 (1962): 275–77; *Mobile Army Argus and Crisis,* Jan. 7, 1865; Cumming, *Kate,* 255–56.

17. Para III, Special Order No. 153, Headquarters Department of Alabama and West Florida, July 1, 1862, General and Special Orders, Department of Alabama and West Florida; Abram M. Glazener to wife, Apr. 27, 1863, in Glazener Papers, Civil War Times Illustrated Collection, United States Army Military History Institute, Carlisle Barracks, Pa.

18. Glazener to R. M. Shuford, May 24, 1863, Glazener Papers.

19. Hamilton, *Mobile of the Five Flags,* 303–4.

20. *Mobile Army Argus and Crisis,* Jan. 7, 1865; Donald, ed., "Alabama Confederate Hospitals," 275–76; Cumming, *Kate,* 255.

21. *Selma Morning Reporter,* Feb. 24, 1863; *Mobile Advertiser and Register,* Oct. 11, 1863; William P. Fidler, *Augusta Evans Wilson, 1835–1900: A Biography* (University, Ala.: University of Alabama Press, 1951), 91.

22. Hamilton, *Mobile of the Five Flags,* 306–7; W. W. Corson, *Two Months in the Confederate States* (London: Richard Bentley, 1863), 110; Mumford Diary, Aug. 13, 1864; Isbell, "Social and Economic History of Mobile."

23. Hamilton, *Mobile of the Five Flags,* 306; Cumming, *Kate,* 189, 248–49.

24. Mumford Diary, Jan. 13, 1864; Cumming, *Kate,* 88, 249; *Home Journal* (Mobile), May 27, Sept. 23, 1864.

25. Jacob Faser to Louisa Mentzinger Faser, Nov. 10, 1861, in "Letters of Jacob Faser, Confederate Armorer," *Alabama Historical Quarterly* 3 (1941): 197; W. A. Smith, William H. Ross, and B. Tardy (?) to Jones, Mar. 24, 1862, in General Samuel Jones Papers, 1861–65, RG 109, NA; General Order No. 20, Headquarters Army of Mobile, Mar. 24, 1862, Special and General Orders, Army of Mobile, Mar.–June 1862, RG 109, NA; *Mobile Daily Tribune,* Apr. 4, 1862; Jones to Shorter, Mar. 25, 1862, Letterbrook, Bragg Papers, Western Reserve; *Mobile Advertiser and Register,* Jan. 18, Mar. 26, 30, 1862.

26. Maury to Seddon, Feb. 2, 1864, Telegrams Received, Secretary of War; Seddon to Maury, Feb. 5, 1864, Telegrams Sent, Secretary of War,

Chap. IX, vol. 35, p. 154; E. Merton Coulter, *The Confederate States of America, 1861–1865* (Baton Rouge: Louisiana State University Press, 1950), 160; Lieutenant James P. Butler to aunt, Mar. 21, 1864, in Thomas Butler and Family Papers, Louisiana State University, Department of Archives and Manuscripts, Hill Memorial Library, Baton Rouge.

27. Faser to Louisa, Nov. 10, 1861, in "Letters of Jacob Faser," 197; Richard Spencer to Mrs. A. R. Holcombe, Sept. 18, 1863, June 2, 1864, in Mrs. Sargent Pitcher, Jr., ed., "Spencer-Holcombe Letters Written in the 1860s," *Louisiana Genealogical Register* 19 (Mar. 1972): 45–46; Corson, *Two Months in the Confederate States*, 115; Mumford Diary, Jan. 19, 1864; *Mobile Daily Tribune*, Oct. 23, 1864; *Mobile Advertiser and Register*, Jan. 29, 1865.

28. Sam Bowers Hilliard, *Hog Meat and Hoecake: Food Supply in the Old South, 1840–1860* (Carbondale: Southern Illinois University Press, 1972), 107–8, 200, 208–9. Hilliard estimates average annual consumption of the four major food items in the diet of antebellum Southerners as follows: pork, 150 pounds; beef, 25 to 30 pounds; corn, 13 bushels; and wheat, 2 bushels (pp. 105, 130, 157, 230). A survey of fragmentary import statistics for Mobile found in extant newspapers reveals that not enough of these four foods reached the city to meet Hilliard's estimates for consumption, especially in view of the needs of the military and the increased population because of refugees.

29. *Vicksburg Daily Whig*, Jan. 10, 1863; OR, 15:937, 971; Campbell to Pemberton, Feb. 10, 1863, and Campbell to Major L. Mims, Feb. 11, 1863, Telegrams Sent, Secretary of War, Chap. IX, vol. 34, pp. 457, 458; McMillan, *Disintegration of a Confederate State*, 45.

30. OR, 15:938, 971, and vol. 24, pt. 3, p. 625; Seddon to Colonel W. M. Wadley, Mar. 23, 1863, Telegrams Sent, Secretary of War, Chap. IX, vol. 35, p. 1.

31. OR, vol. 23, pt. 2, p. 693, and vol. 24, pt. 3, p. 625; Special Order No. 343 (?), District of the Gulf, Feb. 14, 1863, and General Order No. 129, District of the Gulf, Mar. 15, 1863, quoted in *Mobile Advertiser and Register*, Feb. 19, Mar. 20, 1863.

32. *Mobile Daily Tribune*, Mar. 23, 1863; *Vicksburg Daily Whig*, Mar. 31, 1863.

33. Order No. 1, Mackall's Division, Feb. 21, 1863, quoted in *Mobile Advertiser and Register*, Feb. 25, 1863; Buckner to Cooper, Mar. 20, 1863, Buckner Papers; *Montgomery Daily Advertiser*, Mar. 8, 1863.

34. *Mobile Advertiser and Register*, Dec. 18, 1862; Daniel McNeill to Editors, Dec. 19, 1862, quoted in ibid., Dec. 20, 1862; T. A. Hamilton to Johnston, Feb. 19, 1863, Letters and Telegrams Received, Department of

Alabama, Mississippi, and East Louisiana; Campbell to Slough, Nov. 3, 1863, and Campbell to Johnston, Nov. 3, 1863, Telegrams Sent, Secretary of War, Chap. IX, vol. 35, pp. 124, 125; Johnston to Campbell, Nov. 6, 1863, and Johnston to Slough, Nov. 6, 1863, Johnston Papers; Cumming, *Kate,* 190; Peter Joseph Hamilton, *A Little Boy in Confederate Mobile* (Mobile: Colonial Mobile Book Shop, 1947), 12–13.

35. "Alabama," *The American Annual Cyclopedia and Register of Important Events of the Year 1863,* 14 vols. (New York: D. Appleton, 1865), 3:6; *Vicksburg Daily Whig,* Mar. 24, 1863; *OR,* vol. 52, pt. 2, p. 448.

36. Richard D. Goff, *Confederate Supply* (Durham, N.C.: Duke University Press, 1969), 84; Seddon to Buckner, Apr. 4, 1863, Letters Sent, Secretary of War, Chap. IX, vol. 10, pp. 391–92.

37. *New Orleans Times,* Sept. 21, 1863; Colonel Samuel E. Hunter to Stella Bradley Taylor Hunter, Sept. 4, 1863, in Hunter-Taylor Family Papers; Orear to Carrie Orear, Sept. 5, 1863, Weaver Collection; Rix, *Incidents of Life,* [9]; McMillan, *Disintegration of a Confederate State,* 45–46.

38. *Mobile Advertiser and Register,* Sept. 5, 14, 1863.

39. Mumford Diary, Feb. 16, 1864; *Mobile Daily Tribune,* June 5, 1864; *Mobile Advertiser and Register,* Jan. 29, 1865; Cumming, *Kate,* 248.

CHAPTER 8

1. U.S. Bureau of the Census, *Eighth Census, Population,* 8; Ira Berlin, *Slaves without Masters: The Free Negro in the Antebellum South* (New York: Pantheon Books, 1974), 131; Amos, *Cotton City,* 90, 104, 185, 190; *Mobile Advertiser and Register,* Apr. 26, July 28, Sept. 10, 19, 1863.

2. *OR,* Ser. IV, vol. 1, pp. 1087–88, 1111.

3. Ibid., 2:197; *Mobile Advertiser and Register,* Dec. 18, 1862, July 31, 1863.

4. Cooper to Maury, Sept. 28, 1863, Letters and Telegrams Sent, Adjutant and Inspector General, Chap. I, vol. 38, p. 458; *OR,* Ser. IV, vol. 2, p. 941.

5. Major General Franklin Gardner to Cooper, Aug. 19, 1864, Telegrams Received, Secretary of War; Mumford Diary, Aug. 18, 1864; *Mobile Evening News,* Oct. 22, 1864; *Mobile Advertiser and Register,* Mar. 23, 28, Apr. 8, 1865.

6. Richard C. Wade, *Slavery in the Cities: The South, 1820–1860* (New York: Oxford University Press, 1964), 18, 20–24; Amos, *Cotton City,* 88–89; U.S. Bureau of the Census, *Eighth Census, Population,* 8–10; *Mobile Advertiser and Register,* Apr. 1, 1865; Willie F. —— to Sister, Apr. 12, 1865, reproduced in Delaney, *Confederate Mobile,* 321.

7. Wade, *Slavery in the Cities*, 103–4; *Mobile Daily Tribune*, July 8, 1862, Aug. 21, 23, 1864; *Mobile Evening Telegraph*, June 8, 1864; *Mobile Evening News*, Oct. 8, 1864; *Mobile Advertiser and Register*, Apr. 21, June 11, 16, Sept. 2, Dec. 30, 1863.

8. *Mobile Advertiser and Register*, Sept. 8, Dec. 5, 23, 1863, Aug. 7, 14, 1864; Jane [Covington?] to Mrs. Young, Jan. 5, 1864, William Richard Hansford Papers, Duke University, William R. Perkins Library, Durham, N.C.

9. *Mobile Daily Tribune*, July 8, 1862; *Mobile Advertiser and Register*, June 17, 1863.

10. *Mobile Advertiser and Register*, Oct. 23, 1862, Sept. 22, Nov. 6, 1863.

11. Ibid., Mar. 15, Apr. 1, 16, 26, 1863.

12. Robert F. Durden, *The Gray and the Black: The Confederate Debate on Emancipation* (Baton Rouge: Louisiana State University Press, 1972); Bell I. Wiley, *Southern Negroes, 1861–1865* (New Haven: Yale University Press, 1938), 146–60; *Mobile Advertiser and Register*, Feb. 11, 15, 1865.

13. *Mobile Advertiser and Register*, Oct. 22, 29, 1862; *Montgomery Daily Mail*, Oct. 25, 1862.

14. *Montgomery Daily Mail*, Oct. 25, 1862; *Charleston Mercury*, Oct. 28, 1862.

15. General Order No. 3, Engineer Office, Jan. 26, 1863, Letters Sent, Engineer Office, Gulf, Jan. 1863–Apr. 1864, Chap. III, vol. 12, pp. 3–4.

16. Glenn to Leadbetter, Feb. 1, 1863, and Assistant Surgeon D. E. Smith to Surgeon F. A. Ross, Feb. 11, 1863, Leadbetter Papers.

17. Smith to Ross, Feb. 11, 1863, Leadbetter Papers; *Mobile Advertiser and Register*, Feb. 17, 1863; Glenn to Leadbetter, Mar. 3, 1863, Leadbetter Papers.

18. *OR*, vol. 26, pt. 2, p. 27; Notice by Leadbetter, June 11, 1863, Letters Sent, Engineer Office, Gulf, Chap. III, vol. 12, p. 261; Leadbetter to Colonel I. W. Robertson, June 17, 1863, Letters and Telegrams Sent, Engineer Office at Mobile, June–July 1863, Chap. III, vol. 10, p. 2; Orear to Carrie Orear, June 28, 1863, Weaver Collection.

19. Von Sheliha to Garner, Dec. 4, 1863, Letters Sent, Engineer Office, Gulf, Chap. III, vol. 12, p. 504; General Order No. 2, Engineer Office, Department of Mobile [sic], Dec. 9, 1863, quoted in Ross, *Cities and Camps*, 162.

20. *OR*, vol. 26, pt. 2, pp. 503–4; McMillan, *Disintegration of a Confederate State*, 111.

21. Von Sheliha to Senator Clement C. Clay, Dec. 29, 1863, Letters Sent, Engineer Office, Gulf, Chap. III, vol. 12, pp. 525–26.

22. Ibid.; *OR*, vol. 26, pt. 2, p. 503. John Forsyth supported a proposal

similar to von Sheliha's in an editorial, *Mobile Advertiser and Register*, Nov. 13, 1863.

23. Polk to Maury, May 7, 1864, Letters and Telegrams Sent, Department of Alabama, Mississippi, and East Louisiana, 1864–65, Chap. II, vol. 8 3/4, p. 270, RG 109, NA; *OR*, Ser. II, vol. 7, pp. 27, 153, 155–56, and Ser. I, vol. 49, pt. 1, p. 957; Report of Colonel Samuel H. Lockett, Mar. 13, 1865, Letters Sent, Engineer Office at Mobile, Oct. 11, 1864–May 8, 1865, Chap. III, vol. 11, p. 389, RG 109, NA.

24. *OR*, Ser. II, vol. 8, pp. 109, 153, 354–55, 362, 382, 396; Maury to Lieutenant General Richard Taylor, Mar. 14, 1865, Joseph L. Brent Collection, Louisiana Adjutant General's Archives, Jackson Barracks, Chalmette, La.

CHAPTER 9

1. Frank L. Owsley, *King Cotton Diplomacy: Foreign Relations of the Confederate States of America*, 2d ed., rev. (Chicago: University of Chicago Press, 1966), 251–52; Francis B. C. Bradlee, "Blockade Running during the Civil War," *Essex Institute Historical Collections* 60 (1924): 167; Wise, *Lifeline of the Confederacy*, 81; Delaney, *Story of Mobile*, 113–14.

2. James Russell Soley, *The Blockade and the Cruisers* (New York: Charles Scribner's Sons, 1883), 132–34.

3. Ibid., 132; Marcus W. Price, "Ships That Tested the Blockade of the Gulf Ports, 1861–1865," *American Neptune* 11 (1951): 263; Lieutenant Colonel Stewart to Julia Stewart, Apr. 21, 1863, Stewart Letters; von Scheliha, *Treatise on Coast-Defence*, 103.

4. James D. Richardson, comp., *A Compilation of the Messages and Papers of the Presidents, 1789–1897*, 10 vols. (Washington, D.C.: U.S. Government Printing Office, 1896–99), 6:14–15; *ORN*, 4:155, 182, 208, and 16:820; *Mobile Daily Advertiser*, May 28, 1861.

5. Lord Lyons to James Magee, May 8, 1861, quoted in Scharf, *History of the Confederate States Navy*, 437–38; Record Book of Exports of Domestic Produce in Confederate Vessels and Foreign Vessels, 1861–75, RG 36, NA; *ORN*, 4:185, 196, 206; Rix, *Incidents of Life*, [6–7].

6. *ORN*, 16:647; Price, "Ships That Tested the Blockade," 267–69; Wise, *Lifeline of the Confederacy*, 81.

7. Frank E. Vandiver, ed., *Confederate Blockade Running through Bermuda, 1861–1865: Letters and Cargo Manifests* (Austin: University of Texas Press, 1947), xiv.

8. "Weekly Receipts of Cotton at Mobile," *Mobile Advertiser and Register*, June–Sept. 1861, Aug. 30, 1861.

9. Bragg to Cooper, Dec. 31, 1861, Telegrams Received, Secretary of

War; *OR*, 6:498–99; *ORN*, 17:59–60, 62–63; Scharf, *History of the Confederate States Navy*, 536.

10. Butler to Bragg, Mar. 29, 31, 1862, and Jones to Cooper, Apr. 5, 1862, Letterbook, Bragg Papers, Western Reserve; Jones to Randolph, Apr. 4, 1862, Telegrams Received, Secretary of War.

11. Randolph to Jones, Mar. 26, Apr. 14, 1862, Letters Sent, Secretary of War, Chap. IX, vol. 6, pp. 217, 329–30; Randolph to Jones, Apr. 4, 1862, Telegrams Sent, Secretary of War, Chap. IX, vol. 34, p. 171.

12. *ORN*, 1:766; Frank Lawrence Owsley, Jr., *The C.S.S. Florida: Her Building and Operations* (Tuscaloosa: University of Alabama Press, 1987), 37–38; Edward Boykin, *Sea Devil of the Confederacy* (New York: Funk & Wagnalls, 1959), 109, 116–22.

13. *ORN*, 1:436–40, 460–68; Susan G. Perkins, arr. and ed., *Letters of Capt. Geo. Hamilton Perkins, U.S.N.* (Concord, N.H.: Ira C. Evans, 1886), 102–3; Owsley, *C.S.S. Florida*, 38–42; Boykin, *Sea Devil of the Confederacy*, 122–31.

14. *ORN*, 1:767–69, and 2:30–31, 667–68; Owsley, *C.S.S. Florida*, 42–49; Boykin, *Sea Devil of the Confederacy*, 132–40; David D. Porter, *The Naval History of the Civil War* (New York: Sherman 1886), 627.

15. Corson, *Two Months in the Confederate States*, 114–15.

16. *New York Herald*, Feb. 26, 1863.

17. Information on the various arrivals and departures can be found in Record Book of Exports, 1861–75; Entry of Merchandise, Mobile, 1861–65, RG 36, NA; Abstracts of Import Duties, Mobile, 1861–65, ibid.; Bureau of Customs Cargo Manifests, Mobile, 1861–65, ibid.; *ORN*, vols. 17, 18, and 19, passim; and Price, "Ships That Tested the Blockade," 52–59.

18. Owsley, *King Cotton Diplomacy*, 232.

19. *OR*, Ser. IV, vol. 2, pp. 462–63, 472–73; Gift to unknown, June 10, 1863, quoted in Castlen, *Hope Bids Me Onward*, 125.

20. John E. Murrell to Colonel William L. Powell, Apr. 30, 1863, Letters Received, Secretary of War; Vandiver, ed., *Confederate Blockade Running*, xxxv–xxxvi.

21. Seddon to Buckner, Apr. 3, 1863, Letters Sent, Secretary of War, Chap. IX, vol. 10, pp. 390–91.

22. Seddon to Maury, June 8, 1863, Telegrams Sent, Secretary of War, Chap. IX, vol. 35, p. 49; Maury to Seddon, June 13, 24, 1863, Telegrams Received, Secretary of War; *OR*, vol. 26, pt. 2, pp. 112–13, 121.

23. *OR*, vol. 52, pt. 2, pp. 518, 531.

24. *ORN*, 20:583–84; *OR*, vol. 26, pt. 2, p. 244, and vol. 52, pt. 2, p. 531; Maury to [Johnston], Sept. 29, 1863, Letters and Telegrams Re-

ceived, Department of Alabama, Mississippi, and East Louisiana; Wise, *Lifeline of the Confederacy*, 172, 174.

25. Record Book of Exports, 1861–75; Entry of Merchandise, Mobile, 1861–65; Abstracts of Import Duties, Mobile, 1861–65; Bureau of Customs Cargo Manifests, Mobile, 1861–65, RG 36, NA; Wise, *Lifeline of the Confederacy*, 174; Owsley, *King Cotton Diplomacy*, 252–53.

26. Thomas H. Dudley to William H. Seward, Oct. 20, 1863, quoted in Price, "Ships That Tested the Blockade," 271.

27. Thompson and Wainwright, eds., *Confidential Correspondence of Gustavus Vasa Fox*, 1:344; *Mobile Advertiser and Register*, Feb. 4, Mar. 24, 1864.

28. Ellsworth H. Hults, "Aboard the *Galena* at Mobile," 19; Tarleton to Lightfoot, July 10, 12, 1864, in Still, ed., "Civil War Letters of Robert Tarleton," 69–70, 72; Tarleton to Lightfoot, July 21, 1864, Tarleton Letters; *Mobile Daily Tribune*, July 13, 1864.

29. Hults, "Aboard the *Galena* at Mobile," 17–19; *ORN*, 21:355; Sergeant William J. Byrnes to Captain John T. Purves, July 5, 1864, in John T. Purves Papers, Special Collections Division, Tulane University, Howard-Tilton Memorial Library, New Orleans, La.; Tarleton to Lightfoot, July 5, 7, 10, 1864, in Still, ed., "Civil War Letters of Robert Tarleton," 63–64, 66–68; *OR*, vol. 39, pt. 2, p. 693; Tarleton to Lightfoot, July 21, 1864, Tarleton Letters.

30. Tarleton to Lightfoot, July 28, 1864, Tarleton Letters; Seddon to Maury, July 20, Aug. 5, 1864, Telegrams Sent, Secretary of War, Chap. IX, vol. 35, pp. 246, 224–25; Maury to Seddon, Aug. 4, 1864, Maury to Seddon, Aug. 14, 1864, with endorsement by Lieutenant Colonel Thomas L. Bayne, Aug. 16, 1864, and John Scott to G. A. Trenholm, Aug. 17, 1864, Telegrams Received, Secretary of War; Jeanie M. Walker, *Life of Capt. Joseph Fry, the Cuban Martyr* (Hartford, Conn.: J. B. Burr Publishing Co., 1875), 176–78; Bradlee, "Blockade Running," 155; Scharf, *History of the Confederate States Navy*, 595, 598.

31. Vandiver, ed., *Confederate Blockade Running*, xli.

32. Wise, *Lifeline of the Confederacy*, 3; Vandiver, ed., *Confederate Blockade Running*, xli.

33. Wise, *Lifeline of the Confederacy*, 167, 177, 180–81; Owsley, *King Cotton Diplomacy*, 259–60. The figures quoted were compiled by the author from most of the sources cited in this chapter.

CHAPTER 10

1. Folmar, ed., *From That Terrible Field*, 14.

2. *ORN*, 17:xvii, 12; *Mobile Evening News*, Dec. 25, 1861.

3. Still, *Iron Afloat*, 189; Scharf, *History of the Confederate States Navy*, 536; *Mobile Advertiser and Register*, Apr. 4, 1862; *ORN*, 18:691.

4. *ORN*, 18:840, 843; Ed. Harleson Edwards to father, Apr. 11, 1862, in Edwards Letters; Still, *Iron Afloat*, 189.

5. Still, *Iron Afloat*, 80–81; Rix, *Incidents of Life*, [6]; Scharf, *History of the Confederate States Navy*, 534.

6. *ORN*, 19:734; *Mobile Advertiser and Register*, Dec. 16, 1862.

7. *ORN*, 19:627; T. L. Moore to Cousin Blannie, Mar. 7, 1863, in Southall and Bowen Papers.

8. Roll for Feb. 28–Apr. 30, 1863, Record of Events Cards, Company B, First Alabama Artillery Battalion, Compiled Service Records of Confederate Soldiers Who Served in Organizations from Alabama, RG 109, NA; Stewart to Julia Stewart, Apr. 21, 1863, Stewart Letters.

9. Folmar, ed., *From That Terrible Field*, 120, 122, 172.

10. *ORN*, 20:584–85; Roll for July and Aug. 1863, Record of Events Cards, Company D, Twenty-first Alabama Infantry, Compiled Service Records of Confederate Soldiers from Alabama; "Company D, 21st Ala. Regt.," to Editor, Sept. 16, 1863, quoted in *Mobile Daily Tribune*, Sept. 19, 1863.

11. *OR*, vol. 32, pt. 2, pp. 114, 402, and vol. 34, pt. 2, p. 266; *ORN*, 31:90–91, 93; Farragut to Fox, Feb. 8, 1864, in Thompson and Wainwright, eds., *Confidential Correspondence of Gustavus Vasa Fox*, 1:343.

12. *OR*, vol. 32, pt. 1, pp. 175, 335, and pt. 2, pp. 655, 663, 681, 692; Chambers, "My Journal," 299; Smith, *Company K*, 90.

13. Para I, Special Order No. 37, Headquarters Department of the Gulf, Feb. 6, 1864, cited in Compiled Service Record of Francis A. Shoup, Compiled Service Records of Confederate General and Staff Officers; Bob ——— to Hunter, Feb. 5, 1864, Hunter-Taylor Papers; Orear to Carrie Orear, Feb. 6, 1864, Weaver Collection.

14. *OR*, vol. 32, pt. 1, p. 335, and pt. 2, pp. 695, 700, 701; Chambers, "My Journal," 301; *Mobile Advertiser and Register*, Feb. 5, 1864.

15. *Mobile Advertiser and Register*, Feb. 11, 16, 1864; Mumford Diary, Feb. 15, 1864; Chambers, "My Journal," 302; Mary Elizabeth Massey, *Refugee Life in the Confederacy* (Baton Rouge: Louisiana State University Press, 1964), 87.

16. *OR*, vol. 32, pt. 2, pp. 716, 726, 751–52, 738, vol. 52, pt. 2, p. 619, and vol. 35, pt. 1, p. 605; Johnston to Davis, Feb. 11, 1864, Johnston Papers.

17. *OR*, vol. 32, pt. 2, pp. 734, 736, 739; Rives to Seddon, Feb. 15, 1864, Letters and Telegrams Sent, Engineer Bureau, Chap. III, vol. 4, p. 428.

18. *OR*, vol. 32, pt. 2, p. 739; Lieutenant Colonel William E. Burnett to

Judge D. G. Burnett, Mar. 7, 1864, quoted in *New York Daily Tribune*, Apr. 18, 1864.

19. *ORN*, 21:98–102; Lieutenant C. E. Ross to Garner, Feb. 16, 1864, quoted in *Mobile Advertiser and Register*, Feb. 17, 1864; Colonel George A. Smith to Garner, Feb. 16, 1864, quoted in ibid., Feb. 18, 1864; *OR*, vol. 32, pt. 1, p. 401; Tarleton to Lightfoot, Feb. 22, 1864, in Still, ed., "Civil War Letters of Robert Tarleton," 52–53; Folmar, ed., *From That Terrible Field*, 128; *Mobile Advertiser and Register*, Feb. 20, 1864.

20. *OR*, vol. 32, pt. 1, p. 401, and pt. 2, pp. 754, 763; Rives to von Sheliha, Feb. 17, 1864, and Rives to Beauregard, Feb. 18, 22, 1864, Letters and Telegrams Sent, Engineer Bureau, Chap. III, vol. 4, pp. 434, 437, 445; Para IV, Special Order No. 43, Headquarters Department of the Gulf, Feb. 17, 1864, quoted in *Mobile Advertiser and Register*, Feb. 18, 1864; Polk to Maury, Feb. 17, 1864, Letters and Telegrams Sent, Department of Alabama, Mississippi, and East Louisiana, Chap. II, vol. 8 3/4, p. 47; Cooper to Beauregard, Feb. 18, 1864, Letters and Telegrams Sent, Adjutant and Inspector General, Chap. I, vol. 40, p. 81; Folmar, ed., *From That Terrible Field*, 128; Chambers, "My Journal," 304–6.

21. Still, *Iron Afloat*, 195–96, 200–202; Scharf, *History of the Confederate States Navy*, 553–54.

22. *OR*, vol. 32, pt. 2, pp. 755, 769, 771, 785; Smith, *Company K*, 90–91; Edward Young McMorries, *History of the First Regiment Alabama Volunteer Infantry C.S.A.* (Montgomery: Brown Printing Co., 1904), 72; Rives to Gilmer, Feb. 20, 1864, Letters and Telegrams Sent, Engineer Bureau, Chap. III, vol. 4, p. 433.

23. Gee to Major D. W. Flowerree, Feb. 23, 1864, and Lieutenant Colonel James M. Williams to Flowerree, Feb. 23, 1864, quoted in *Mobile Advertiser and Register*, Feb. 24, 1864; Tarleton to Lightfoot, Feb. 25, 1864, in Still, ed., "Civil War Letters of Robert Tarleton," 54; *OR*, vol. 32, pt. 1, p. 401, and vol. 52, pt. 2, p. 631; *Mobile Advertiser and Register*, Feb. 26, 1864; Folmar, ed., *From That Terrible Field*, 128–92; Tarleton to Lightfoot, Feb. 26, 1864, Tarleton Letters.

24. *ORN*, 21:95.

25. Ibid., 96–97, 880–81; *OR*, vol. 52, pt. 2, p. 631; *Mobile Advertiser and Register*, Mar. 2, 1864; Tarleton to Lightfoot, Mar. 2, 1864, in Still, ed., "Civil War Letters of Robert Tarleton," 55; *OR*, vol. 32, pt. 1, p. 402.

26. Farragut to Fox, Feb. 28, 1864, in Thompson and Wainwright, eds., *Confidential Correspondence of Gustavus Vasa Fox*, 1:345; *ORN*, 21:96–98.

27. *OR*, vol. 32, pt. 1, pp. 173, 175–76, 252–53, 257, and pt. 2, p. 12; Hattaway and Jones, *How the North Won*, 509–10.

28. *OR,* vol. 32, pt. 1, p. 402; von Scheliha, *Treatise on Coast-Defence,* 36, 38, 229.

29. Still, *Iron Afloat,* 200–203; *ORN,* 21:267, 935; Mumford Diary, May 19, 24, 25, 1864; Tarleton to Lightfoot, May 18, 20, 27, 1864, in Still, ed., "Civil War Letters of Robert Tarleton," 59, 61–62; C. Carter Smith, Jr., ed., *Two Naval Journals: 1864* (Chicago: Wyvern Press, 1964), 2–3.

CHAPTER 11

1. *ORN,* 21:378, 380, 386, 388, 397–98.

2. *OR,* vol. 39, pt. 2, p. 216, pt. 1, pp. 428, 441, and vol. 41, pt. 2, p. 449; Andrews, *History of the Campaign of Mobile,* 14; Benjamin B. Cox, "Mobile in the War between the States," *Confederate Veteran* 24 (1916): 212; Bernard A. Reynolds, *Sketches of Mobile, from 1814 to the Present* (Mobile: B. H. Richardson, 1868), 75; *Mobile Register,* Aug. 9, 1908.

3. Cox, "Mobile in the War," 212; Hurieosco Austill, "Fort Morgan in the Confederacy," *Alabama Historical Quarterly* 7 (1945): 256–57; Diary of First Lieutenant James Biddle Wilkinson, Aug. 5, 1864, photostatic copy in Mobile Museum Department, Mobile, Ala.; *ORN,* 21:378, 416–18, 479, 570; *OR,* vol. 39, pt. 1, pp. 435–36.

4. *ORN,* 21:417, 489–90, 569–70, 505–7, 584; Perry, *Infernal Machines,* 161.

5. *ORN,* 21:576–78, 583–85, 587–90; George S. Waterman, "Afloat—Afield—Afloat," *Confederate Veteran* 7 (1899): 16–21.

6. *ORN,* 21:417–18, 577–81; John C. Kinney, "Farragut at Mobile Bay," in Robert U. Johnson and Clarence C. Buel, eds., *Battles and Leaders of the Civil War,* 4 vols. (New York: Century, 1887–88), 4:379–99; Harrie Webster, "An August Morning with Farragut at Mobile Bay," in U.S. Navy Department, *Civil War Naval Chronology,* 6:85–98; Hults, "Aboard the *Galena* at Mobile," 29–31; Perkins, ed. and arr., *Letters of Perkins,* 130–40; James D. Johnston, "The Ram 'Tennessee' at Mobile Bay," in Johnson and Buel, eds., *Battles and Leaders,* 4:401–4; R. C. Bowles, "The Ship Tennessee," *Southern Historical Society Papers* 21 (1893): 291–94; James D. Johnston, "The Battle of Mobile Bay," ibid. 9 (1881): 471–76.

7. *ORN,* 21:407, 578–79, 585, 588; *OR,* vol. 39, pt. 1, p. 442.

8. Von Scheliha, *Treatise on Coast-Defence,* 178, 104–5; Waterman, "Afloat—Afield—Afloat," 17; *OR,* vol. 39, pt. 1, p. 433; *ORN,* 21:559, 570.

9. *ORN,* 21:397–98, 417; Kinney, "Farragut at Mobile Bay," 390–91; Perry, *Infernal Machines,* 161; Daniel B. Conrad, "Capture of the C.S. Ram

Tennessee in Mobile Bay, August, 1864," *Southern Historical Society Papers*
19 (1891): 74.

10. *ORN*, 21:905–6, 785–86; Perry, *Infernal Machines*, 161, 44; von
Scheliha, *Treatise on Coast-Defence*, 105.

11. Charles M. Todorich, "Franklin Buchanan: Symbol for Two Navies,"
in *Captains of the Old Steam Navy*, ed. Bradford, 108, *ORN*, 21:418, 425;
Conrad, "Capture of the Tennessee," 75, 80.

12. *ORN*, 21:500, 503–4, 786–87; Perkins, ed. and arr., *Letters of Perkins*, 140–41; Folmar, ed., *From That Terrible Field*, 136; John Kent Folmar,
"Lt. Col. James M. Williams and the Ft. Powell Incident," *Alabama Review*
17 (1964): 127–29; *OR*, vol. 39, pt. 1, pp. 441–42.

13. *OR*, vol 39, pt. 1, pp. 441–42; von Scheliha to Gilmer, Aug. 11,
1864, Letters Sent, Engineer Office, Gulf, Chap. III, vol. 16, p. 164, *Mobile
Advertiser and Register*, Aug. 9, 10, 1864; *Mobile Daily Tribune*, Aug. 7, 1864.

14. *OR*, vol. 52, pt. 2, pp. 741–42; Williams to Seddon, Sept. 14, 1864,
Letters Received, Secretary of War; Folmar, "Lt. Col. Williams," 130–34.

15. Von Scheliha to Gilmer, Aug. 11, 1864, Letters Sent, Engineer Office,
Gulf, Chap. III, vol. 16, p. 164; *OR*, vol. 39, pt. 1, p. 428.

16. *OR*, vol. 39, pt. 1, pp. 410, 428–29, and vol. 52, pt. 2, p. 715;
Mumford Diary, Aug. 5, 1864; Reynolds, *Sketches of Mobile*, 75; Roll for July
and Aug. 1864, Record of Events Cards, Company F, Twenty-second Louisiana Consolidated Infantry, Compiled Service Records of Confederate Soldiers Who Served in Organizations from Louisiana, RG 109, NA.

17. *ORN*, 21:403–4, 512, 824; Reynolds, *Sketches of Mobile*, 75; Andrews, *Campaign of Mobile*, 15.

18. *OR*, vol. 39, pt. 1, p. 429; *ORN*, 21:521; Roll for July and Aug.
1864, Company F, Twenty-second Louisiana, Compiled Service Records of
Confederate Soldiers from Louisiana.

19. *OR*, vol. 39, pt. 1, pp. 410, 436; *ORN*, 21:519.

20. *ORN*, 21:414–15, 524, 561–62, 787; *OR*, vol. 39, pt. 1, p. 437,
and vol. 52, pt. 2, pp. 743–44; Perkins, ed. and arr., *Letters of Perkins*, 142;
Reynolds, *Sketches of Mobile*, 76–79; Wilkinson Diary, Aug. 7, 8, 1864.

21. *OR*, vol. 39, pt. 1, pp. 437, 426, 428; Maury to Bragg, Aug. 14, 1864,
Bragg Papers, Western Reserve.

22. Austill, "Fort Morgan," 259; Wilkinson Diary, Aug. 8, 1864.

23. Reynolds, *Sketches of Mobile*, 77–79.

24. Andrews, *Campaign of Mobile*, 17; *ORN*, 21:523, 821, 563; *OR*,
vol. 39, pt. 1, pp. 438–39, and vol. 52, pt. 2, p. 720; Richard L. Page, "The
Defense of Fort Morgan," in Johnson and Buel, eds., *Battles and Leaders*,
4:409; Austill, "Fort Morgan," 259; Wilkinson Diary, Aug. 9, 1864.

25. Andrews, *Campaign of Mobile*, 17; OR, vol. 39, pt. 1, p. 439; Wilkinson Diary, Aug. 10, 12, 13, 14, 1864; Austill, "Fort Morgan," 260–61.

26. OR, vol. 39, pt. 1, p. 439; Austill, "Fort Morgan," 261–65; Wilkinson Diary, Aug. 15, 16, 1864.

27. Wilkinson Diary, Aug. 9, 15, 16, 1864; Austill, "Fort Morgan," 261, 264–65.

28. Andrews, *Campaign of Mobile*, 18; Austill, "Fort Morgan," 266–67; OR, vol. 39, pt. 1, p. 440.

29. George H. Gordon, *A War Diary of Events in the War of the Great Rebellion, 1861–1865* (Boston: James R. Osgood, 1882), 337.

30. ORN, 21:537–38, 571; OR, vol. 39, pt. 1, p. 440; Austill, "Fort Morgan," 267–68; Gordon, *War Diary*, 410.

31. Page, "Defense of Fort Morgan," 410.

32. OR, vol. 39, pt. 1, pp. 440, 404, 419–20, 430, and vol. 52, pt. 2, p. 716; von Scheliha, *Treatise on Coast-Defence*, 19–20; *Mobile Daily Tribune*, Aug. 31, 1864; Wilkinson Diary, Aug. 9–18, 1864; Austill, "Fort Morgan," 259–67.

33. OR, vol. 38, pt. 5, p. 610, and vol. 39, pt. 2, pp. 299, 344.

CHAPTER 12

1. Arthur W. Bergeron, Jr., "The Twenty-Second Louisiana Consolidated Infantry in the Defense of Mobile, 1864–1865," *Alabama Historical Quarterly* 38 (1976): 207; OR, vol. 52, pt. 2, pp. 716, 719; Mumford Diary, Aug. 5, 6, 1864; Rolls for July and Aug. 1864, Record of Events Cards, First Mississippi Light Artillery, Compiled Service Records of Confederate Soldiers Who Served in Organizations from Mississippi, RG 109, NA; Waterman, "Afloat—Afield—Afloat," 21; Maury to Bragg, Aug. 14, 1864, Bragg Papers, Western Reserve.

2. General Order No. 96, Headquarters District of the Gulf, Aug. 4, 1864, quoted in *Mobile Advertiser and Register*, Aug. 7, 1864; *Mobile Daily Tribune*, Aug. 6, 7, 1864.

3. Special Order No. 228, Headquarters District of the Gulf, Aug. 10, 1864, Para II, Special Order No. 234, Headquarters Provost Marshal's Office, Aug. 10, 1864, and Special Order No. 1, Headquarters Post Commandant, Aug. 11, 1864, quoted in *Mobile Evening News*, Aug. 12, 1864; *Mobile Daily Tribune*, Aug. 7, 1864; Mumford Diary, Aug. 8, 11, 1864; OR, vol. 52, pt. 2, p. 721.

4. ORN, 21:913; General Order No. 1, Naval Commandant's Office, Aug. 7, 1864, quoted in *Mobile Daily Tribune*, Aug. 12, 1864; U.S. Navy Department, *Officers of the Confederate States Navy*, 41; Still, *Iron Afloat*, 190, 198.

5. Still, *Iron Afloat*, 204, 212; *ORN*, 21:903–4.

6. Maury to Bragg, Aug. 14, 1864, Bragg Papers, Western Reserve; Para VII, Special Order No. 193, Headquarters Department of South Carolina, Georgia, and Florida, Aug. 4, 1864, quoted in Compiled Service Record of Gardner; Maury to Cooper, Aug. 12, 1864, Telegrams Received, Secretary of War.

7. Seddon to Maury, Aug. 13, 1864, Telegrams Sent, Secretary of War, Chap. IX, vol. 35, p. 228; General Order No. —, Headquarters Department of Alabama, Mississippi, and East Louisiana, Aug. 17, 1864, quoted in Compiled Service Record of Gardner; *Mobile Evening News*, Oct. 8, 1864; *OR*, vol. 39, pt. 2, p. 795.

8. *OR*, vol. 39, pt. 2, pp. 767, 780, and vol. 52, pt. 2, p. 721; Maury to Bragg, Aug. 14, 1864, Bragg Papers, Western Reserve; Clay to Maury, Aug. 8, 1864, Letters and Telegrams Sent, Adjutant and Inspector General, Chap. I, vol. 40, p. 527; Hughes, ed., *Liddell's Record*, 189.

9. *OR*, vol. 39, pt. 2, pp. 759, 760, 769, 772, 776; von Sheliha to Gilmer, Aug. 12, 13, 1864, and von Sheliha to Gindrat, Aug. 12, 1864, Letters Sent, Engineer Office, Gulf, Chap. III, vol. 16, pp. 169, 173, 170.

10. *ORN*, 21:555–56, 558; *OR*, vol. 39, pt. 2, pp. 764, 775; Gilmer to Maury, Aug. 9, 1864, and Gilmer to von Sheliha, Aug. 9, 1864, Letters and Telegrams Sent, Engineer Bureau, Chap. III, vol. 5, p. 605.

11. *OR*, vol. 39, pt. 2, pp. 768, 775–76; Para V, Special Order No. 226, Headquarters District of the Gulf, Aug. 13, 1864, quoted in *Mobile Daily Tribune*, Aug. 14, 1864; Mumford Diary, Aug. 8, 13, 1864; von Sheliha to Gilmer, Aug. 12, 1864, Letters Sent, Engineer Office, Gulf, Chap. III, vol. 16, p. 169.

12. *OR*, vol. 35, pt. 1, pp. 426–27, and vol. 39, pt. 2, pp. 798, 800; Mumford Diary, Aug. 11, 1864; Rolls for July and Aug. 1864, First Mississippi Light Artillery, Record of Events Cards, Compiled Service Records of Confederate Soldiers Who Served in Organizations from Mississippi, RG 109, NA.

13. *ORN*, 21:528–30, 828; Mumford Diary, Aug. 15, 1864; von Scheliha, *Treatise on Coast-Defence*, 189–90; Rix, *Incidents of Life*, [17].

14. Von Sheliha to Captain John B. Grayson, Aug. 16, 1864, and von Sheliha to Gilmer, Aug. 17, 1864, Letters Sent, Engineer Office, Gulf, Chap. III, vol. 16, pp. 190, 193; Mumford Diary, Aug. 16, 27, 1864; Waterman, "Afloat—Afield—Afloat," 449; *OR*, vol. 39, pt. 2, p. 782.

15. Von Sheliha to Gilmer, Aug. 16, 17, 1864, Letters Sent, Engineer Office, Gulf, Chap. III, vol. 16, pp. 188, 193.

16. Gilmer to Seddon, Aug. 17, 1864, in Compiled Service Record of Lockett; Para III, Special Order No. 106, Headquarters Department of Ala-

bama, Mississippi, and East Louisiana, Aug. 20, 1864, quoted in ibid.; von Sheliha to Gilmer, Aug. 20, 1864, von Sheliha to Gindrat, Aug. 20, 1864, and von Sheliha to Seddon, Aug. 20, 1864, Letters Sent, Engineer Office, Gulf, Chap. III, vol. 16, pp. 206, 208–9.

17. OR, vol. 39, pt. 2, pp. 780, 796, 803; Maury to Watts, Aug. 28, 1864, Letters Sent, Department of Alabama, Mississippi, and East Louisiana, 1864–65, Chap. II, vol. 14, p. 81; Seddon to Watts, Sept. 2, 1864, Telegrams Sent, Secretary of War, Chap. IX, vol. 35, p. 237; Maury to Cooper, Aug. 24, 1864, Telegrams Received, Secretary of War; History of Company B, 82–83; McMillan, Disintegration of a Confederate State, 113.

18. OR, vol. 39, pt. 2, pp. 796–97, 815, 818, and vol. 52, pt. 2, pp. 731–32; Davis to Maury, Sept. 2, 4, 1864, in Rowland, ed., Jefferson Davis, 6:330, 331; Taylor, Destruction and Reconstruction, 242.

19. Maury to Captain W. F. Bullock, Sept. 26, 27, 1864, in George W. Brent Collection (LSM 8932.1), Louisiana State Museum Archives and Manuscript Collection, New Orleans; OR, vol. 39, pt. 2, p. 886, and vol. 52, pt. 2, pp. 746, 748.

20. OR, vol. 39, pt. 2, p. 815, and pt. 3, p. 793; Weekly Report of Operations for the Defence of Mobile, Sept. 17, 1864, Letters Sent, Engineer Office, Department of the Gulf, Aug. 1864–May 1865, Chap. III, vol. 13, p. 61, RG 109, NA; Home Journal (Mobile), Sept. 23, 1864.

21. OR, vol. 39, pt. 3, pp. 793–94; Mumford Diary, Sept. 5, 1864; Weekly Report, Sept. 17, 1864, Letters Sent, Engineer Office, Gulf, Chap. III, vol. 13, p. 62.

22. OR, vol. 39, pt. 2, pp. 815, 819, 841–42, and pt. 3, p. 794; von Sheliha to Gindrat, Sept. 6, 1864, and Weekly Report, Sept. 17, 1864, Letters Sent, Engineer Office, Gulf, Chap. III, vol. 13, pp. 29, 62–63.

23. Maury to Surget, Oct. 4, 1864, in Richard Taylor Papers, Louisiana Adjutant General's Library, Jackson Barracks, Chalmette, La.; OR, vol. 39, pt. 3, pp. 910–11, and vol. 45, pt. 2, p. 632.

24. OR, vol. 39, pt. 3, p. 910; Surget to Maury, Oct. 1, 1864, Letters Sent, Department of Alabama, Mississippi, and East Louisiana, Chap. II, vol. 14, p. 109.

25. Maury to Watts, Nov. 23, 1864, Letters Sent, Department of Alabama, Mississippi, and East Louisiana, Chap. II, vol. 14, p. 197; OR, vol. 45, pt. 2, pp. 683–84, 724.

26. OR, vol. 39, pt. 3, p. 786, and vol. 52, pt. 2, p. 747; General Order No. 126, Headquarters Department of Alabama, Mississippi, and East Louisiana, Oct. 4, 1864, General Orders, Department of Alabama, Mississippi, and East Louisiana, 1861–65, RG 109, NA; Mumford Diary, Oct. 4, 1864.

27. Mumford Diary, Sept. 24, 1864; *OR*, vol. 39, pt. 3, p. 847.

28. *OR*, vol. 45, pt. 1, pp. 1213, 1239, 1248, and vol. 52, pt. 2, p. 791; Maury to Brent, Nov. 28, Dec. 1, 1864, Letters Sent, Department of Alabama, Mississippi, and East Louisiana, Chap. II, vol. 14, pp. 198, 206.

29. *OR*, vol. 39, pt. 3, pp. 839–40, 850–51, 884, 895, 916, and vol. 45, pt. 1, pp. 1230, 1250; von Sheliha to Captain W. D. Morris, Nov. 23, 1864, Letters Sent, Engineer Office, Gulf, Chap. III, vol. 13, p. 208; Levy to Maury, Dec. 25, 1864, Letters Sent, Department of Alabama, Mississippi, and East Louisiana, Chap. II, vol. 14, p. 247.

30. *OR*, vol. 45, pt. 2, pp. 678, 707–8, 734; Smith to Lockett, Dec. 29, 1864, Letters Sent, Engineer Office at Mobile, Oct. 11, 1864–May 8, 1865, Chap. III, vol. 11, p. 177.

31. *OR*, vol. 39, pt. 3, pp. 840, 851, 885, 895, 916, 1229, vol. 45, pt. 1, pp. 1231, 1250, and pt. 2, pp. 678, 708, 735; Lockett to von Sheliha, Dec. 14, 1864, Letters Sent, Engineer Office, Mobile, Chap. III, vol. 11, p. 128.

32. *OR*, vol. 39, pt. 3, pp. 840, 851, 885, 895, 916, vol. 45, pt. 1, pp. 1231, 1250, and pt. 2, pp. 678, 708,

33. *OR*, vol. 39, pt. 3, pp. 840, 851, 885, 895, 916, and vol. 45, pt. 2, pp. 678, 708, 735; Lockett to Lieutenant E. A. Ford, Dec. 17, 1864, Letters Sent, Engineer Office, Mobile, Chap. III, vol. 11, p. 139.

34. *OR*, vol. 39, pt. 3, pp. 840, 851, 885, and vol. 45, pt. 2, pp. 678, 708, 735, 746–47; Maury to Lockett, Nov. 27, 1864, Letters Sent, Engineer Office, Mobile, Chap. III, vol. 11, p. 70.

35. *OR*, 44:449, and vol. 45, pt. 2, pp. 688, 695, 697, 699, 709; Hughes, ed., *Liddell's Record,* 191–92; *Mobile Army Argus and Crisis,* Dec. 24, 1865.

36. *O.R.*, vol. 41, pt. 4, pp. 686–87, vol. 45, pt. 1, pp. 787–89, and pt. 2, pp. 661–62.

37. *OR*, vol. 41, pt. 4, pp. 752, 853, 862–63, 875–76, and vol. 45, pt. 2, pp. 291–92.

38. Maury, *Recollections of a Virginian,* 200; *OR*, vol. 45, pt. 2, pp. 723–25.

39. *OR*, vol. 49, pt. 1, p. 311; Chambers, "My Journal," 367; Confederate Diary, Apr. 1, 1865, quoted in Andrews, *Campaign of Mobile,* 91, n. 1; Bradley, *Confederate Mail Carrier,* 224–25; Account of Lieutenant G. W. Sent, Department of Alabama, Mississippi, and East Louisiana, Chap. II, vol. 14, p. 225; Endorsement of Major John J. Walker, Dec. 17, 1864, on Levy to Maury, Dec. 15, 1864, Letters and Telegrams Received, Department of Alabama, Mississippi, and East Louisiana; Maury to Watt, Dec. 28, 1864, Brent Collection.

41. Beringer et al., *Why the South Lost the Civil War,* 334.

42. Para I, Special Field Order No. —, Headquarters Military Division of the West, Jan. 19, 1865, Special Field Orders, Military Division of the West, Oct. 1864–Mar. 1865, RG 109, NA; *OR*, vol. 45, pt. 2, p. 801, and vol. 49, pt. 1, pp. 938, 940; Maury to Taylor, Jan. 25, 1865, Maury to Surget, Jan. 27, 1865, and Maury to Bullock, Feb. 16, 1865, Brent Collection; *History of Company B, 40th Alabama*, 86.

43. Surget to Maury, Jan. 21, 1865, Letters Sent, Department of Alabama, Mississippi, and East Louisiana, Chap. II, vol. 14, p. 285; Para IV, Special Order No. 19, Headquarters Army of Tennessee, Jan. 24, 1865, in Compiled Service Record of Randall L. Gibson, Compiled Service Records of Confederate General and Staff Officers; Rolls for Jan. and Feb. 1865, Record of Events Cards, First Louisiana (Strawbridge's) Infantry, and Rolls for Jan. and Feb. 1865, Record of Events Cards, Fourth Louisiana Infantry, Compiled Service Records of Confederate Soldiers from Louisiana.

44. Robert S. Bevier, *History of the First and Second Missouri Confederate Brigades, 1861–1865* (St. Louis: Bryan, Brand, 1879), 261–62; Chambers, "My Journal," 360; *OR*, vol. 49, pt. 1, pp. 943, 951, 1045.

45. *OR*, vol. 49, pt. 1, pp. 947, 951; Maury to Taylor, Feb. 3, 1865, Brent Collection; Little and Maxwell, *History of Lumsden's Battery*, 63; Captain Stouten H. Dent to Anna Beall Young Dent, Feb. 10, 1865, in Dent Confederate Collection, Auburn University Archives, Auburn, Ala.; William Miller Owen, *In Camp and Battle with the Washington Artillery of New Orleans* (Boston: Ticknor, 1885), 420; Captain John B. Grayson to Major John A. A. West, Feb. 26, 1865, in Compiled Service Record of John B. Grayson, Compiled Service Records of Confederate General and Staff Officers.

46. *ORN*, 21:902–3; Perry, *Infernal Machines*, 183.

47. Gilmer to Maury, Aug. 13, 1864, and Gilmer to J. P. Halligan, Aug. 13, 1864, Letters and Telegrams Sent, Engineer Bureau, Chap. III, vol. 5, p. 631; *ORN*, 21:568; *OR*, vol. 45, pt. 2, pp. 649, 720, 781.

48. *OR*, vol. 49, pt. 1, p. 13; Lockett to Capt. T. J. Fremaux, Feb. 2, 1865, Letters Sent, Engineer Office, Mobile, Chap. III, vol. 11, p. 286; Perry, *Infernal Machines*, 183–84.

49. Maury to Surget, Jan. 26, 1865, Brent Collection.

50. *ORN*, 22:269.

51. Maury to Taylor, Mar. 14, 1865, and Commander E. Farrand to Maury, Mar. 16, 1865, Brent Collection.

52. Surget to Maury, Jan. 11, 1865, and Taylor to Maury, Feb. 5, 1865, Letters Sent, Department of Alabama, Mississippi, and East Louisiana, Chap. II, vol. 14, pp. 271, 312–13; Maury to Surget, Jan. 27, 1865, and Maury to Taylor, Feb. 3, 7, Mar. 14, 1865, Brent Collection.

53. Maury to Surget, Jan. 27, 1865, Brent Collection; Lieutenant Colonel J. R. Waddy to Brent, Jan. 21, 1865, in George W. Brent Papers, Duke University, William R. Perkins Library, Durham, N.C.; Chambers, "My Journal," 364.

54. Waddy to Brent, Jan. 21, 1865, Brent Papers; "Tabular Statement of the Artillery in the District of the Gulf, Mobile, Ala., Jan. 10th, 1865," Palmer Civil War Collection.

55. Circular, Headquarters District of the Gulf, Mar. 3, 1865, quoted in *Mobile Advertiser and Register*, Mar. 4, 1865; General Order No. 8, Headquarters District of the Gulf, Mar. 12, 1865, ibid., Mar. 14, 1865; Surget to Maury, Feb. 6, Mar. 14, 1865, Letters Sent, Department of Alabama, Mississippi, and East Louisiana, Chap. II, vol. 14, pp. 314, 385; Lockett to Myers, Mar. 14, 1865, Letters Sent, Engineer Office, Mobile, Chap. III, vol. 11, p. 394; von Sheliha to Garner, Mar. 16, 1865, ibid., vol. 13, p. 344; Maury to Surget, Feb. 10, 1865, and Maury to Taylor, Mar. 14, 1865, Brent Collection; Bullock to Maury, Mar. 12, 1865, Telegrams Sent, Department of Alabama, Mississippi, and East Louisiana, Feb. 1–Mar. 21, 1865, Chap. II, vol. 196, p. 115, RG 109, NA.

56. Butler to sister, Mar. 13, 1865, Butler Family Papers; Para IV, General Order No. 8, Headquarters District of the Gulf, Mar. 12, 1865, quoted in *Mobile Advertiser and Register*, Mar. 14, 1865.

CHAPTER 13

1. *OR*, vol. 45, pt. 2, p. 506, vol. 48, pt. 1, p. 580, and vol. 49, pt. 1, pp. 91–92, 593; Andrews, *Campaign of Mobile*, 21, 31–32; Hattaway and Jones, *How the North Won*, 662; B. L. Roberson, "Valor on the Eastern Shore: The Mobile Campaign of 1865" (research paper, 1965), 6–7.

2. *OR*, vol. 49, pt. 1, pp. 91–92, 584; Andrews, *Campaign of Mobile*, 21–22, 25–26, 31; Hattaway and Jones, *How the North Won*, 668.

3. *OR*, vol. 49, pt. 1, p. 1045; Dabney H. Maury, "Defence of Mobile in 1865," *Southern Historical Society Papers* 3 (1877): 4; Maury to Davis, Dec. 25, 1871, quoted in ibid., 6.

4. General Robert E. Lee to Taylor, Mar. 15, 1865, Taylor Papers.

5. *OR*, vol. 49, pt. 2, pp. 1139, 1161; Taylor, *Destruction and Reconstruction*, 267–69.

6. Circular, Headquarters Military Post, Mobile, Mar. 20, 1865, quoted in *Mobile Advertiser and Register*, Mar. 21, 1865; Circular, Headquarters Military Post, Mar. 21, 1865, quoted in *Mobile Army Argus and Crisis*, Mar. 25, 1865.

7. General Order No. 11, Headquarters District of the Gulf, Mar. 21,

1865, quoted in *Mobile Advertiser and Register*, Mar. 22, 1865; Order, Mayor's Office, Mar. 21, 1865, ibid., Mar. 23, 1865; Hughes, ed., *Liddell's Record*, 194.

8. *OR*, vol. 49, pt. 1, pp. 313–14, and pt. 2, pp. 1129, 1153, 1157; Chambers, "My Journal," 366; Little and Maxwell, *History of Lumsden's Battery*, 65–66; Maury to Surget, Apr. 15, 1865, Records of the Department of the Gulf, Louisiana Historical Association Collection; Maury to Beauregard, June 1, 1865, Dabney H. Maury Letter, Louisiana State University Department of Archives and Manuscripts, Hill Memorial Library, Baton Rouge. Coehorn mortars were small bronze mortars used in trench warfare.

9. Stephenson, "Defence of Spanish Fort," 121.

10. Andrews, *Campaign of Mobile*, 49–50; *OR*, vol. 49, pt. 1, pp. 314–15; Gibson to Liddell, Mar. 26 [27?], 1865, in Randall Lee Gibson Papers, Louisiana State University, Department of Archives and Manuscripts, Hill Memorial Library, Baton Rouge; Gibson to John McGrath, Sept. 26, 1884, in Randall Lee Gibson Letters, Tulane University, Special Collections Division, Howard-Tilton Memorial Library, New Orleans; *Mobile Army Argus and Crisis*, Apr. 1, 1865.

11. *OR*, vol. 49, pt. 1, pp. 1162–64; Holt, ed., *Miss Waring's Journal*, 9; Maury to Taylor, Mar. 27, 1865, Brent Collection; *Mobile Advertiser and Register*, Mar. 26, 1865; *Mobile Army Argus and Crisis*, Apr. 1, 1865.

12. *OR*, vol. 49, pt. 2, p. 1161; Stephenson, "Defence of Spanish Fort," 122.

13. *OR*, vol. 49, pt. 2, pp. 1162–63; Circular, Headquarters Forces at Spanish Fort, Mar. 27, 1865, in Record Books of Brigadier General Daniel W. Adams' and Brigadier General Randall L. Gibson's Brigade, 1862–65, Chap. II, vol. 304, p. 301, RG 109, NA (hereafter cited as Adams-Gibson Record Books); Gibson to Liddell, Mar. 27, 1865 (two items), Gibson to Maury, Mar. 27, 1865, and Gibson to Myers, Mar. 27, 1865, ibid., vol. 302, pp. 359, 361, 362.

14. *Mobile Army Argus and Crisis*, Apr. 1, 1865; Diary of a Confederate officer, Mar. 28, 29, 1865, quoted in Andrews, *Campaign of Mobile*, 68, n. 2, 77, n. 1; Maury, "Defence of Mobile," 12.

15. Maury to Taylor, Mar. 28, 1865, 4 P.M., Brent Collection; Lewis to Brigadier General James T. Holtzclaw, Mar. 28, 1865, Lewis to Brigadier General Francis M. Cockrell, Mar. 28, 1865, and Liddell to Gibson, Mar. 28, 1865, Letters Sent, Eastern Division, District of the Gulf, Mar.–Apr. 1865, Chap. II, vol. 99, pp. 43, 100, RG 109, NA.

16. Confederate Diary, Mar. 30, 1865, quoted in Andrews, *Campaign of Mobile*, 80, n. 2; *Mobile Army Argus and Crisis*, Apr. 1, 1865.

17. Confederate Diary, Mar. 30, 1865, quoted in Andrews, *Campaign of Mobile*, 80, n. 2; Liddell to Gibson, Mar. 30, 1865, quoted in ibid., 80, n. 1; Report of casualties to Mar. 29, 1865, dated Mar. 29, 1865, Gibson Papers; Casualty report, Mar. 29–Apr. 8, 1865, Adams-Gibson Record Books, Chap. II, vol. 302, p. 397; Special Order No. 6, Headquarters Forces at Spanish Fort, Mar. 31, 1865, ibid., vol. 304, p. 305; Lewis to [Holtzclaw], Mar. 30, 1865, Letters Sent, Eastern Division, Gulf, Chap. II, vol. 99, p. 46; Liddell to Maury, Mar. 31, 1865, Telegrams Sent, Eastern Division, District of the Gulf, Mar.-Apr. 1865, Chap. II, vol. 100, p. 77, RG 109, NA.

18. Confederate Diary, Mar. 31, 1865, quoted in Andrews, *Campaign of Mobile*, 87, n. 1; OR, vol. 49, pt. 1, pp. 225–26, and pt. 2, pp. 1178–79; Maury, "Defence of Mobile," 12; Dabney H. Maury, "Defence of Spanish Fort," *Southern Historical Society Papers* 39 (1914): 135; *Mobile Army Argus and Crisis*, Apr. 8, 1865; Para IV, General Order No. 17, Headquarters District of the Gulf, Apr. 1, 1865, Gibson, Papers.

19. Stephenson, "Defence of Spanish Fort," 122–23.

20. Waterman, "Afloat—Afield—Afloat," 23.

21. "H.A.J." to Editors, Apr. 1, 1865, in *Mobile Advertiser and Register*, Apr. 4, 1865; Circular, [Headquarters Spanish Fort], Apr. 6, 1865, Gibson Papers; Circular, Headquarters Forces at Spanish Fort, Apr. 5, 1865, Adams-Gibson Record Books, Chap. II, vol. 304, p. 310.

22. Waterman, "Afloat—Afield—Afloat," 23; Maury, "Defence of Spanish Fort," 135.

23. OR, vol. 49, pt. 2, pp. 1184–85; Gibson to Maury, Apr. 5, 1865, quoted in Andrews, *Campaign of Mobile*, 142, n. 2; Gibson to Maury, Apr. 6, 1865, Adams-Gibson Record Books, Chap. II, vol. 302, p. 378; Special Order No. 7, Headquarters Forces at Spanish Fort, Apr. 3, 1865, Circular, Headquarters Forces at Spanish Fort, Apr. 4, 1865, and Circular, Headquarters Forces at Spanish Fort, Apr. 5, 1865, ibid., vol. 304, pp. 307, 308, 311.

24. OR, vol. 49, pt. 2, pp. 1192; Circular, [Headquarters Spanish Fort], Apr. 5, 1865, Gibson Papers.

25. Circular, Headquarters Forces at Spanish Fort, Apr. 2, 1865, Adams-Gibson Record Books, Chap. II, vol. 304, p. 306; OR, vol. 49, pt. 2, pp. 1200–1201.

26. Confederate Diary, Apr. 4, 1865, quoted in Andrews, *Campaign of Mobile*, 137, n. 1; Holt, ed., *Miss Waring's Journal*, 12.

27. OR, vol. 49, pt. 2, p. 1199; Confederate Diary, Apr. 4, 1865, quoted in Andrews, *Campaign of Mobile*, 137, n. 1; Waterman, "Afloat—Afield—Afloat," 23; J. A. Chalaron, "Battle Echoes from Shiloh," *Southern Historical Society Papers* 21 (1893): 220–21; Maury, "Defence of Spanish Fort," 132.

28. *OR*, vol. 49, pt. 1, pp. 316, 319–20, and pt. 2, p. 1184; Confederate Diary, Apr. 1, 1865, quoted in Andrews, *Campaign of Mobile*, 91, n. 1.

29. *OR*, vol. 49, pt. 2, pp. 1192, 1200, 1209–10; Gibson to Maury, Apr. 2, 1865, Gibson Papers; Lewis to Captain Joseph Fry, Apr. 4, 1865, Letters Sent, Eastern Division, Gulf, Chap. II, vol. 99, p. 53; Liddell to Gibson, Apr. 4, 1865, ibid., vol. 100, p. 98.

30. Confederate Diary, Apr. 7, 1865, quoted in Andrews, *Campaign of Mobile*, 147, n. 1; Circular, Headquarters Spanish Fort, Apr. 7, 1865, Adams-Gibson Record Books, Chap. II, vol. 304, p. 314; *OR*, vol. 49, pt. 2, pp. 1214–15.

31. *OR*, vol. 49, pt. 2, pp. 1217, 1219; Rix, *Incidents of Life*, [19].

32. *OR*, vol. 49, pt. 1, p. 316, and pt. 2, p. 1218.

33. Ibid., pt. 1, pp. 96, 316; Stephenson, "Defence of Spanish Fort," 123–25.

34. *OR*, vol. 49, pt. 1, pp. 275–78, 316, and pt. 2, p. 1218; W. Bailey, "The Star Company of Ector's Texas Brigade," *Confederate Veteran* 22 (1914): 405.

35. *OR*, vol. 49, pt. 1, pp. 275, 316–17; Gibson to McGrath, Sept. 26, 1884, Gibson Letters; Stephenson, "Defence of Spanish Fort," 125–26; Andrews, *Campaign of Mobile*, 155–58.

36. *OR*, vol. 49, pt. 1, p. 317, and pt. 2, p. 1219; Stephenson, "Defence of Spanish Fort," 126–28; Maury, "Defence of Spanish Fort," 131; Maury to Taylor, Apr. 8, 1865, Taylor Papers; Maury to Taylor, Apr. 9, 1865, Brent Collection; Holt, ed., *Miss Waring's Journal*, 13.

37. *OR*, vol. 49, pt. 1, pp. 318, 102, 317–18; Casualty List, Adams-Gibson Record Books, Chap. II, vol. 302, p. 397; Taylor, *Destruction and Reconstruction*, 270; Maury, "Defence of Spanish Fort," 130; Hughes, ed., *Liddell's Record*, 194.

38. Maury to Davis, Dec. 25, 1871, quoted in Maury, "Defence of Mobile," 8; Maury to Beauregard, June 1, 1865, Maury Letter; James Bradley, *The Confederate Mail Carrier* (Mexico, Mo.: N.p., 1894), 224; Chambers, "My Journal," 367; Edward W. Tarrant, "Siege and Capture of Fort Blakely," *Confederate Veteran* 23 (1915): 457; Liddell to Garner, Apr. 1, 1865, Telegrams Sent, Eastern Division, Gulf, Chap. II, vol. 100, p. 84.

39. *OR*, vol. 49, pt. 1, p. 311; Chambers, "My Journal," 367; Confederate Diary, Apr. 1, 1865, quoted in Andrews, *Campaign of Mobile*, 91, n. 1; Bradley, *Confederate Mail Carrier*, 224–25; Account of Lieutenant G. W. Warren, quoted in Bevier, *History of the Missouri Brigades*, 262.

40. Liddell to Maury, Apr. 1, 1865, Telegrams Sent, Eastern Division, Gulf, Chap. II, vol. 100, p. 87; *OR*, vol. 49, pt. 2, pp. 1188, 1185, 1187.

41. *OR*, vol. 49, pt. 1, pp. 282, 287, and pt. 2, p. 1190; Bradley, *Confederate Mail Carrier*, 225; Liddell to Maury, Apr. 2, 1865, Telegrams Sent, Eastern Division, Gulf, Chap. II, vol. 100, p. 90.

42. *OR*, vol. 49, pt. 1, pp. 283, 320–21; Bradley, *Confederate Mail Carrier*, 225.

43. Liddell to Maury, Apr. 3, 1865, Liddell to Garner, Apr. 3, 1865, and Liddell to Myers, Apr. 5, 1865, Telegrams Sent, Eastern Division, Gulf, Chap. II, Vol. 100, pp. 91, 93, 100; Liddell to Maury, Apr. 3, 1865, quoted in Andrews, *Campaign of Mobile*, 171, n. 1; Liddell to Maury, Apr. 7, 1865, quoted in ibid., 183, n. 1.

44. Maury to Taylor, Apr. 7, 1865, Taylor Papers; *OR*, vol. 49, pt. 1, pp. 261, 264, and pt. 2, pp. 282, 284.

45. Liddell to Maury, Apr. 7, 1865, quoted in Andrews, *Campaign of Mobile*, 183, n. 1.

46. Captain J. L. Bradford to mother, Apr. 8, 1865, typed copy in Confederate Pension Application file of Sallie Slatten, Louisiana State Archives and Records Service, Baton Rouge; Hughes, ed., *Liddell's Record*, 194–95.

47. Liddell to Gibson, Apr. 5, 1865, Telegrams Sent, Eastern Division, Gulf, Chap. II, vol. 100, p. 100; Bradford to mother, Apr. 8, 1865, Slatten Pension Application.

48. *OR*, vol. 49, pt. 1, p. 321, and pt. 2, p. 1217; Lewis to Cockrell and Thomas, Apr. 7, 1865, Letters Sent, Eastern Division, Gulf, Chap. II, vol. 99, p. 60; Walker, *Life of Capt. Joseph Fry*, 180–84.

49. *OR*, vol. 49, pt. 2, pp. 1222–23; Hughes, ed., *Liddell's Record*, 196; Lewis to Cockrell and Thomas, Apr. 8, 1865, quoted in Andrews, *Campaign of Mobile*, 188, n. 2.

50. *OR*, vol. 49, pt. 1, pp. 97–98, 321–22; Maury to Davis, Dec. 25, 1871, quoted in Maury, "Defence of Mobile," 8; Bradley, *Confederate Mail Carrier*, 225; Tarrant, "Siege and Capture of Fort Blakely," 457–58; Anderson, *Memoirs*, 399–400; Bevier, *History of the Missouri Brigades*, 265–67.

51. Hughes, ed., *Liddell's Record*, 196; *OR*, vol. 49, pt. 1, pp. 101–2.

52. Hughes, ed., *Liddell's Record*, 196.

53. Waterman, "Afloat—Afield—Afloat," 23, 55; Liddell to Colonel Isaac W. Patton, Apr. 3, 1865, Telegrams Sent, Eastern Division, Gulf, Chap. II, vol. 100, p. 93.

54. Maury to Davis, Dec. 25, 1871, quoted in Maury, "Defence of Mobile," 9–10; "Ebenezer R. F. S." to Editor, Mar. 31, 1865, quoted in *Mobile Advertiser and Register*, Apr. 4, 1865; Confederate Diary, Apr. 2–7, 1865, quoted in Andrews, *Campaign of Mobile*, 135, n. 1, 136, n. 1, 137, n. 1, 143, n. 2, 145, n. 1.

55. OR, vol. 49, pt. 2, p. 1219; Mumford Diary, Apr. 9–11, 1865; Rix, *Incidents of Life*, [20]; Maury to Davis, Dec. 25, 1871, quoted in Maury, "Defence of Mobile," 10; Waterman, "Afield—Afloat—Afield," 55.

56. Para II, General Order No. 15, Headquarters District of the Gulf, Mar. 30, 1865, Gibson Papers; Major Joseph D. Sayers to Colonel Thomas Taylor, Mar. 31, 1865, Letters Sent, Department of Alabama, Mississippi, and East Louisiana, Chap. II, vol. 14, p. 423; Surget to T. Taylor, Apr. 5, 1865, Telegrams Sent, Department of Alabama, Mississippi, and East Louisiana, Chap. II, vol. II, p. 63; General Order No. 16, Headquarters District of the Gulf, Mar. 31, 1865, quoted in *Mobile Army Argus and Crisis*, Apr. 8, 1865; Circular, Headquarters Military Post, Mobile, Apr. 1, 1865, quoted in *Mobile Advertiser and Register*, Apr. 2, 1865; Major William H. Ketchum to T. Taylor, Apr. 20, 1865, Brent Collection; Rix, *Incidents of Life*, [20].

57. Maury to Surget, Apr. 15, 1865, Department of the Gulf Records, Louisiana Historical Association Collection; Maury to Beauregard, June 1, 1865, Maury Letter; Maury to Taylor, Apr. 9, 10, 1865, and Bullock to Maury, Apr. 10, 1865, Taylor Papers.

58. Mumford Diary, Apr. 10, 1865.

59. Maury, "Defence of Mobile," 1–2.

60. Holt, ed., *Miss Waring's Journal*, 13; Mumford Diary, Apr. 10, 1865; Ketchum to T. Taylor, Apr. 20, 1865, Brent Collection; Account of Sister Gabriella, quoted in Oscar H. Lipscomb, "The Administration of John Quinlan, Second Bishop of Mobile, 1859–1883" (M.A. thesis, Catholic University of America, 1959), 92.

61. Maury to Taylor, Apr. 11, 1865 (several items), Taylor Papers; Holt, ed., *Miss Waring's Journal*, 14; Diary, Apr. 11, 1865, Geary Papers.

62. Scharf, *History of the Confederate States Navy*, 595–96; Still, *Iron Afloat*, 224–26; Taylor, *Destruction and Reconstruction*, 271.

63. Rix, *Incidents of Life*, [21]; Mumford Diary, Apr. 11, 1865.

64. Maury to Taylor, Apr. 12, 1865, Taylor Papers; Maury to Surget, Apr. 15, 1865, Department of the Gulf Records, Louisiana Historical Association Collection; Maury, "Defence of Mobile," 8; Maury to Beauregard, June 1, 1865, Maury Letter; Ketchum to T. Taylor, Apr. 20, 1865, with endorsements by R. Taylor, Apr. 20, 1865, and Maury to Taylor, Apr. 13, 1865, Brent Collection; Rix, *Incidents of Life*, [21–22]; Holt, ed., *Miss Waring's Journal*, 15.

65. OR, vol. 49, pt. 1, pp. 143–44, 146; Maury to Taylor, Apr. 13, 1865, Brent Collection; Holt, ed., *Miss Waring's Journal*, 15; Hamilton, *Little Boy in Confederate Mobile*, 26; Cox, "Mobile in the War between the States," 210.

66. OR, vol. 49, pt. 1, p. 175; Cox, "Mobile in the War between the States," 210–11; Rix, *Incidents of Life,* [24].

67. Holt, ed., *Miss Waring's Journal,* 15.

68. Roberson, "Valor on the Eastern Shore," 39.

69. James Pickett Jones, *Yankee Blitzkrieg: Wilson's Raid through Alabama and Georgia* (Athens: University of Georgia Press, 1976), 185–86.

70. *Cincinnati Daily Commercial,* May 10, 1865.

EPILOGUE

1. Richard M. McMurry, *Two Great Rebel Armies: An Essay in Confederate Military History* (Chapel Hill: University of North Carolina Press, 1989), 151.

2. Ibid., 152.

Bibliography

PRIMARY SOURCES

MANUSCRIPT COLLECTIONS
Auburn University Archives, Auburn, Ala.
  Dent Confederate Collection, 1861–65
Duke University, William R. Perkins Library, Durham, N.C.
  Braxton Bragg Papers, 1861–65
  George W. Brent Papers, 1861–65
  Jefferson Davis Papers, 1861–65
  William Richard Hansford Papers, 1861–65
Federal Records Center, East Point, Ga.
  Minute Book, Confederate District Court, Southern Division of Alabama,
    1861–65
Fort Morgan Museum, Gulf Shores, Ala.
  Charles S. Stewart Letters, 1862–63
Fredericksburg-Spotsylvania National Military Park Library, Fredericks-
  burg, Va.
  Daniel Ruggles Papers, 1862–65
Henry E. Huntington Library, San Marino, Calif.
  Simon B. Buckner Papers, 1862–63
  James W. Eldridge Collection, 1861–65
  Mansfield Lovell Papers, 1861–62
Louisiana Adjutant General's Archives, Jackson Barracks, Chalmette, La.
  Joseph L. Brent Collection
  Richard Taylor Papers, 1863–65
Louisiana State Archives and Records Service, Baton Rouge
  Confederate Pension Application Files

Louisiana State Museum Archives and Manuscripts Collection, New Orleans
George W. Brent Collection, 1863–65
Louisiana State University, Department of Archives and Manuscripts, Hill
Memorial Library, Baton Rouge
Michel Thomassin Andry Family Papers, 1864–65
Thomas Butler and Family Papers, 1861–65
Randall Lee Gibson Papers, 1865
John Achilles Harris Letters, 1861–64
Hunter-Taylor Family Papers, 1861–65
Dabney H. Maury Letter, 1865
Thomas O. Moore Papers, 1861–62
Mobile Museum Department, Mobile, Ala.
Fort Gaines Collection
Lee F. Irwin Collection
Dr. Thomas M. McMillan Collection
William T. Mumford Collection
James Biddle Wilkinson Diary
Mobile Public Library, Local History Department, Mobile, Ala.
Daniel Geary Papers, 1862–65
National Archives, Washington, D.C.
Record Group 36, Records of the Bureau of Customs
Abstracts of Import Duties, Mobile, 1861–65
Bureau of Customs Cargo Manifests, Mobile, 1861–65
Entry of Merchandise, Mobile, 1861–65
Record Book of Exports of Domestic Produce in Confederate Vessels and
Foreign Vessels, 1861–75
Record Group 109, War Department Collection of Confederate Archives
Letters and Telegrams Sent by the Confederate Adjutant and Inspector
General, 1861–65, Chap. I, Vols. 35–41, 43–44
Letters and Telegrams Sent, Department of Alabama, Mississippi, and East
Louisiana, Feb. 2–May 7, 1864, Chap. II, Vol. 8 3/4
Telegrams Sent, Department of Alabama, Mississippi, and East Louisiana,
1864–65, Chap. II, Vol. 10
Telegrams Sent, Department of Alabama, Mississippi, and East Louisiana,
1865, Chap. II, Vol. 11
Letters Sent, Department of Alabama, Mississippi, and East Louisiana,
1864–65, Chap. II, Vol. 14
Letters Sent, Eastern Division, District of the Gulf, Mar.–Apr. 1865,
Chap. II, Vol. 99

Telegrams Sent, Eastern Division, District of the Gulf, Mar.–Apr. 1865, Chap. II, Vol. 100

Telegrams Sent, Department of Alabama, Mississippi, and East Louisiana, Feb. 1–Mar. 21, 1865, Chap. II, Vol. 196

Telegrams Sent, Department of Alabama, Mississippi, and East Louisiana, Jan.–Feb. 1864, Chap. II, Vol. 236 1/4

Record Books of Brigadier General Daniel W. Adams' and Brigadier General Randall L. Gibson's Brigade, 1862–65, Chap. II, Vols. 302 and 304

Letters and Telegrams Sent by the Engineer Bureau of the Confederate War Department, 1861–64, Chap. III, Vols. 1–5

Letters and Telegrams Sent, Engineer Office at Mobile, June–July 1863, Chap. III, Vol. 10

Letters Sent, Engineer Office at Mobile, Oct. 11, 1864–May 8, 1865, Chap. III, Vol. 11

Letters Sent, Engineer Office, Department of the Gulf, Jan. 1863–Apr. 1864, Chap. III, Vol. 12

Letters Sent, Engineer Office, Department of the Gulf, Aug. 1864–May 1865, Chap. III, Vol. 13

Letters Sent, Engineer Office, Department of Alabama and West Florida, Apr.–May 1862, Chap. III, Vol. 15

Letters Sent, Engineer Office, Department of the Gulf, Apr.–Sept. 1864, Chap. III, Vol. 16

Letters Sent by the Confederate Secretary of War, 1861–65, Chap. IX, Vols. 1–4, 6–19

Telegrams Sent by the Confederate Secretary of War, 1861–65, Chap. IX, Vols. 33–35

Compiled Service Records of Confederate General and Staff Officers and Non-regimental Enlisted Men

Compiled Service Records of Confederate Soldiers Who Served in Organizations from Alabama

Compiled Service Records of Confederate Soldiers Who Served in Organizations from Louisiana

Compiled Service Records of Confederate Soldiers Who Served in Organizations from Mississippi

Compiled Service Records of Confederate Soldiers Who Served in Organizations from Tennessee

General and Special Orders, Department of Alabama and West Florida, Oct. 15, 1861–Feb. 28, 1862

General and Special Orders, Department of Alabama and West Florida, Mar. 3–Apr. 26, 1862

General and Special Orders, Department of Alabama and West Florida, Apr. 28–July 5, 1862

General Orders, Department of Alabama, Mississippi, and East Louisiana, 1861–65

General Orders, Department of Alabama and West Florida, Oct. 14, 1861–Feb. 28, 1862

General Samuel Jones Papers, 1861–65

Letters and Telegrams Received, Department of Alabama, Mississippi, and East Louisiana, Nov. 1862–Apr. 1865

Letters Received by the Confederate Secretary of War, 1861–65

Letters Received, Confederate Adjutant and Inspector General's Office, 1861–65

Orders, District of the Gulf, 1862–65

Special and General Orders, Army of Mobile, Mar.–June 1862

Special Field Orders, Military Division of the West, Oct. 1864–Mar. 1865

Special Orders, Military Division of the West, Oct. 1864–Mar. 1865

Telegrams Received by the Confederate Secretary of War, 1861–65

Telegrams Received, Confederate Adjutant and Inspector General's Office, 1861–65

South Carolina Historical Society, Charleston

    Chestnut-Miller-Manning Collection, 1861–65

South Caroliniana Library, University of South Carolina, Columbia

    E. H. Edwards Letters, 1861–65

Southern Historical Collection, University of North Carolina, Chapel Hill

    Thomas Bragg Diary, 1861–62

    Leonidas Polk Papers, 1767–1934

    Edmund Kirby Smith Papers, 1776–1906

    Southall and Bowen Papers, 1861–65

    Samuel H. Stout Papers, 1847–1903

Sallie L. Tarleton Letters in possession of Grace DuValle, Mobile, Ala.

Tulane University, Special Collections Division, Howard-Tilton Memorial Library, New Orleans, La.

    Randall Lee Gibson Letters, 1877–93

    Louisiana Historical Association Collection

    John T. Purves Papers

    A. C. Van Benthuysen Papers, 1861–65

    Eldridge Virgil Weaver III Collection, 1861–68

United States Army Military History Institute, Carlisle Barracks, Pa.
  Civil War Times Illustrated Collection
Western Reserve Historical Society, Cleveland, Ohio
  William P. Palmer Collection of Braxton Bragg Papers, 1861–65
  William P. Palmer Collection of Civil War Manuscripts, 1861–65
College of William and Mary Library, Williamsburg, Va.
  Joseph E. Johnston Papers, 1863–64

NEWSPAPERS
Aberdeen (Miss.) *Examiner*, Feb. 7, 1890
Charleston Mercury, Apr. 2, Oct. 28, 1862
Cincinnati Daily Commercial, May 10, 1865
Home Journal (Mobile), 1863–65
Index (London, Eng.), 1861–63
Mobile Advertiser and Register, 1861–65
Mobile Army Argus and Crisis, 1864–65
Mobile Daily Advertiser, 1860–61
Mobile Daily Tribune, 1861–65
Mobile Evening News, 1862–65
Mobile Evening Telegraph, June 8, 1864
Mobile Press Register, Oct. 17, 1948
Mobile Register, Aug. 9, 1908
Montgomery Daily Mail, 1862–63
Montgomery Weekly Post, 1860–61
New Orleans Daily Picayune, 1861–62
New Orleans Times, 1863–65
New York Daily Tribune, Apr. 18, 1864
New York Herald, Feb. 26, 1863
Selma Morning Reporter, Feb. 24, 1863
Weekly Thibodaux (La.) *Sentinel*, July 1868
Vicksburg Daily Whig, 1862–63

GOVERNMENT PUBLICATIONS
Agriculture of the United States in 1860; Compiled from the Original Returns of the Eighth Census. Washington, D.C.: U.S. Government Printing Office, 1864.
American State Papers, Military Affairs. Vol. 5, 22d Cong., 2d sess., No. 551.
Report of the Secretary of War. Senate Executive Document No. 1, 37th Cong., 2d sess., vol. 2.

Richardson, James D., comp. *A Compilation of the Messages and Papers of the Presidents, 1789–1897.* 10 vols. Washington, D.C.: U.S. Government Printing Office, 1896–99.

U.S. Bureau of the Census. *Eighth Census of the United States, 1860, Population.* Washington, D.C.: U.S. Government Printing Office, 1864.

U.S. Navy Department. *Civil War Naval Chronology, 1861–1865.* 6 parts. Washington, D.C.: U.S. Government Printing Office, 1961–66.

———. *Officers of the Confederate States Navy, 1861–1865.* Washington, D.C.: U.S. Government Printing Office, 1898.

———. *War of the Rebellion: Official Records of the Union and Confederate Navies.* 30 vols. Washington, D.C.: U.S. Government Printing Office, 1894–1922.

U.S. Treasury Department. *Commerce and Navigation of the United States, 1860.* Washington, D.C.: George W. Bowman, Printer, 1860.

U.S. War Department. *War of the Rebellion: Official Records of Union and Confederate Armies.* 128 parts in 70 vols. Washington, D.C.: U.S. Government Printing Office, 1880–1901.

CONTEMPORARY ACCOUNTS, DIARIES, MEMOIRS,
REMINISCENCES

Books

The American Annual Cyclopedia and Register of Important Events of the Year 1863. 14 vols. New York: D. Appleton, 1865.

The American Annual Cyclopedia and Register of Important Events of the Year 1865. New York: D. Appleton, 1866.

Anderson, Ephraim McD. *Memoirs: Historical and Personal; Including the Campaigns of the First Missouri Brigade.* St. Louis: Times Printing Co., 1868.

Bevier, Robert S. *History of the First and Second Missouri Confederate Brigades, 1861–1865.* St. Louis: Bryan, Brand, 1879.

Bradley, James. *The Confederate Mail Carrier.* Mexico, Mo.: N.p., 1894.

Corson, W. W. *Two Months in the Confederate States.* London: Richard Bentley, 1863.

Cumming, Kate. *Kate: The Journal of a Confederate Nurse.* Edited by Richard B. Harwell. Baton Rouge: Louisiana State University Press, 1959.

DeLeon, Thomas C. *Belles, Beaux and Brains of the Sixties.* New York: Dillingham, 1907.

———. *Four Years In Rebel Capitals: An Inside View of Life in the Southern*

Confederacy, from Birth to Death. Edited by E. B. Long. New York: Collier Books, 1962.

Folmar, John Kent, ed. *From That Terrible Field: Civil War Letters of James M. Williams, Twenty-First Alabama Infantry Volunteers.* University, Ala.: University of Alabama Press, 1981.

Fremantle, Arthur J. L. *The Fremantle Diary.* Edited by Walter Lord. Boston: Little, Brown, 1954.

Gordon, George H. *A War Diary of Events in the War of the Great Rebellion, 1861–1865.* Boston: James R. Osgood, 1882.

Holt, Thad, ed. *Miss Waring's Journal, 1863 and 1865.* Chicago: Wyvern Press, 1964.

Hotze, Henry. *Three Months in the Confederate Army.* Edited by Richard B. Harwell. University, Ala.: University of Alabama Press, 1952.

Hughes, Nathaniel C., ed. *Liddell's Record.* Dayton, Ohio: Morningside House, 1985.

Johnston, Joseph E. *Narrative of Military Operations.* New York: D. Appleton, 1874.

Jones, J. B. *A Rebel War Clerk's Diary.* Edited by Howard Swiggett. 2 vols. New York: Old Hickory Bookshop, 1935.

Kirwan, A. D., ed. *Johnny Green of the Orphan Brigade: The Journal of a Confederate Soldier.* Lexington: University of Kentucky Press, 1956.

Little, George, and James R. Maxwell. *A History of Lumsden's Battery, C.S.A.* Tuscaloosa: United Daughters of the Confederacy, 1905.

Marshall, Jessie Ames, ed. *Private and Official Correspondence of Gen. Benjamin F. Butler during the Period of the Civil War.* 5 vols. Norwood, Mass.: Plimpton Press, 1917.

Maury, Dabney H. *Recollections of a Virginian.* New York: Charles Scribner's Sons, 1894.

Owen, William Miller. *In Camp and Battle with the Washington Artillery of New Orleans.* Boston: Ticknor, 1885.

Perkins, Susan G., ed. and arr. *Letters of Capt. Geo. Hamilton Perkins, U.S.N.* Concord, N.H.: Ira C. Evans, 1886.

Porter, David D. *Incidents and Anecdotes of the Civil War.* New York: D. Appleton, 1885.

——. *The Naval History of the Civil War.* New York: Sherman, 1886.

Richardson, Albert D. *The Secret Service, the Field, the Dungeon, and the Escape.* Hartford, Conn.: American Publishing Co., 1865.

Rix, William. *Incidents of Life in a Southern City during the War.* Mobile: Iberville Historical Society Papers, 1865.

Ross, FitzGerald. *Cities and Camps of the Confederate States.* Edited by Richard B. Harwell. Urbana: University of Illinois Press, 1958.

Rowland, Dunbar, ed. *Jefferson Davis, Constitutionalist: His Letters, Papers and Speeches.* 10 vols. Jackson, Miss.: Department of Archives and History, 1923.

Russell, William Howard. *My Diary North and South.* Edited by Fletcher Pratt. New York: Harper & Row, 1965.

St. Paul, Henry. *Our Home and Foreign Policy.* Mobile: *Daily Register & Advertiser,* 1863.

Semmes, Raphael. *Memoirs of Service Afloat during the War between the States.* Baltimore: Kelly, Piet & Co., 1869.

Smith, C. Carter, Jr., ed. *Two Naval Journals: 1864.* Chicago: Wyvern Press, 1964.

Smith, Daniel P. *Company K, First Alabama Regiment, or Three Years in the Confederate Service.* Prattville, Ala.: Published by the Survivors, 1885.

Taylor, F. Jay, ed. *Reluctant Rebel: The Secret Diary of Robert Patrick, 1861–1865.* Baton Rouge: Louisiana State University Press, 1959.

Taylor, Richard. *Destruction and Reconstruction: Personal Experiences of the Late War.* Edited by Richard B. Harwell. New York: Longmans, Green, 1955.

Thompson, Robert M., and Richard Wainwright, eds. *Confidential Correspondence of Gustavus Vasa Fox.* 2 vols. New York: Printed for the Naval History Society, 1918–19.

Vandiver, Frank E., ed. *Confederate Blockade Running through Bermuda, 1861–1865: Letters and Cargo Manifests.* Austin: University of Texas Press, 1947.

Von Scheliha, Victor K. R. *A Treatise on Coast-Defence.* London: E. & F. N. Spon, 1868.

Articles

Austill, Hurieosco. "Fort Morgan in the Confederacy." *Alabama Historical Quarterly* 7 (1945): 254–68.

Bailey, W. "The Star Company of Ector's Texas Brigade." *Confederate Veteran* 22 (1914): 404–5.

Bowles, R. C. "The Ship Tennessee." *Southern Historical Society Papers* 21 (1893): 291–94.

[Brother, Charles]. "The Journal of Private Charles Brother." In U.S. Navy Department, Naval History Division, *Civil War Naval Chronology.* 6 vols., 6:47–89. Washington, D.C.: U.S. Government Printing Office, 1961–66.

Buchanan, Franklin. "Official Report of the Fight in Mobile Bay." *Southern Historical Society Papers* 6 (1878): 220–24.

Cameron, William L. "The Battles Opposite Mobile." *Confederate Veteran* 23 (1915): 305–8.

Chalaron, J. A. "Battle Echoes from Shiloh." *Southern Historical Society Papers* 21 (1893): 219–22.

Chambers, William Pitt. "My Journal: The Story of a Soldier's Life Told by Himself." *Publications of the Mississippi Historical Society*, Centenary Series, 5 (1925): 227–386.

Conrad, Daniel B. "Capture of the C.S. Ram Tennessee in Mobile Bay, August, 1864." *Southern Historical Society Papers* 19 (1891): 72–82.

Cox, Benjamin B. "Mobile in the War between the States." *Confederate Veteran* 24 (1916): 209–12.

"Diary of Captain Edward Crenshaw of the Confederate States Army." *Alabama Historical Quarterly* 1 (1930): 438–52.

[Graves, Charles I.]. "A Confederate Sailor's Lament." Edited by William B. Hesseltine. *Civil War History* 5 (1959): 99–102.

Hults, Ellsworth H. "Aboard the *Galena* at Mobile." *Civil War Times Illustrated* 10 (Apr. 1971): 12–21; (May 1971) 28–40.

Johnston, James D. "The Battle of Mobile Bay." *Southern Historical Society Papers* 9 (1881): 471–76.

———. "The Fight in Mobile Bay." *Southern Historical Society Papers* 6 (1878): 224–27.

———. "The Ram 'Tennessee' at Mobile Bay." In Robert U. Johnson and Clarence C. Buel, eds., *Battles and Leaders of the Civil War*. 4 vols., 4:401–5. New York: Century, 1887–88.

Kinney, John C. "Farragut at Mobile Bay." In Robert U. Johnson and Clarence C. Buel, eds., *Battles and Leaders of the Civil War*. 4 vols., 4:379–99. New York: Century, 1887–88.

"Letters of Jacob Faser, Confederate Armorer." *Alabama Historical Quarterly* 3 (1941): 193–202.

Maury, Dabney H. "Defence of Mobile in 1865." *Southern Historical Society Papers* 3 (1877): 1–13.

———. "Defence of Spanish Fort." *Southern Historical Society Papers* 39 (1914): 130–36.

"Mobile—Its Past and Its Present." *DeBow's Review* 28 (1860): 310–11.

Padgett, James A., ed. "Some Letters of George Stanton Denison, 1854–1866: Observations of a Yankee on Conditions in Louisiana and Texas." *Louisiana Historical Quarterly* 23 (1940): 3–111.

Page, Richard L. "The Defense of Fort Morgan." In Robert U. Johnson and Clarence C. Buel, eds., *Battles and Leaders of the Civil War*. 4 vols., 4:408–9. New York: Century, 1887–88.

Pitcher, Mrs. Sargent, Jr., ed. "Spencer-Holcombe Letters Written in the 1860s." *Louisiana Genealogical Register* 19 (Mar. 1972): 44–47.

Ryan, Harriet Fitts, arr. "The Letters of Harden Perkins Cockrane, 1862–1864." *Alabama Review* 7 (1954): 277–94.

Stephenson, P. D. "Defence of Spanish Fort." *Southern Historical Society Papers* 39 (1914): 118–29.

Still, William N., Jr., ed. "The Civil War Letters of Robert Tarleton." *Alabama Historical Quarterly* 32 (1970): 51–80.

Tarrant, Edward W. "Siege and Capture of Fort Blakely." *Confederate Veteran* 23 (1915): 457–58.

Walker, Anne Kendrick. "Governor John Gill Shorter: Miscellaneous Papers, 1861–1863." *Alabama Review* 11 (1958): 208–32.

Waterman, George S. "Afloat—Afield—Afloat." *Confederate Veteran* 7 (1899): 16–21, 449–52, 490–92; 8 (1900): 21–24, 53–55; 9 (1901): 24–29.

Webster, Harrie. "An August Morning with Farragut at Mobile Bay." In U.S. Navy Department, *Civil War Naval Chronology, 1861–1865*. 6 parts, 6:85–98. Washington, D.C.: U.S. Government Printing Office, 1961–66.

SECONDARY WORKS

BOOKS

Amos, Harriet E. *Cotton City: Urban Development in Antebellum Mobile*. University, Ala.: University of Alabama Press, 1985.

Andrews, Christopher C. *History of the Campaign of Mobile; Including the Cooperative Operations of General Wilson's Cavalry in Alabama*. New York: D. Van Nostrand, 1867.

Barney, William L. *The Secessionist Impulse: Alabama and Mississippi in 1860*. Princeton: Princeton University Press, 1974.

Bearss, Edwin C. *Rebel Victory at Vicksburg*. Little Rock, Ark.: Pioneer Press, 1963.

Beringer, Richard E., Herman Hattaway, Archer Jones, and William N. Still, Jr. *Why the South Lost the Civil War*. Athens: University of Georgia Press, 1986.

Berlin, Ira. *Slaves without Masters: The Free Negro in the Antebellum South*. New York: Pantheon Books, 1974.

Black, Robert C., III. *The Railroads of the Confederacy.* Chapel Hill: University of North Carolina Press, 1952.

Boatner, Mark M., III. *The Civil War Dictionary.* New York: David McKay, 1959.

Boykin, Edward. *Sea Devil of the Confederacy.* New York: Funk & Wagnalls, 1959.

Bradford, James C., ed. *Captains of the Old Steam Navy: Makers of the American Naval Tradition, 1840–1880.* Annapolis, Md.: Naval Institute Press, 1986.

Brewer, Willis. *Alabama: Her History, Resources, War Record, and Public Men, from 1540 to 1872.* Montgomery: Barrett & Brown, 1872.

Carter, Samuel, III. *The Final Fortress: The Campaign for Vicksburg, 1862–1863.* New York: St. Martin's Press, 1980.

Castlen, Harriet Gift. *Hope Bids Me Onward.* Savannah, Ga.: Chatham Publishing Co., 1945.

Chandler, Hatchett. *Little Gems from Fort Morgan: The Cradle of American History.* Boston: Christopher Publishing House, 1961.

Cochran, Hamilton. *Blockade Runners of the Confederacy.* New York: Bobbs-Merrill, 1958.

Connelly, Thomas Lawrence. *Army of the Heartland: The Army of Tennessee, 1861–1862.* Baton Rouge: Louisiana State University Press, 1967.

———. *Autumn of Glory: The Army of Tennessee, 1862–1865.* Baton Rouge: Louisiana State University Press, 1971.

Connelly, Thomas Lawrence, and Archer Jones. *The Politics of Command: Factions and Ideas in Confederate Strategy.* Baton Rouge: Louisiana State University Press, 1973.

Cooling, Benjamin Franklin. *Forts Henry and Donelson: The Key to the Confederate Heartland.* Knoxville: University of Tennessee Press, 1987.

Coulter, E. Merton. *The Confederate States of America, 1861–1865.* Baton Rouge: Louisiana State University Press, 1950.

Craighead, Erwin. *From Mobile's Past.* Mobile: Powers Printing Co., 1925.

Daniel, Larry J., and Riley W. Gunter. *Confederate Cannon Foundries.* Union City, Tenn.: Pioneer Press, 1977.

Delaney, Caldwell. *Confederate Mobile: A Pictorial History.* Mobile: Haunted Book Shop, 1971.

———. *The Story of Mobile.* Mobile: Gill Printing Co., 1953.

Denman, Clarence P. *The Secession Movement in Alabama.* Montgomery: Alabama State Department of Archives and History, 1933.

Dorman, Leavy. *Party Politics in Alabama from 1850 through 1860.* Wetumpka, Ala.: Wetumpka Printing Co., 1935.

Dufour, Charles L. *The Night the War Was Lost.* New York: Doubleday, 1960.

Durden, Robert F. *The Gray and the Black: The Confederate Debate on Emancipation.* Baton Rouge: Louisiana State University Press, 1972.

Dyer, John P. *From Shiloh to San Juan: The Life of "Fightin' Joe" Wheeler.* Baton Rouge: Louisiana State University Press, 1961.

Evans, Clement A., ed. *Confederate Military History.* 12 vols. Atlanta: Confederate Publishing Co., 1899.

Fidler, William P. *Augusta Evans Wilson, 1835–1900: A Biography.* University, Ala.: University of Alabama Press, 1951.

Fitzgerald, W. Norman. *President Lincoln's Blockade and the Defense of Mobile.* Lincoln Fellowship of Wisconsin, Historical Bulletin No. 12. Madison, 1954.

Fleming, Walter L. *Civil War and Reconstruction in Alabama.* New York: Columbia University Press, 1905.

Goff, Richard D. *Confederate Supply.* Durham, N.C.: Duke University Press, 1969.

Goodrow, Sister Esther Marie. *Mobile during the Civil War.* Mobile: Historic Mobile Preservation Society, 1950.

Hamilton, Peter J. *A Little Boy in Confederate Mobile.* Mobile: Colonial Mobile Book Shop, 1947.

———. *Mobile of the Five Flags.* Mobile: Gill Printing Co., 1913.

Hattaway, Herman, and Archer Jones. *How the North Won: A Military History of the Civil War.* Urbana: University of Illinois Press, 1983.

Hazlett, James C., Edwin Olmstead, and M. Hume Parks. *Field Artillery Weapons of the Civil War.* Newark: University of Delaware Press, 1983.

Hewitt, Lawrence L. *Port Hudson: Confederate Bastion on the Mississippi.* Baton Rouge: Louisiana State University Press, 1987.

Hilliard, Sam Bowers. *Hog Meat and Hoecake: Food Supply in the Old South, 1840–1860.* Carbondale: Southern Illinois University Press, 1972.

History of Company B, 40th Alabama Regiment, Confederate States Army, 1862 to 1865. [Anniston, Ala.]: Colonial Press, 1963.

Johnson, Ludwell H. *Red River Campaign: Politics and Cotton in the Civil War.* Baltimore: Johns Hopkins Press, 1958.

Jones, James Pickett. *Yankee Blitzkrieg: Wilson's Raid through Alabama and Georgia.* Athens: University of Georgia Press, 1976.

Lewis, Charles L. *Admiral Franklin Buchanan, Fearless Man of Action.* Baltimore: Norman, Remington, 1929.

Mackall, William W. *A Son's Recollections of His Father.* New York: E. P. Dutton, 1930.

McMillan, Malcolm C. *The Disintegration of a Confederate State: Three Governors and Alabama's Wartime Home Front, 1861–1865.* Macon, Ga.: Mercer University Press, 1986.

McMorries, Edward Young. *History of the First Regiment Alabama Volunteer Infantry C.S.A.* Montgomery: Brown Printing Co., 1904.

McMurry, Richard M. *Two Great Rebel Armies: An Essay in Confederate Military History.* Chapel Hill: University of North Carolina Press, 1989.

McPherson, James M. *Battle Cry of Freedom: The Civil War Era.* New York: Oxford University Press, 1988.

McWhiney, Grady. *Braxton Bragg and Confederate Defeat: Field Command.* New York: Columbia University Press, 1969.

Martin, Bessie. *Desertion of Alabama Troops from the Confederate Army.* New York: AMS Press, 1966.

Massey, Mary Elizabeth. *Refugee Life in the Confederacy.* Baton Rouge: Louisiana State University Press, 1964.

Nichols, James L. *Confederate Engineers.* Tuscaloosa, Ala.: Confederate Publishing Co., 1957.

Owen, Thomas M. *History of Alabama and Dictionary of Alabama Biography.* 4 vols. Chicago: S. J. Clarke, 1921.

Owsley, Frank L. *King Cotton Diplomacy: Foreign Relations of the Confederate States of America.* 2d ed., rev. Chicago: University of Chicago Press, 1966.

Owsley, Frank Lawrence, Jr. *The C.S.S. Florida: Her Building and Operations.* Tuscaloosa: University of Alabama Press, 1987.

Parks, Joseph H. *General Leonidas Polk, C.S.A.: The Fighting Bishop.* Baton Rouge: Louisiana State University Press, 1962.

Perry, Milton F. *Infernal Machines: The Story of Confederate Submarine and Mine Warfare.* Baton Rouge: Louisiana State University Press, 1965.

Reed, Rowena. *Combined Operations in the Civil War.* Annapolis, Md.: Naval Institute Press, 1978.

Reynolds, Bernard A. *Sketches of Mobile, from 1814 to the Present Time.* Mobile: B. H. Richardson, 1868.

Ripley, Warren. *Artillery and Ammunition of the Civil War.* 4th rev. ed. Charleston, S.C.: Battery Press, 1984.

Scharf, J. Thomas. *History of the Confederate States Navy.* 2d ed. Albany, N.Y.: Joseph McDonough, 1894.

Soley, James Russell. *The Blockade and the Cruisers.* New York: Charles Scribner's Sons, 1883.

Spiller, Roger J., ed. *Dictionary of American Military Biography.* 3 vols. Westport, Conn.: Greenwood Press, 1984.

Sterkx, H. E. *Partners in Rebellion: Alabama Women in the Civil War.* Rutherford, N.J.: Fairleigh Dickinson University Press, 1970.

Still, William N., Jr. *Iron Afloat: The Story of the Confederate Armorclads.* Nashville: Vanderbilt University Press, 1971.

Summersell, Charles G. *Mobile: History of a Seaport Town.* University Ala.: University of Alabama Press, 1949.

Wade, Richard C. *Slavery in the Cities: The South, 1820–1860.* New York: Oxford University Press, 1964.

Walker, Jeanie M. *Life of Capt. Joseph Fry, the Cuban Martyr.* Hartford, Conn.: J. B. Burr Publishing Co., 1875.

Warner, Ezra J. *Generals in Gray: Lives of the Confederate Commanders.* Baton Rouge: Louisiana State University Press, 1959.

West, Richard S., Jr. *Gideon Welles: Lincoln's Navy Department.* Indianapolis: Bobbs-Merrill, 1943.

Wiley, Bill I. *Southern Negroes, 1861–1865.* New Haven: Yale University Press, 1938.

Wise, Stephen R. *Lifeline of the Confederacy: Blockade Running during the Civil War.* Columbia: University of South Carolina Press, 1988.

Yearns, W. Buck, ed. *The Confederate Governors.* Athens: University of Georgia Press, 1985.

ARTICLES

Bergeron, Arthur W., Jr. "'They Bore Themselves with Distinguished Gallantry': The Twenty-Second Louisiana Infantry." *Louisiana History* 13 (1972): 253–82.

———. "The Twenty-Second Louisiana Consolidated Infantry in the Defense of Mobile, 1864–1865." *Alabama Historical Quarterly* 38 (1976): 204–13.

Bradlee, Francis B. C. "Blockade Running during the Civil War." *Essex Institute Historical Collections* 60 (1924): 1–16, 153–76, 233–56, 349–72.

Donald, W. J., ed. "Alabama Confederate Hospitals." *Alabama Review* 15 (1962): 275–77.

Folmar, John Kent. "Lt. Col. James M. Williams and the Ft. Powell Incident." *Alabama Review* 17 (1964): 123–36.

Fornell, Earl W. "Confederate Seaport Strategy." *Civil War History* 2 (1956): 61–68.

———. "Mobile during the Blockade." *Alabama Historical Quarterly* 23 (1961): 29–43.

Jordan, Weymouth T. "Ante-Bellum Mobile: Alabama's Agricultural Emporium." *Alabama Review* 1 (1948): 180–202.

Nichols, James L. "Confederate Engineers and the Defense of Mobile." *Alabama Review* 12 (1959): 181–95.

Preu, James A. "The First Phase of Naval Action against Mobile." *Florida State University Studies* 14 (1954): 41–69.

Price, Marcus W. "Ships That Tested the Blockade of the Gulf Ports, 1861–1865." *American Neptune* 11 (1951): 262–90; 12 (1952): 52–59, 154–61, 229–38.

Still, William N., Jr. "The Confederate States Navy at Mobile, 1861 to August 1864." *Alabama Historical Quarterly* 30 (1968): 127–44.

Swartz, Oretha D. "Franklin Buchanan: A Study in Divided Loyalties." *United States Naval Institute Proceedings* 88 (1962): 61–71.

THESES AND MANUSCRIPTS

Bright, Samuel R., Jr. "Confederate Coast Defense." Ph.D. dissertation, Duke University, 1961.

Buchanan, Robert Patrick. "The Military Campaign for Mobile, 1864–1865." M.A. thesis, Auburn University, 1963.

Hewitt, Lawrence L. "Braxton Bragg and the Invasion of Kentucky: A Campaign of Maneuver." Seminar paper, Louisiana State University, 1975.

Isbell, Frances Annette. "A Social and Economic History of Mobile, 1865–1875." M.A. thesis, University of Alabama, 1951.

Lipscomb, Oscar H. "The Administration of John Quinlan, Second Bishop of Mobile, 1859–1883." M.A. thesis, Catholic University of America, 1959.

Roberson, B. L. "Valor on the Eastern Shore: The Mobile Campaign of 1865." Research paper, 1965.

Robinson, Robert L. "Mobile in the 1850s: A Social, Cultural and Economic History." M.A. thesis, University of Alabama, 1955.

Smith, Thomas A. "Mobilization of the Army in Alabama, 1859–1865." M.A. thesis, Auburn University, 1953.

INDEX